CONGLOMERATES UNLIMITED

CONGLOMERATES

UNLIMITED

THE FAILURE OF REGULATION

JOHN F. WINSLOW

INDIANA UNIVERSITY PRESS

BLOOMINGTON AND LONDON

Published in Canada by Fitzhenry & Whiteside Limited,
Don Mills, Ontario
Library of Congress catalog number: 73-80381
ISBN: 0-253-11335-0
Manufactured in the United States of America

CONTENTS

INTRODUCTION

An Overview of the Current Merger Movement

In a decade marked by far-reaching economic, political, and social changes, the merger movement of the 1960s stands out as one of its most important features. This movement has already greatly altered the structure of American industry, led to important changes in a number of business practices, and redistributed on a large scale both economic and political power. It has caught many business firms by surprise and introduced new elements of uncertainty and insecurity into what might be called the business establishment. It has been marked by the development of new techniques in both the acquisition process and defense against take-over attempts. It has puzzled economists, government officials, financial analysts, accountants, and others whose job it is to monitor the economy and shape economic policy, both private and public. There are still debates as to why this merger movement began, whether it is desirable or undesirable, whether it will continue into the future on the same scale, what its full consequences will be.

The degree of merger activity appeared to have reached its apex in 1968, and as a result the general concern with mergers has somewhat diminished in the last few years. This lessening of concern, however, is quite ill advised. The decrease in merger activity has all the marks of a temporary phenomenon that could be attributed to the recession starting in 1969, the depressed stock market accompanying that recession, and a number of threats to the merger movement made in the early years of the first Nixon administration. But, with economic activity increasing, a buoyant stock market, and a downgrading of antitrust opposition to mergers by the Nixon administration, it is clear that the merger movement, as of 1973, is again gathering strength and momentum. There is, therefore, much more reason to study and understand the workings of the merger movement than would be dictated by pure academic interest.

Magnitude and Form

There is very little question about the magnitude of this recent, and apparently ongoing, merger wave. The Bureau of Economics of the Federal Trade Commission, which dated this merger wave as beginning in 1948, has provided information with which to measure its magnitude, although most comprehensively only for those companies classified in manufacturing and mining industries.[1] The data show that the merger trend was continuously upward from 1948 to 1968, with very sharp rises in 1967 and 1968 (1968 was the last full year in this study). Over the 1948–1968 period, there were no fewer than 15,445 acquisitions large enough to be reported in *Standard's Corporation Records* and *Moody's Industrial Manual*. These acquisitions involved assets valued at over $67 billion. Many of the acquisitions were of very large companies. Of the 15,445 acquisitions, 1,276 were of firms with assets greater than $10 million. A most startling finding was that, of the 1,000 largest manufacturing and mining companies of 1950, 327 were acquired. A calculation in this study led to the conclusion that by 1968 there were about 850 fewer corporations with assets of $25 million or greater than there would have been had there been no mergers.

Some figures assembled on nonmanufacturing and nonmining acquisitions, although incomplete, are nevertheless impressive. From 1949 to 1968 some 760 retail grocery concerns, with annual sales estimated at $7.7 billion, were acquired. During 1967, 1968, and the first nine months of 1969, the 200 largest manufacturing firms acquired some 40 firms in retailing, service, finance, and construction, each having assets of at least $10 million. The total value of these acquired assets during this short period was about $10 billion.

Mergers can be classified in several different ways. From a legal viewpoint, they can be divided into two categories: consolidations and acquisitions. The acquisition route, where one firm takes over another, generally by acquiring a controlling interest in its common stock, has been much more important in the recent merger wave than that of consolidation, in which a new legal entity is formed from two or more companies. A much more meaningful classification of mergers can also be made on the basis of the relation between the products and services of the acquiring and acquired firms. A merger is called horizontal if the products and services of the two firms compete for markets. A merger is said to be vertical if the two firms have an actual or potential supplier-customer relationship. Mergers are said to be conglomerate if there are neither horizontal nor vertical relationships between the merging firms. Conglomerate mergers are generally subdivided into three further categories: market extension, in which the products of the two firms are closely competitive, but are sold in different geographic markets; product extension, in which the products have similarities, but are not closely competitive, such as cans and bottles; and "pure," in which the products and services are virtually completely unrelated. It is worth noting that a merger of two diversified firms can have horizontal, vertical, and conglomerate aspects.

An important attribute of the recent merger wave has been its increasingly conglomerate nature. The FTC's Bureau of Economics classified 37.5% of the large acquisitions ($10 million or more in terms of acquired assets) as conglomerate in the 1948–1957 period. But by 1968, some 88% of such acquisitions were of the conglomerate type. Although product extension mergers continued to be important, the "pure" conglomerate mergers became increasingly dominant through the 1960s.

New Elements in the Current Merger Wave

Mergers are not, of course, a new phenomenon. There were two earlier and comparable merger waves: from 1898 to 1903, and during the late 1920s. All three merger waves have some characteristics in common and some characteristics that are unique.[2] The unique features of the merger wave which began to intensify in the 1960s are so important and incongruous with what had happened before that they have forced reappraisals of status, power, how a business should be run, the meanings of value, and so forth.

One obviously important feature of the ongoing merger wave is the "conglomerateness" of the firms after the mergers. Critical observers have taken delight in pointing out that one firm may be in helicopters and ladies' underwear, another in cigars and railroads. It is not that diversification is by itself undesirable: indeed it is a wise strategy in an era of rapidly-changing markets, technologies, and needs. But the more traditional business sense expects diversification to take some kind of logical path. Many have questioned whether it is possible for the management of one firm to evaluate and run an acquisition in a completely different line of work. Those engaged in building conglomerates, not unmindful of the effect of such criticism on their common stock prices, have found it necessary to try to give at least some semblance of logic to their pattern of acquisition. Thus, such disparate activities as boat building and motion picture making are grouped together as catering to the "leisure" market, while coal mining and potato farming both become "extractive" industries. Whether the techniques of management have been sufficiently developed so that a widely diversified enterprise can in fact be efficiently managed is a question to which there is no definite answer yet.

A second novel feature of the current merger wave is the demonstrated capability of a small, virtually unknown firm, often with some meaningless name (such as National General) to acquire control of a very large, well-established company. Even more important, such acquisitions have been made despite the opposition of the management of the large take-over target. Sometimes large firms have been acquired without the management's even knowing that the acquisition had been taking place: there have been instances in which the president or chairman of a large firm has received a telephone call from a heretofore unknown individual informing him that the caller owns a controlling interest in "his" firm.

It is difficult to overestimate the impact that this feature of the current merger wave is having on business attitudes and behavior. Surprise acquisitions go completely counter to our general expectations of power, in which big firms are supposed to take over small firms. It is fair to speculate that many high-ranking managers have felt severely threatened by the ever-present possibility of their firms' being acquired, and the remark has been made that GM and AT&T are the only American firms large enough so that their managers do not have to worry about becoming take-over targets.[3] I do not want to leave the impression that all or most of the take-overs are by small unknown firms — the big firms are still the major acquirers — but the possibility of the surprise take-over by the small firm has injected a unique element into the current business scene.

The development of the take-over arts to new heights is another characteristic of this merger wave. The acquiring firm often works with allies — banks, brokers, mutual funds, investment houses — in quietly obtaining the stock of the take-over target. In this way the element of surprise can be used, for if any one purchaser acquired more than 10% of the stock of the target, the facts of the sale would have to be made public. Another aspect of the art of taking over is the ability of the acquiring firm to pay for the take-over with the target's own assets. To do so, it is only necessary to find a publicly held corporation whose stock price is below the market value of its assets; and there seems to be an abundance of such firms. One merely borrows money to acquire the stock of such a firm and, after control is achieved, one sells off some of the assets (sometimes they are in cash) and uses the proceeds to repay the loans. Two professors of finance at Columbia University, Benjamin Graham and David Dodd, some thirty years ago pioneered in these techniques by acquiring control of companies whose stock prices were lower than their asset values and then liquidating these companies. A biography of M. Riklis, one of the earlier "conglomerators," reports how astounded he was when, as a student of finance at The Ohio State University, an assignment led him to the discovery that the stock market frequently places a lower value on a firm than the value of its liquid assets.[4] One must agree with Riklis that it is incredible indeed that stock market prices could be so low.

The acquiring firm may profit greatly even when it does not actually acquire the target company. The formula for doing so is simple. The potential acquirer first purchases a large number of shares in the target company. It must do so quietly, often with allies in financial institutions, so that the price of the stock does not rise substantially. The acquirer can then make a public tender offer for more of the stock, or better still, just leak the news that it intends to make such an offer. In either case, the price of the stock in the target company will rise. If others com-

pete for the target company, or if the target company enlists
allies to buy its stock in order to keep control from falling to the
acquiring company, the latter company can make a substantial
gain from selling its stock holdings in the target company. A collection of articles from *Fortune* reports that Loew's made over
$30 million this way in its unsuccessful bid to take over Commer-
cial Credit, while Gulf & Western made a stock profit of $50
million while losing out in its attempt to acquire Sinclair Oil.[5]
One may suppose that a great deal of money has been made by
buying stock, leaking news that there will be a take-over attempt,
and then selling this stock, with no real intention of acquiring
the target firm.

Another interesting feature of the current merger wave is the
growth of what could be called a merger industry. Most large
firms now have staffs concerned exclusively with acquisitions.
Management consultant, law, and accounting firms have been
very active, not only in giving technical advice on mergers, but
in promoting them.[6] Mutual funds, stockbrokers, banks, and
other financial institutions are known to work closely with
acquisition-minded firms in arranging, promoting, and aiding
the take-over process. Seminars have been widely offered in the
techniques of acquisition. There is even a trade journal in the
field—the hallmark of any self-respecting industry—called
Mergers and Acquisitions.

Motives

To understand the current merger movement, it is necessary
to delve into the motives of those who promote and oppose mergers. It is, of course, naive to take at face value the announced
reasons for any particular merger. Businessmen and financiers
are not so crass as to make public such motives as personal gain,
the dumping of ineffective management, ego satisfaction, the
gain of monopoly power, the gain of political power, or the eva-
sion of laws. Instead they talk about planned diversification,
synergy, asset deployment, growth patterns, and other terms
that have recently become part of the business lexicon.

One cannot overestimate the possibility of personal gain as a motive for merger. Insiders in both the acquiring and the target companies, and those in financial, legal, and accounting firms privy to merger intentions, are in excellent positions to reap personal gains. The main source of these gains is the almost certain rise in the price of the target firm's stock as a result of the acquiring firm's buying it on the open market (publicly offering a premium over the current market price in a tender bid) or simply leaking to the press its intention to acquire the stock of the takeover target. It is even possible for the insiders of the acquiring firm to make personal gains at the expense of their own stockholders. First, they purchase stock in the target company for their personal accounts; then, when their firm offers a high price for that stock, they sell their personal holdings of target company stock at the higher price. Insiders in the target company can gain by the same means, and may be induced to cooperate with, and provide information to, the acquiring firm. These personal gains can come about by promises of good jobs as well as profiting in the stock market. Insiders of the acquiring firm can also personally profit, after obtaining control, by "looting" or "milking" the target firm by having the target firm sell its assets at low prices to closely held firms controlled by the insiders. There are, clearly, endless possibilities for personal gains along these lines.

There are a number of powerful motives for acquisitions on the part of the acquiring firm, some of them perfectly legitimate, others of questionable legality. First, the acquisition route is an easy way to grow and to diversify into new markets. The acquiring firm immediately obtains, in addition to the tangible assets, the managerial and technical know-how, the trade connections, the brand names that might take many years to develop if the acquirer were to enter the market from scratch. Sometimes the strengths of the acquiring and acquired firms complement each other—as when a firm that is strong in marketing acquires a firm that is strong in research and product development. Sometimes, as the acquisitors often claim, the capability and profitability of the acquired firm can be enhanced by new management and financing provided by the acquiring firm.

The merger may also be a cheap way of obtaining productive assets. It has already been noted that stock prices are frequently lower than the value of the target firm's assets. In addition, the acquiring company can obtain assets cheaply if the merger takes the form of an exchange of stock. It has been amply demonstrated that when the price-earnings ratio of the acquiring firm is, say, twice that of the acquired firm, the acquiring firm can get control of $2 worth of assets for every $1 worth of its own assets if the stocks are exchanged on the basis of market values. The acquiring firm may also, once it gains control of the acquired company, "milk" the latter of its assets by the methods described earlier.

Taxes may also provide an important motive. A firm that has lost money in the last few years is an attractive target because its losses can be carried forward to offset the profits of the acquiring firm, thus reducing the latter's taxes. Tax considerations have also played an important role in the forms of mergers because those who exchange the stock of the acquired firm for debt securities of the acquiring firm do not have to pay capital gains taxes on the transaction. Taxes are very important in mergers involving foreign firms, since the acquiring firm has latitude in intrafirm transfer pricing that would reduce profits in countries with high profit taxes and increase them in countries with low profit tax rates.

The merged entity will frequently have greater bargaining power in the marketplace than smaller, specialized firms. The large diversified firm is in a position to insist on "reciprocity" — a practice in which one firm pressures another to buy from it as a condition for the first one's being a customer of the second. The diversified firm is in a better position to bargain with labor unions than the specialized firm because the income it receives from activities that are not the target of a strike enable it to hold out against wage demands in the affected parts of its business. It is also a well-known tenet in oligopoly theory that the diversified firm has the advantage over the specialized firm in a price war.

Political power can also accrue to large diversified firms. It is no secret that businesses seek help from members of Congress to obtain government contracts and favorable rulings by regulators and the executive branch. The large firm, with many locations throughout the country, obviously has an advantage over the smaller, single-location firm in this respect.

Last, but far from least, mergers provide a means for the acquiring firm to enhance its stock prices in the stock market. An aggressive, acquisition-minded firm projects a most favorable image on Wall Street. "Pooling-of-interest" accounting methods enable the acquiring firm to recalculate its history of earnings, thus projecting to the stock market a company with rapidly rising earnings per share — a valuable image indeed. By controlling the dividend policies of its subsidiaries, the acquiring company can also make sure that its profits per share show steady, rather than fluctuating, growth.

Many entities other than the direct parties stand to gain or lose as the result of a merger. The current suppliers of various inputs to the acquired firm may be replaced, after the merger, by a new group of suppliers. Bankers, lawyers, accountants, and consultants of the acquired firm may be replaced by others. Even cities and states stand to gain or lose from a merger, since the administrative headquarters of the acquired firm is frequently shifted to that of the acquiring firm.[7] Thus, an acquiring firm may have many allies in its attempt to take over another firm; but the target, if it chooses to resist a take-over might also have allies.

The take-over targets may also benefit from a merger. The stockholders are usually paid more for their stock than current market prices. The owners of closely held corporations may benefit from trading their difficult-to-market stock for the stock of a well-known, nationally traded firm. The top managers, it has been noted, may be induced to help in the take-over by being promised jobs in the larger firm. Mergers may also be a way for firms to rid themselves of deadwood and incompetent personnel: it is well known that a shake-up is in store for an acquired firm after the merger takes effect.

In addition to the fired or demoted personnel and the suppliers who lose their customers, the public may also be a loser as a result of conglomerate mergers. The entry into industries via mergers may replace entry by investment in new productive capacity, therefore leading to lower investment than might otherwise be the case. The political power of the large diversified firms may also act against the interest of the public. Finally, the reciprocity that is common between diversified firms may lead to higher prices.

Why the Intensification in the 1960s?

What was there in the 1960s that contributed to the magnitude
and special character of the merger wave? We know that two
elements were present in that decade that were also present at
the turn of the century and in the late 1920s, namely, a rapidly
expanding economy and a buoyant stock market. A buoyant
stock market is a necessary condition for a merger wave because
speculative psychology is high, and the new securities generally
created in mergers are easily sold. Stock market prices move up
rapidly and potential earnings growth resulting from mergers is
immediately and generously rewarded.

It is fairly easy to explain why the conglomerate type of merger
became dominant in the 1960s. The Celler-Kefauver amendment
to Section 7 of the Clayton Act, which was designed to prohibit
mergers that might substantially lessen competition, together
with a series of court decisions favorable to the antitrust authorities, gave the antitrust agencies powerful weapons with which
to oppose horizontal and vertical mergers. Economic theory is
now quite clear concerning the anticompetitive effects of horizontal and vertical mergers. But the question of the anticompeti-
tiveness of conglomerate mergers is more complicated, mainly
because we traditionally think of monopolization with regard
to a particular market, while the nature of the conglomerate
merger is that it brings together operations in a number of different markets. At any rate, the antitrust authorities have not
seriously opposed the conglomerate merger—an attitude which
in effect condoned it.

Another important factor in this merger movement are the
low prices on the stock market of many firms that have solid, but
not spectacular, earnings records and valuable assets. These
low stock prices in a way reflect a triumph for modern economic
and financial theory, which teaches that the value of an asset
should be calculated on the basis of the stream of income that
asset will produce in the future. Those teachings are in contrast
to older views in which assets were also valued by their liquid
values—what they could be sold for. The result has been that
the stocks of companies with growing earnings (even if manipu-

lated) and prospects for continued growth in earnings (and there is room for manipulation of these future earnings expectations) command high prices, while the stocks of other companies frequently sell at prices below the book value of their assets. Furthermore, the book value of these assets often understates their liquid market value, the result of conservative accounting techniques that value assets at their original cost instead of at the higher amounts they would currently cost in an inflationary period.

In this context the conglomerators, in contrast to their image as bold financial innovators, were as a group old-fashioned in their ways of valuing assets. Whereas most of us look only at earnings per share in evaluating the prices of stocks, the conglomerators were shrewd enough to analyze balance sheets and the liquidation values of companies. With this approach they were able to acquire companies with valuable assets at low prices, even while paying the stockholders premiums over the market prices of these undervalued companies.

A factor partly responsible for the low market prices of the stocks of companies laden with valuable assets is that capital gains income is held in higher regard than dividend income. Stocks with a chance of showing strong upward movement because of expected increases in earnings per share are thus bid up in price, while the stock prices of conservatively run companies with solid earnings and dividend records are allowed to languish.

The knowledge that the stock market prices of many companies are low in relation to the value of their assets was a necessary but not a sufficient condition for the size of the merger movement. In addition, there had to be the financial capability and know-how to take over a company. I think this capability began to come about in the 1960s as the result of the concentration of financial securities among relatively few people. This concentration was largely brought about by the growth of mutual funds, which enabled a comparatively small number of individuals to control billions of dollars' worth of securities. The growth of the major banks, with their huge trust departments, also contributed to this concentration of financial power. These developments, along with other sources of financial concentration, made it pos-

sible for a small group of men working together to readily amass
the huge amounts of money and establish the new issuances of
securities that are necessary to obtain control of a major corporation.

Neil Jacoby cites one more reason why the conglomerate
merger became possible. Management principles, Jacoby argues,
have gradually become more abstract, so that once these principles are understood, any type of business firm can be managed.[8]
Thus, it is not difficult for a firm with money and good management to go into virtually any kind of business.

Some Implications for Business Behavior

In the early 1930s, Berle and Means argued that in most major
corporations there is a split between managers and owners.[9]
Economists have since developed alternative models of the firm
that have challenged the traditional one, which was built on the
assumption that the firm seeks to maximize profits. These alternative models are based on the thesis that the managers often
have de facto control of corporations and that profit maximiza-
tion is not in the interest of the managers.[10] Rather managers run
firms in order to maximize sales growth and technological vir-
tuosity, since success in those areas leads to more and better-paid
managerial jobs, large staffs, and managerial security. Managers
are viewed as wishing to earn only "acceptable" profits—that
is, just enough to keep the stockholders from overthrowing them.
The best-known recent development of this thesis is Galbraith's
The New Industrial State.[11]

The power of managers to act in their own, rather than in the
stockholders', interest ultimately rests on the wide dispersion of
stockholders, with the resulting inability of any single stockholder or group of stockholders to challenge the management
and, if necessary, remove them from their jobs. The current
merger movement has shown that this dispersion of stockholders
is no longer the case; that because of mutual funds and the concentration of financial interests, managers may no longer go un-
challenged when they run firms in their own interests. Put quite
plainly, the financial interests are back in the saddle. It should
be made clear that, contrary to what others have suggested,

those in charge of the conglomerate firms—the Geneens, Lings, Bluhdorns, and Thorntons—should not be considered industrial managers. Rather, they are financiers, primarily concerned with the buying and selling of companies, who operate out of an industrial firm rather than a financial institution.

If my thesis that power has shifted from the managers to the financial interests is correct, managers will be under renewed pressure to maximize profits. One victim of the profit-oriented outlook is likely to be the general paternalism toward white-collar workers and other managerial personnel that had characterized many large corporations. All operations are now more ruthlessly tested by the profit criterion, and such socially desirable corporate activity as basic research is likely to be diminished, along with public-minded attitudes toward minority groups and environmental problems. We will surely be seeing "tougher" corporations in the future than we saw in the past.

To avoid becoming take-over targets, corporation managers will have to pay greater attention to two items: the market prices of their stocks and their holdings of attractive assets. These concerns have already led to an important and growing phenomenon: corporations are going into the market to buy up their common stock. The purchase of one's own stock accomplishes a number of things for a manager worried about a take-over. It raises earnings per share; it tends to drive the price of the stock up; it gets rid of the "idle" cash balances that are so attractive to acquisition-minded companies.

There are other things managers can do to avoid being taken over. They can threaten to quit en masse in the event of a take-over. They can ally themselves with "friendly" financial interests, in an attempt to provide alternative acquirers when threatened by the take-over of an unfriendly, or unknown, acquirer. They can even bring the government into the picture. B. F. Goodrich, for example, when threatened with a take-over by Northwest Industries, acquired subsidiaries that competed with Northwest in order to get the antitrust authorities to oppose the merger.[12] Along these lines, by entering fields that are regulated by governmental agencies—such as transportation or banking—the regulatory agencies can be brought in to oppose a take-over effort.

Public Policy

The conglomerate merger wave has also been marked by a failure of government agencies — particularly the antitrust authorities — to take strong action to stop these mergers. However, conglomerate mergers are not as blatantly anticompetitive as the horizontal and vertical ones that characterized earlier merger movements. Two aspects of the conglomerate mergers might actually have had a positive appeal to the antitrust agencies. First, they might not have been too unhappy about outsiders challenging the entrenched managerial establishment. Second, the entry of a profit-minded conglomerate into an industry via the acquisition of an existing firm might shake up the subtle collusion among the firms. Thus, the acquisition of Jones & Laughlin by Ling's LTV could well have introduced an element of competition, or at least uncertainty, into the steel industry. At any rate, Donald Turner, the Antitrust chief in the Johnson administration, was not sure he had the legal authority to challenge the pure conglomerate mergers — although others thought the Celler-Kefauver Amendment gave him ample authority to do so — and in fact he exhibited very little opposition to the conglomerate merger.[13]

Somewhat paradoxically, the Nixon administration has acted more strongly to oppose the conglomerate merger. (I use the term "paradoxically" because the Republicans are popularly thought to be "softer" on antitrust.) One may wonder, however, if the actions of the Nixon administration may not have been more in response to a beleaguered managerial establishment concerned about take-overs and their loss of power than to a desire to maintain a competitive economy. A number of challenges were made — the most important were to LTV's take-over of J & L Steel and to ITT's take-over of Hartford Insurance and Canteen Corporation — but they were settled out of court by consent decrees and, as a consequence, the law regarding conglomerate mergers is still neither tested nor clear. Since the departure of Richard W. McLaren as the Nixon administration's Antitrust chief, there has not been much activity on conglomerates.

The broad review of the current merger movement that I have sketched out, although helpful I hope to an understanding of that movement, cannot by itself provide a complete understanding of what has happened. Each individual merger has its unique characteristics, is shaped by the personalities involved, develops new twists in the art of the take-over, and has its own dose of drama. Many of these mergers also explore the limits of the law and of ethical business behavior. To appreciate fully the current merger movement and what might be store in the future, one must study individual mergers in detail. John F. Winslow provides us with such a study in a clear, forceful, and at times dramatic manner. And there is plenty of drama. In addition to the histories of these mergers, he points up the failure of various public agencies to enforce existing laws.

Mr. Winslow served as counsel to the Antitrust Subcommittee of the House Committee on the Judiciary, which investigated the current trend of corporate consolidation for two years in order to ascertain if new legislation was needed and if the public agencies had adequately performed their tasks. These investigations, together with other sources, provide the materials which enable us to learn about the merger movement from the lips of many of its dominant figures. Winslow has strong feelings about the undesirability of this merger movement. The reader interested in the financial and political machinations of big business will have spent his time well in learning what he has to say.

Indiana University   Irvin M. Grossack
March 1973   PROFESSOR OF BUSINESS ECONOMICS
     AND PUBLIC POLICY

PART **I**

The Forces of Concentration

CHAPTER **1**

The Offensive Intensifies

> My power would fall were I not to support it by new ex-
> pansion. Conquest has made me what I am, and conquest
> must sustain me.
>
> Napoleon

Conglomerate corporations sustain their expansion not by production but by the conquest of more companies in dissimilar
industries. So rapidly have conglomerates expanded that one
quarter of all major independent U. S. industrial enterprises in
existence between 1960 and 1968 are no more.[1]

Only 200 independent corporations will exist by the end of
the decade, according to one authoritative estimate. Those 200,
allegedly, will be conglomerate acquirers of all other major corporations (those with assets over $10 million) now independent.[2]

Bold as that draconian prediction is, it may nevertheless un-
derstate the force of the current trend of corporate concentration
resulting from acquisitions and mergers. The 100 largest U. S.
industrial corporations now control a greater share of the nation's
manufacturing facilities than did the 200 largest in 1950. The
200 largest industrial corporations in 1972 in turn held more
than 60% of all manufacturing plants and equipment—a greater
share than the 1,000 largest companies owned three decades
before.[3] The vast increase of assets controlled by those corporations comes not from building new plants and equipment but
rather from acquisition of other companies.

The 25 conglomerate acquirers which have expanded most
into multifarious industries by purchasing other companies

1

TABLE 1

Assets Acquired by 25 Most Active Acquiring Companies
among the 200 Largest[1] Manufacturing Corporations, 1961–1968

Company	Acquisitions 1961–1968 incl.[2]		Change in assets of company in millions of dollars			Acquired assets as % of change in assets	Rank among largest industrial companies according to assets[3]	
	Number of corporations acquired	Assets of acquired companies (millions)	1960	1968	Change		1960	1968
Gulf & Western Industries, Inc.	67	$ 2,882	$ 12	$ 3,455[4]	$ 3,443	84	–	34(17)[5]
Ling-Temco-Vought, Inc.	23	1,901	94	2,648	2,554	74	335	22
International Telephone & Telegraph Corp.	47	1,487	924	4,022	3,098	48	35	15
Tenneco, Inc.	31	1,196	1,734[6]	3,888	2,154	56	–	16
Teledyne, Inc.	125	1,026	0	1,146[4]	1,146	90	–	136(74)[5]
McDonnell Douglas Corp.	8	864	141	1,237	1,096	79	242(92)[7]	62
Union Oil Company of Cal.	11	825	734	2,298	1,564	53	56	30
Sun Oil Company	3	808	760	2,363	1,603	50	54	28
Signal Companies, Inc.	10	770	306	1,228	922	84	126	66
Occidental Petroleum Corp.	15	767	7	1,788	1,781	43	–	41
Continental Oil Co.	19	686	832	2,537	1,705	40	45	24
General Telephone & Electronics Corp.	40	679	2,205	6,157	3,952	17	13	9
U. S. Plywood–Champion Papers, Inc.	27	649	210	1,123	913	71	176	74

Litton Industries, Inc.	79	609	119	1,421[4]	1,302	47	275	67(55)[5]
Atlantic Richfield Co.	9	543	820	2,451	1,631	33	46	25
North American Rockwell Corp.	6	534	386	1,362	976	55	103	58
FMC Corp.	13	497	313	974	661	75	121	89
Studebaker-Worthington, Inc.	13	480	164	602	438	100+	222	138
General American Transportation Corp.	4	453	414	1,204[4]	790	57	94	123(68)[5]
Textron, Inc.	50	453	272	892	620	73	132	98
White Consolidated Industries, Inc.	28	443	19	620	601	74	–	133
Phillips Petroleum Co.	11	440	1,647	2,889	1,242	35	17	20
Colt Industries, Inc.	9	437	143	588	445	98	238	140
Radio Corporation of America	2	402	816	2,366	1,550	26	47	27
Georgia-Pacific Corp.	45	396	295	1,269	974	41	128	64
Total 25 companies	695	$20,227	$13,367	$50,528	$37,161	54		

1. Ranks refer to FTC 200 largest manufacturing companies, except where noted, by asset size.

2. It should be emphasized that the data shown are compilations based on publicly announced acquisitions of U. S. and Canadian companies. Foreign acquisitions are not included and asset data are not available for many smaller acquired companies. When a particular company is subject to litigation, it is often found that a number of acquisitions have not been publicly reported. For example, subsequent to the preparation of this table, the Justice Department introduced an exhibit in the ITT-Hartford hearings (*U. S. v. International Telephone & Telegraph Corp. and The Hartford Fire Insurance Company*, Civil Action No. 13320) showing ITT as having made 120 acquisitions from 1961 through 1968. Of this total, 52 were of domestic firms. This number is somewhat larger than the 47 shown above. However, the additional firms included in the Justice list were all small: all had assets of less than $10 million and with one exception had assets of less than $1 million.

3. Source: *Fortune* ranking.

4. Including non-consolidated subsidiaries.

5. Rank in parenthesis based on consolidated assets.

6. Tennessee Gas Transmission Co.

7. Acquiring and acquired company, respectively.

SOURCE: *Economic Report on Corporate Mergers*, p.260.

since 1960 are listed in Table 1 in order of the aggregate size of
their purchases. The calculation includes only purchases of
corporations which cost more than $10 million. In eight years
these 25 acquirers alone purchased 695 companies costing altogether over $20 billion. Those billions of dollars of assets,
rather than being spread among 695 independent owners as
before, are now concentrated in the hands of the 25 acquirers.

As the "rank among largest industrial companies according to
assets" (from the *Fortune* list) shows, the 25 acquirers generally
rose astronomically over other corporations between 1960 and
1969. Their rise, however, came merely from shifting plants,
machinery, and other production facilities from the former owners to themselves — not from the creation of new facilities which
provide for industrial expansion, greater production, and increased employment.

The entire cost of acquired companies amounted to $15 billion
in the single year 1968. In early 1969 the momentum of corporate
acquisitions was surpassing the annual rate of $20 billion, but it
declined during the last six months.[4]

Between 1948 and 1952, the cost of acquiring other corporations was less than 3% of the total expenditure on new capital
investment. By 1968 that figure had risen to 55%.[5] Thus, U. S.
corporations were expending on the purchase of existing facilities an increasing proportion of the funds which they might
otherwise have invested in the creation of new production facilities (see Figure 1). Without that investment the economy does
not grow. And without increased production capacity, rising
consumer demand results in rising inflation.

The pretext given for the conglomeration of formerly autonomous enterprises into fewer and fewer industrial giants controlling diverse and unrelated subsidiaries is the advantage
those giants claim results from operating in myriad directions
simultaneously. The present phenomenon of consolidation
would baffle masters of earlier eras of notorious corporate concentration, such as John D. Rockefeller, Andrew Carnegie, and
J. P. Morgan. For they formed their industrial trusts and combinations each to monopolize a distinct field of industry. Standard Oil Company would scarcely have bothered to acquire 37
other companies by 1911 had those companies functioned out-

FIGURE 1

Acquired Assets[1] Compared with New Investment,[2]
in Manufacturing and Mining, 1948–1968

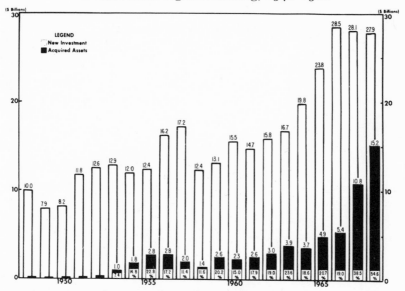

1. Acquisitions of mining and manufacturing firms with assets of $10 million or more.

2. Total new investment for plant and equipment by mining and manufacturing firms.

SOURCE: *Economic Report on Corporate Mergers*, p.41, from data of the Bureau of Economics, Federal Trade Commission.

side Standard's target industry for monopolization. The same singleness of purpose—elimination of competitors—gave rise to other monolithic combinations, such as the steel and railroad trusts. The American Tobacco Company's acquisition of its competitors was so devoid of any purpose other than the elimination of rivals that it promptly scrapped their plants, warehouses, and equipment upon purchase. Present-day acquisitors hold the assets of their acquired companies in far higher esteem.

By monopolizing an entire industry, and hence expelling competition, the dominant company can set prices and standards of performance at its whim. Legislation beginning in 1890 and culminating with the 1950 amendments to the Clayton Antitrust Act largely prevents monopolization of fields of industry by the merger of corporations engaged in similar activity. Generally,

FIGURE 2
Three Merger Movements Compared:
Manufacturing and Mining Acquisitions

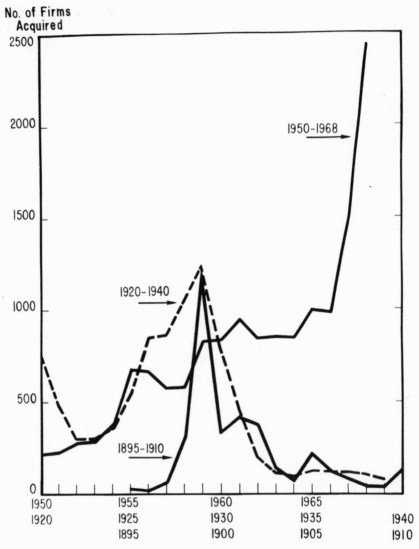

SOURCE: *Economic Report on Corporate Mergers*, p.32, from data of the Bureau of Economics, Federal Trade Commission.

only corporations functioning in unrelated activity may now merge or acquire one another.

Why the present and greatest era of industrial concentration results essentially from the conglomeration of dissimilar enterprises is, then, no mystery. The question, rather, is why the amalgamation of companies in unrelated fields occurs at all. And more specifically, whether the acclaimed rewards of diversification resulting from the acquisition of diverse corporations are the true cause. Roy Ash, former president of Litton Industries (in 1967 and 1968 the acquirer of companies at the rate of almost two a month), likened that reward to the advantage enjoyed by a fleet of diverse ocean vessels:

> I like the analogy of the aircraft carrier and the destroyers. Think of a larger, centralized company as an aircraft carrier. If a man falls overboard, you'd have to turn the whole ship around to go back after him. Litton is more like a fleet of smaller destroyers. If a man falls overboard, only one destroyer has to turn back to pick him up. The others can continue unimpeded with their mission.[6]

In 1969 and 1970, ten investigations of national scope were attempting to find explanations other than Ash's for corporate conglomeration. The Senate Antitrust and Monopoly Subcommittee, the Federal Trade Commission, the Federal Communications Commission, the Securities and Exchange Commission, the New York Stock Exchange, the House Ways and Means Committee, the Department of Justice, the Interstate Commerce Commission, the Cabinet Committee on Price Stability, and the House Antitrust Subcommittee were all conducting separate inquiries.

In 1964 conglomerate acquirers absorbed 89 major manufacturing corporations (each possessing assets of over $10 million). Together, the assets of those acquired companies amounted to $2.707 billion. The corresponding 1965 figure exceeded that amount by more than one third. The annual amount of acquired assets still rose, the 1967 figure more than doubling the increased 1966 amount. In 1968 the amount of assets of the largest corporations (each possessing assets of over $10 million) absorbed by conglomerates reached still another historic record, totaling $12.8 billion, up from $9.062 billion in 1967 (see Tables 2 and 3).

TABLE 2

Trends in Large[1] Firms Acquired Compared with Total
Large Corporations in Manufacturing and Mining, 1960–1968

	Number of large mergers		Total acquired assets		Total number of large corps.		Total assets of large corps.	
Year	Number	Index[2]	Millions	Index[2]	Number	Index[2]	Millions	Index[2]
1960	62	100	$1,708	100	2,106	100	$202,787	100
1961	55	89	2,056	120	2,100	100	210,186	104
1962	72	116	2,174	127	2,178	103	225,114	111
1963	71	115	2,956	173	2,244	107	236,656	117
1964	89	144	2,707	158	2,307	110	251,865	124
1965	90	145	3,827	224	2,396	114	273,492	135
1966	99	160	4,167	244	2,535	120	307,323	152
1967	167	269	9,062	531	2,685	127	344,235	170
1968	201	324	12,800	749	2,692	128	383,903	189

1. Firms with assets of $10 million or more.
2. Index numbers: 1960 = 100.
SOURCE: *Economic Report on Corporate Mergers*, p.669, from data of the Bureau of Economics, Federal Trade Commission.

The acquisition pace in early 1969 again exceeded previous
years' rates, spiraling toward another consecutive all-time high.
But in the second half of the year, with the advent of high interest rates and a declining stock market, the acquisition pace
likewise declined. It has not since equaled its records of the
late 1960s.

Some observers contend that the decline means that the greatest merger wave of the century has ended, and with it the threat
of undue industrial concentration. But other commentators believe that the unprecedented momentum of corporate consolidation has only receded and not subsided. According to their
reasoning, in a time of rising stock market prices and greater
corporate profitability, the trend toward industrial concentration
must resume.

Representative of the latter belief is the departing comment
by Walker B. Comegys, acting assistant attorney general of the
Antitrust Division, on July 9, 1972, his last day in office. The
first of his "two prime concerns," *The Washington Post* reported
the next day, was, "Watch for a developing merger movement
that is anti-competitive as the economy begins to pick up."
He then briefly restated the warning he had given the New York
Bar Association on January 26, 1972:

TABLE 3
Number and Total Assets of Manufacturing and
Mining Firms Acquired, 1948–1968

	No. of acquisitions	Assets ($Millions)
1948	223	156
1949	126	103
1950	219	262
1951	235	288
1952	288	452
1953	295	953
1954	387	1,782
1955	683	2,825
1956	673	2,777
1957	585	1,963
1958	589	1,435
1959	835	2,642
1960	844	2,326
1961	954	2,630
1962	853	2,990
1963	861	3,947
1964	854	3,670
1965	1,008	4,914
1966	995	5,416
1967	1,496	10,815
1968	2,442	15,200
Total	15,445	67,546

SOURCE: *Economic Report on Corporate Mergers*, p.667, from
data of the Bureau of Economics, Federal Trade Commission.

the merger wave of 1969 has substantially receded for a number
of reasons—our enforcement program, stock and money market
conditions, and the like. Nevertheless, major mergers have not
disappeared entirely: witness for example, the Wells Fargo Bank
case which we filed last week. As the economy picks up steam in
1972, it is possible that we will see a revival of major merger activity.

Two weeks later, Mr. Comegys' successor, Thomas E. Kauper,
voiced the same fear: "We are concerned that the up-turn in the
economy may spur more of these mergers that we need to worry
about."

The fact that the Antitrust Division of the Justice Department
consented (in return for certain divestitures) in 1971 to the largest merger of all time, between the eleventh largest American

industrial corporation, International Telephone & Telegraph, and the sixth largest property/liability insurance company, Hartford Fire Insurance Co., and in 1970 to the merger of the fourteenth largest industrial corporation, Ling-Temco-Vought, and the sixth largest steel producer, Jones & Laughlin — while asserting that the mergers clearly violated antitrust legislation and expressing confidence that the Supreme Court would not allow the consolidations — adds to the plausibility of the two Antitrust chiefs' concern.

The accuracy of their forecast was borne out by a report in *The Wall Street Journal* of March 30, 1973:

> NEW YORK — Executives at scores of U. S. corporations are pre-paring — and with good reason — for the possibility of a hostile takeover attempt.
>
> Many of these companies are profitable and laden with cash. The depressed levels of their stock prices have made them ripe plums. A surge in tender offers in the past six months has spot-lighted their vulnerability. Now, many of the companies are map-ping defensive proxy fights and other plans to forestall takeovers.
>
> "We've got a dozen clients operating on a day-to-day basis, wondering when they're going to get hit," says Richard B. Nye Sr., senior partner of Georgeson & Co., a large proxy-solicitation firm. "We're being called at least twice a week by someone who is thinking of making a tender offer."

The article went on to explain that "Tender offers are solicita-tions by a buyer directly to a corporation's shareholders to turn in their shares, usually for cash, in order to give control to the buying company," and concluded: "there are plenty of U. S. and foreign concerns with sufficient cash resources to pursue take-overs even if they cost more [now than in previous years]."

For perspective on that issue — recurrence of the merger spiral — this book examines three areas of the present trend of cor-porate concentration: the methods and motives for building conglomerate corporations; the function of the central, acquiring management; and the role of government agencies. Public dis-closures of national investigations are an abundant source of in-formation.

Of particular value is the *Investigation of Conglomerate Corporations,* 1969–1970, prepared by the Antitrust Subcommittee of the House Judiciary Committee. It was based on the actual internal corporate documents generated by acquisitors while they acquired. The investigation findings were issued as a report of the staff, not of the committee. Similarly, the Federal Trade Commission's *Economic Report on Corporate Mergers,* 1969, was issued as a report of the commission staff. The commission itself, created to protect the public from undue economic concentration, disclaimed the report with the introductory comment: "The Commission as a whole and the individual Commissioners neither necessarily endorse nor adopt the report or its recommendations." Especially underrated is the prescient Interstate Commerce Committee staff report which warned the commissioners more than a year in advance of the impending largest bankruptcy in history, the collapse of Penn Central.

The Federal Trade Commission staff prepared a second study, *Conglomerate Merger Performance—An Empirical Analysis of Nine Corporations,* January 3, 1973. The staff then collected performance data of 348 acquired subsidiaries. That information, however, revealing whether specific acquiring managements enhance or hinder the U. S. economy, was deleted from the publicly distributed *Analysis.* The Federal Trade Commission thus "protected conglomerate managers from their stockholders by keeping specific mistakes secret,"[7] according to one of the three staff economists. "The commission destroyed all copies of the 'hot report' by putting them through a shredding machine."[8]

But the most reticent of the conglomerate investigators is the Federal Communications Commission. Beginning in 1970 it employed a diligent staff to investigate conglomeration in the communications industry. By mid-1973, a year and a half after completion of the study, the commission had given no explanation for not having released a single word of its investigation findings. Nor has it indicated that it ever intends to. Why the public must be spared the findings, the commission does not say.

The disclosures examined should offer, in accordance with the purpose of the investigations, proof or disproof of the acquirers' claims that:

Concentration of unrelated enterprises under central ownership produces corporate strength through diversification.
Management by conglomerate headquarters is superior to the
formerly independent managements which successfully operated the acquired companies prior to merger.
Membership in the conglomerate provides acquired subsidiaries with added financial and technological resources.

Likewise, the examination should test the charges that:

1. The word "diversification" by its mere resonance stifles
common sense. Under its influence men mistake the shifting of
wealth (assets and earnings of acquired companies) for the creation of wealth (after it is added to the conglomerate total). Only
when the acquisitions cease do they see that the conglomerates'
inflated earnings reports come not from heightened performance
but from acquiring other companies' assets. Conglomerates
falsely claim success for diversification by simply adding to
their own income the earnings of acquired companies.

2. Excuses given for acquisition often are objectives which
managements could patently better accomplish without merger.
Acquisitors even promise shareholders of target companies, in
return for their consent to be bought out, payment which only
the assets they surrender can produce.

3. Many acquiring conglomerates must acquire to survive.
Shareholders of healthy corporations, nevertheless, rush to
shackle their assets to moribund corporations which exist only
from the strength of their acquired companies.

4. The more prosperous the enterprise the greater its chances
to be acquired. More than one third of the thousand largest
American manufacturing corporations of 1950 were acquired by
other companies by 1970.[9] Traditionally, less prosperous companies were the object of merger. The purpose, theoretically,
has been to transfer assets, usually of smaller companies, to a
more successful management. The current merger era shatters
that tradition. Former Assistant Attorney General of the Antitrust
Division, Professor Donald Turner, told the Senate Antitrust and
Monopoly Subcommittee that good management is a company's
best protection against being acquired.[10] As prevention against
acquisition, he thus prescribes the exact quality which drasti-

cally increases a company's chances of becoming an acquisition target.

5. Conglomerate acquirers are loath to reveal whether their acquired companies benefit from merger. Information which they are required to supply, however, indicates that the performance of acquired companies declines under conglomerate control.

6. The undisclosed declines of the acquired parts draw the acquisitor into a vicious cycle. It can show increased earnings and claim improved performance only by acquiring still more companies and adding their earnings to the total. Automatic Sprinkler, for one, was in that cycle in 1968 when the decreasing earnings of its acquisitions were insufficient to purchase more companies. Then, for the first time, it could not inflate conglomerate earnings with acquired earnings. Profits went from $1.43 to ten cents a share.[11]

7. Another device conglomerates use in claiming success for acquisition programs is a change in accounting methods. After acquiring John Morrell & Co., AMK Corporation changed Morrell's depreciation and inventory accounting and thereby reported a 74-cent-per-share profit increase although the profits of the acquired company had actually declined. Gulf & Western Industries likewise, by shifting accounting methods, showed a 1966 earnings increase of $1.6 million for New Jersey Zinc and a 1967 multimillion-dollar earnings increase for Paramount Pictures.[12] Those delusive reports exemplify the accounting gimmickry sanctioned by federal regulatory agencies and the accounting profession.

8. Conglomerate managers, masters of finance rather than of industry operations, by securing such paper profits from acquired companies inflate the market value of their conglomerate stock and thereby secure more resources for acquiring more companies.

9. Corporate acquirers resort to explanations of declining profits which absolve themselves from blame — explanations which their own internal management documents specifically refute.

10. Unable to rely on the competitive quality of their products and services, conglomerate managers acquire other companies to manipulate customers through reciprocal and tie-in sales.

Their practices do not add credibility to their public disclaimers of such anticompetitive intent.

11. The acquisition process deprives stockholders and the public generally of insight into corporate operations and performance. The Securities and Exchange Commission exempts acquired corporations from disclosure requirements upon their exchange of autonomy for conglomerate control. Ingalls Shipbuilding Corp., for one, is not required as a Litton Industries subsidiary to reveal performance data required of it when it was independent. Thus, the public did not learn of the failure of the most colossal shipbuilding contract of all time until it received the bill for Ingalls' cost overruns. A 15-volume claims "summation" to the navy is only the beginning of that bill.

12. The trend toward industrial concentration could not flourish if the regulatory agencies performed the elementary duties entrusted to them. Government administrators, however, often reject the findings of their own staffs in order to allow special dispensations to permit conglomeration. Frequently, the larger the illegal transaction the greater the chance of governmental acquiescence.

The Securities and Exchange Commission declines to answer public inquiries of which specific investment companies escape, contrary to Congress' intent, public protection requirements of the Investment Company Act (which the SEC enforces). The commission did not decline, however, to consider and approve an acquisitor's reporting to the public a spurious $2.3 million profit in the place of an actual $80 million annual loss.

Not every conglomerate engages in all the practices at which the charges are leveled. All those practices, however, stem from the condition which gives rise to the conglomeration phenomenon.

CHAPTER **2**

Mounting the Counterattack

United States Attorney General John N. Mitchell was skeptical of the purported benefits from conglomeration. He feared that communities throughout the country were losing their control of native industries purchased by conglomerates, and hence of their economic destiny. That control was being transferred, he said in 1969, away from the localities of the acquired industries to the cities of the corporate acquirers. The communities of the formerly autonomous acquired enterprises faced the risk, he explained, of becoming "'branch store' communities":

> one of the great benefits of an open marketplace is the active participation and control by as many of our citizens as possible in their own economic well-being—not just a small segment of our population in certain cities.
>
> An urban area should have a substantial influence over its local economy. Its businessmen should have an opportunity to be suppliers. Its lawyers should have an opportunity of negotiating in their own community, for their workers. And its consumers should have the opportunity to exercise local economic options in their choice of competing goods and services. . . .
>
> We do not want our middle-sized and smaller cities to be merely "branch store" communities; nor do we want our average consumers to be "second class" economic citizens.[1]

The number of corporate headquarters which acquirers removed from each state during the period 1955–1968 is indicated by the negative numbers in the far right column in Table 4. The attorney general's term "'branch store' communities" might

15

TABLE 4
Total Acquisitions[1] by Headquarters State of
Acquired and Acquiring Company, 1955–1968

State	Companies headquartered in state that were acquired			Acquisitions made by companies headquartered in state			Net gain or loss
	Total	By firms outside state	By firms within state	Total	Of firms outside state	Of firms within state	
Alabama	135	120	15	61	46	15	−74
Alaska	9	9	−	−	−	−	−9
Arizona	102	86	16	46	30	16	−56
Arkansas	56	49	7	30	23	7	−26
California	2,593	1,541	1,052	2,082	1,030	1,052	−511
Colorado	201	187	14	69	55	14	−132
Connecticut	464	392	72	382	310	72	−82
Delaware	49	45	4	112	108	4	63
Dist. of Columbia	83	67	16	103	87	16	20
Florida	477	367	110	301	191	110	−176
Georgia	284	240	44	180	136	44	−104
Hawaii	45	33	12	31	19	12	−14
Idaho	27	22	5	59	54	5	32
Illinois	1,345	910	435	1,829	1,394	435	484
Indiana	339	296	43	257	214	43	−82
Iowa	120	110	10	52	42	10	−68
Kansas	127	121	6	38	32	6	−89
Kentucky	141	126	15	169	154	15	28
Louisiana	123	107	16	48	32	16	−75
Maine	49	47	2	20	18	2	−29
Maryland	238	218	20	168	148	20	−70
Massachusetts	757	578	179	673	494	179	−84
Michigan	755	567	188	644	456	188	−111
Minnesota	249	190	59	339	280	59	90
Mississippi	62	58	4	14	10	4	−48
Missouri	361	290	71	382	311	71	21

Montana	18	18	2	2	—	−16
Nebraska	76	70	60	54	6	−16
Nevada	27	27	1	1	—	−26
New Hampshire	58	54	22	18	4	−36
New Jersey	863	727	763	627	136	−100
New Mexico	37	32	13	8	5	−24
New York	2,732	1,346	4,464	3,078	1,386	1,732
North Carolina	239	198	117	76	41	−122
North Dakota	7	7	1	1	—	−6
Ohio	1,105	788	1,225	908	317	120
Oklahoma	179	149	154	124	30	−25
Oregon	121	106	78	63	15	−43
Pennsylvania	1,103	842	1,190	929	261	87
Rhode Island	102	92	122	112	10	20
South Carolina	92	81	29	18	11	−63
South Dakota	13	13	1	1	—	−12
Tennessee	207	176	151	120	31	−56
Texas	854	552	822	520	302	−32
Utah	52	48	32	28	4	−20
Vermont	29	25	9	5	4	−20
Virginia	208	191	124	107	17	−84
Washington	152	132	74	54	20	−78
West Virginia	75	72	13	10	3	−62
Wisconsin	338	260	333	255	78	−5
Wyoming	16	16	5	5	—	−11
Total, all States	17,894	12,798	17,894	12,798	5,096	0
Regions						
Northeast	6,157	4,103	7,645	5,591	2,054	1,488
North Central	4,835	3,622	5,161	3,948	1,213	326
South	3,502	2,816	2,596	1,910	686	−906
West	3,400	2,257	2,492	1,349	1,143	−908
Total	17,894	12,798	17,894	12,798	5,096	0

1. Includes only acquisitions for which state of headquarters was known for both companies.
SOURCE: *Economic Report on Corporate Mergers*, p.697, from data of the Bureau of Economics, Federal Trade Commission.

apply, then, to the cities in Alabama, the first listing, from which
74 corporate headquarters were removed. California, the column
shows, lost the greatest number of corporate headquarters—511
—to out-of-state acquirers.

Mr. Mitchell and his chief lieutenant for antitrust enforcement, Assistant Attorney General Richard L. McLaren, expressed
"deep concern over the current merger movement" and promised to assert their statutory antitrust authority to an unprecedented extent "to meet all threats to competition" posed by the
conglomeration phenomenon.[2] To halt the merger trend is worth
the "risk of losing some cases," Mr. McLaren said. Reliance on
"merger guidelines" issued by his predecessor, which explain
the circumstances under which the Justice Department challenges a merger, could be to their detriment, he told would-be
acquirers. Those guidelines were outmoded, Mr. McLaren explained to the House Ways and Means Committee on March 12,
1969:

> I have tried to warn businessmen and their lawyers that we may
> sue even though particular mergers appear to satisfy those guide-
> lines. . . . I have also stated that I am by no means opposed to
> amendatory legislation, but I feel that the matter is too pressing
> to wait. We are willing to risk losing some cases to find out how
> far [antitrust legislation] will take us in halting the current ac-
> celerated trend toward concentration by merger and—as I see it—
> the severe economic and social dislocations attendant thereon.[3]

The broad purpose of the antitrust legislation to which he
referred is the "promotion of competition in open markets,"
i.e., "opportunity for market access and fostering of market rivalry." The economic, social, and political functions of those
laws are thus inseparable. For to deny market access is to fore-
close means of livelihood, which in turn is to thwart creativity
and independence:

> Competition is also desirable on principle and for its own sake,
> like political liberty and because political liberty is jeopardized
> if economic power drifts into relatively few hands. Antitrust also
> performs the functions of keeping governing power in the hands
> of politically responsible persons. Power to exclude someone from
> trade, to regulate prices, to determine what shall be produced, is

governing power, whether exercised by public officials or by private groups. In a democracy, such powers are entrusted only to elected representatives of the governed. . . . Antitrust opposition to overwhelming Bigness serves still another purpose. Intellectual and artistic creativeness can be imperiled by the quality of sameness imposed on us when standards of thought and form are delivered into the hands of a few businessmen. . . .[4]

Rivalry among competitors in the marketplace is a guarantor of the worth of their goods and services, and is thus a natural regulator of prices consumers pay. Enforcement of the few laws which protect competition, therefore, serves in the stead of vast artificial regulation which would be necessary without it. Referring to such artificiality on March 22, 1973, Federal Reserve Board Chairman Arthur F. Burns stated to the Senate Antitrust and Monopoly Subcommittee that "Selective controls on wages and prices for a limited period will be helpful, but they are no substitute for vigorous competition." Failure of competitive market structure leads to inflation, which leads to balance of payments crises, which in turn lead to devaluation of the dollar. Chairman Burns explained:

> Structural reforms [of the market] are also needed. Not a few of our corporations and trade unions now have the power to exact rewards that exceed what could be achieved under conditions of active competition.[5]

He recommended more stringent antitrust enforcement and thus opposed other officials who follow the advice that anti-competitive trade practices somehow correct inflation and foreign trade imbalances (see chapter 13).

Besides "maximum choice and utility for consumers," freedom of competition provides "optimum use of economic resources":

> [antitrust law] assumes that the preservation of a large number and variety of decision-making units in the economy is important to ensure innovation, experimentation and continuous adaptation to new conditions. While consumer welfare is thus in the forefront of antitrust policy, important corollary values support the policy. Not only consumers, but those who control the factors of production – labor, capital and entrepreneurial ability – benefit

when resources are permitted to move into the fields of greatest economic return, competition induces such movement . . . competition . . . minimizes the necessity for direct Government intervention in the operation of business, whether by comprehensive regulation of the public utilities type or by informal and sporadic interference such as price guidelines and other ad hoc measures.[6]

Three statutes constitute the basic antitrust law. The first, the Sherman Act of 1890 (26 Stat.209), outlaws "every . . . combination" or trust which inhibits market access and thus restrains commerce. Proscribed are attempts to monopolize "any part" of interstate trade. "As a charter of freedom," Chief Justice Hughes wrote in 1933 (*Appalachian Coals, Inc.* v. *United States,* 288 U. S. 344):

> The act has a generality and adaptability comparable to that found to be desirable in constitutional provisions. It does not go into detailed definitions which might either work injury to legitimate enterprise or through particularization defeat its purposes by providing loopholes for escape.

The Supreme Court did not use the full force of the Sherman Act to prevent concentrated control of industry. Rather than outlawing "every . . . combination" which restrains trade—the act's stated purpose—the Court enunciated in the Standard Oil decision of 1911 (221 U. S. 1) the controversial "Rule of Reason," whereby it allowed the existence of an industrial combination if the resulting restraint of trade was "reasonable." Representative of the dissension over the Court's leniency was Justice Harlan's separate opinion to the decision:

> Congress . . . said that there should be *no* restraint of trade, *in any form,* and this court solemnly adjudged many years ago that Congress meant what it thus said in clear and explicit words of an act. But . . . now . . . the Courts will allow such restraints of interstate commerce as are shown not to be unreasonable or undue.

The "Rule of Reason," legislators said, was a usurpation of congressional power. In the words of the Senate Committee on Interstate Commerce, "It is inconceivable that in a country governed by a written Constitution and statute law the courts can be permitted to test each restraint of trade by the economic standard which the individual members of the court may happen to approve."[7]

By the time of the presidential election of 1912 the issue was clear-cut. The New Nationism platform headed by Theodore Roosevelt held that continued corporate concentration was a fact of life and that American industry could be controlled not by competition among its units but only by the imposition of extensive government regulations. Woodrow Wilson's New Freedom policy rejected that concept of an industrialized system composed of regulated trusts and combinations. Wilson proposed to combat the trend of giant corporate consolidations by stricter enforcement and expansion of antitrust laws. He explained his opposition to concentrated corporate control:

> No country can afford to have its prosperity originated by a small controlling class. The treasury of America does not lie in the brains of the small body of men now in control of the great enterprises. . . . It depends upon the inventions of unknown men, upon the originations of unknown men, upon the ambitions of unknown men. Every country is renewed out of the ranks of the unknown, not out of the ranks of the already famous and powerful in control.[8]

The policy of opposition to crystallization of U. S. industry into larger and larger trusts and combinations at least ostensibly won out. Acting on the assumption that true competition in the marketplace affords better protection to consumers than any elaborate system of government regulations, Congress enacted the other two basic antitrust statutes to prevent restraint of trade.

The Federal Trade Commission Act (38 Stat. 717) protects competition by prohibiting practices which result in unfair trade advantages. The "unfair methods of competition" it renders unlawful may be monopolistic practices and restraints of trade proscribed by the Sherman Act. The act reaches threats to competition which are only incipient, as well as fully developed violations of the Sherman Act.

While the Federal Trade Commission Act is concerned with competitive behavior, a primary function of the Clayton Act (38 Stat. 730) is to protect competition by protecting market structure. The act prohibits specific transactions such as price discrimination, exclusive arrangements, tie-in sales contracts, and corporate acquisitions if the "effect may be substantially to lessen competition or tend to create a monopoly."

However, narrow judicial decisions again restricted the effect of antitrust legislation. The courts "frustrated . . . Congressional design and, as a result . . . (the Clayton Act) fell short of its intended purpose to stop in its incipiency undue concentration of economic power or monopoly."[9] Soon after World War II a new trend of corporate concentration arose which the restrained application of the Clayton Act failed to contain. Corporations engaged in the same industries were combining (by merger or acquisition) with one another at an accelerating rate. Competition suffered because fewer independent rivals were left in the marketplace to compete against one another. Similarly, the rate of mergers between suppliers and their customers was increasing. Many corporations, consequently, were acquiring captive customers whose patronage they secured not because they produced the better product but because they controlled those customers. Thus, sales to the growing number of acquired corporations were lost to former suppliers regardless of the competitive quality of their product.

Between 1948 and 1951, 62% of all corporate combinations involved such anticompetitive market restructuring.[10] Industrial concentration was at one of its highest levels, the House of Representatives reported in 1949, as it amended the Clayton Act "to prevent those acquisitions which substantially lessen competition or tend to create a monopoly. . . ."[11] Congress thus acted "to restrain trends of concentration in their incipiency and well before they have attained such proportions as would justify a Sherman Act proceeding."[12] That legislation, the Celler-Kefauver Amendment of 1950, generally prohibits mergers of competing corporations (horizontal—such as of two companies which both produce cement, or of two car rental agencies) and mergers of suppliers with their customers (vertical—such as of an automobile manufacturer and a paint supplier).

The amendment was demonstrably effective in protecting the competitive quality of the market structure against vertical and horizontal mergers of product-related companies. Combinations of corporations engaged in the same industry amounted to 48% of all mergers between 1952 and 1959. The ratio steadily fell, amounting to 22% between 1964 and 1967. In 1968, mergers of industrially related corporations amounted to only 9% of total mergers.[13]

The current of corporate concentration, however, had only changed courses. Because the Celler-Kefauver Amendment blocked the channel of combinations of enterprises operating in the same industry, the current merely shifted and overflowed with even greater velocity into the channel of mergers of corporations in unrelated industries, i.e., conglomerate mergers. As Assistant Attorney General McLaren explained in 1969, "Merger activity . . . has been redirected, not reduced."[14]

That industrial concentration had not abated during the two decades since the 1950 amendment to the Clayton Act was an understatement. The number of corporate mergers (or acquisitions) increased from 295 in 1953, to 844 in 1960, to 1,008 in 1965. Three years later the number of mergers annually had more than doubled, amounting to 2,442 in 1968. Assets acquired from other companies amounted to $953 million in 1953, $2,326 million in 1960, and $4,914 million in 1965. In three years that annual figure more than tripled, amounting to $15,200 million in 1968.[15]

The current wave of concentration threatens such restructuring of industry, Attorney General John N. Mitchell told the Georgia Bar Association in June 1969, that the "future vitality of our free economy may be in danger." He warned:

> The danger that this super-concentration poses to our economic, political and social structure cannot be overestimated. Concentration of this magnitude is likely to eliminate existing and potential competition. It increases the possibility for reciprocity and other forms of unfair buyer-seller leverage. It creates nation-wide marketing, managerial and financial structures whose enormous physical and psychological resources pose substantial barriers to smaller firms wishing to participate in a competitive market.
>
> And finally, super-concentration creates a "community of interest" which discourages competition among large firms and establishes a tone in the marketplace for more and more mergers.[16]

Continued concentration of the nation's industrial assets "in the hands of fewer and fewer people," Mr. Mitchell explained, is the exact "evil" which the Sherman Act, the Clayton Act, and the Celler-Kefauver Amendment sought to eliminate.

However, the conglomeration phenomenon of which he spoke, as seen, does not involve the merger of competitors. For that reason, application of the antitrust laws to the phenomenon had not been proven, as that application had been to earlier eras of industrial combination. Although the rise of conglomerates transfers greater and greater assets to fewer and fewer corporate holders, such transfer does not, according to most statistics, result in monopolization of fields of industry. A conglomerate is a jack of many trades but usually a monopolizer of none.

Nevertheless, Attorney General Mitchell declared, the Department of Justice would invoke the present antitrust laws, namely the Sherman Act and the amended Clayton Act, to restrain conglomerate mergers. He cited the Procter & Gamble decision of 1967 (386 U. S. 568) as authority that the government, in order to protect a market structure amenable and conducive to competition, need not prove specific anticompetitive behavior. The Supreme Court decided then:

> The Clayton Act was intended to arrest anti-competitive effects in their incipiency. The core question is whether a merger may substantially lessen competition, and necessarily requires a prediction of the merger's impact on competition, present and future . . . [Section 7 of Clayton Act] can deal only with probabilities, not certainties . . . and there is certainly no requirement that the anti-competitive power manifest itself in anti-competitive action before Section 7 can be called into play. If enforcement of Section 7 turned on the existence of actual anti-competitive practices, the congressional policy of thwarting such practices in their incipiency would be frustrated.

He then updated the merger guidelines (which Assistant Attorney General McLaren had said a few weeks earlier were outmoded) and warned that the Department of Justice "will probably oppose any merger by one of the top 200 manufacturing firms of any leading producer in any concentrated industry."[17]

A primary threat posed by conglomerate mergers to competitive market structure, as the attorney general and his Antitrust chief explained, is reciprocal dealing. By that system, one corporation patronizes another in return for its patronage. A bank, for example, indulging in reciprocal practices, awards its contract for building construction to the concern which happens to be its biggest customer among the bidding contractors. Reciprocity of patronage thus renders futile any competition among the bidders.

If a supplier of goods has no occasion to purchase from one of its customers, of course no possibility of reciprocal sales between the two concerns exists. Reciprocity should not be expected to occur, therefore, between a newspaper publisher and its supplier of pulp wood because, presumably, the latter spends not much more than ten cents a day on newspapers. Likewise, reciprocal sales should not be expected to arise between a specialty food processor and a cattle ranch from which the processor purchases beef, if the rancher has no need of the specialized processed food and never buys it from anyone. But if the pulp wood producer acquires the food processor, and the newspaper and cattle ranch likewise come under common management, the pulp producer can secure or augment its sales to the newspaper by threatening to curtail its purchases of beef for the food processor subsidiary unless the publisher-rancher syndicate reciprocally purchases the pulp wood. Thus, a combination of companies in unrelated industries gives rise to reciprocity from contexts in which such practices would be impossible but for the combination. The example is not hypothetical. The pulp wood producer is Rayonier Corporation, and the food producer is the nation's largest baker, Continental Baking, both owned by International Telephone & Telegraph (see chapter 7).

Through reciprocity a producer secures sales by the force of his purchasing power, not by improving his product or by lowering his prices to meet competition. Thus, widespread reciprocity might well necessitate government controls for the protection of consumers, for rivalry in the marketplace would cease to function as a natural insurer of quality and regulator of price. As the attorney general warned, if the conglomeration of industries continues, "we may soon be in a position where demands for more government regulation could be called for."[18]

The phenomenon of conglomerate acquisitions poses a second threat to market structure (as distinguished from outright anticompetitive behavior) because it can curtail future rivalry by reducing the number of entrants into an industry. Many corporations which enter new fields of industry by purchasing enterprises already functioning would otherwise enter by establishing new operations—and thus add to the number of competitors in those industries. As an illustration of how even the possibility of new competition in a market benefits consumers, the attorney general cited the natural gas industry. A certain retailer of gas theretofore unrivaled easily and quickly lowered prices 25% on the mere expectation that a competitor was about to enter his market area. "Elimination of potential competition," Mr. Mitchell said, "tends to maintain the inflated price structure in the concentrated industry."

A third broad effect of concentration on competitive quality of market structure is denominated "community of interest." As more and more formerly independent corporations fall under the control of acquiring managements the greater is the possibility of gentlemen's agreements among those managements to forebear from competition. *Studies by the Staff of the Cabinet Committee on Price Stability* of January 1969 (p.83) observed that as more diversifying corporations encounter one another in more industries the chances increase that competitive aggressiveness in one field will encounter retaliation in another:

> [Loss of independence by acquired corporations] create[s] the probability that a community of interest will develop among the leading actual or potential competitors in many industries. There is also a danger that industries once standing as separate arenas of competition will have their competitive zeal diluted as conglomerate firms operating across many industries meet the rivals in many markets.
>
> If they engage in aggressive acts in particular markets they may anticipate retaliatory measures elsewhere. . . .

Attorney General Mitchell envisioned "community of interest" as follows:

> if the food subsidiary of corporation A aggressively competes with the food subsidiary of corporation B, then the electrical subsidiary of corporation B may start a price war with the electrical subsidiary of corporation A. Thus, it may be in both A's and B's

interest to maintain the status quo and not to engage in the type of aggressive competition which we expect in a free marketplace.[19]

A DuPont official once explained his company's conciliation and forebearance toward Imperial Chemical Industries of Great Britain. The companies encountered each other in more than one field of industry. The official wrote:

> It is not good business sense to attempt an expansion in certain directions if such an act is bound to result as a boomerang of retaliations. It has been the DuPont's policy to follow such lines of common sense procedure. . . :
>
>> This was done on the broad theory that cooperation is wiser than antagonism and that in the matter of detail the chances in the long run were that the boot was just as likely to be on the one leg as on the other.[20]

Obviously then, the matter of "community of interests" is as well explained by "common sense procedure" as by economic theory.

True to the words of its two spokesmen, the Department of Justice filed five suits to prevent exactly the anticompetitive effects of which Mr. Mitchell and Mr. McLaren warned. The suits were based not primarily on the conventional antitrust conception of monopolistic dangers arising from combination of enterprises engaged in the same industry, but rather on the more untried theories of the dangers of reciprocal practices which Mr. Mitchell had fully described earlier in the year. The complaint of August 1969, initiating the suit to prevent the merger of International Telephone & Telegraph Company and Hartford Fire Insurance Co., restates those very warnings. The merger would violate the Clayton Act and lessen competition, the complaint charged, because ITT and Hartford could reciprocally trade with each other and thus "narrow" the markets of their competitors. From such a giant merger a chain reaction of similar consolidation could result as those competitors in turn sought defensively to secure like advantage through merger:

(a) The power of ITT and Hartford to employ reciprocity and benefit from reciprocity effect in the sale of insurance will be

substantially increased and the markets for Hartford's competitors will be correspondingly narrowed;

(b) Actual and potential competitors of Hartford may be foreclosed from competing for the insurance purchases of ITT
and its subsidiaries;

(c) Actual and potential independent competition by ITT and
Hartford may be eliminated or diminished in numerous
markets;

(d) The competitive advantages which will accrue to the defendants, which are leading firms in several industries, as a
result of this merger will raise barriers to entry and discourage
smaller firms from competing in these industries;

(e) This merger will tend to trigger other mergers by companies
seeking to protect themselves from the impact of this acquisition or to obtain similar competitive advantages. . . .[21]

ITT's acquisition of Hartford could not have been designed to
fit more squarely into the guidelines for Justice Department antitrust action enunciated by Mr. Mitchell to the Georgia Bar Association two months earlier. First, the combination was between two of the 200 largest U. S. corporations. ITT, with assets
of over $4 billion, was the 11th largest industrial concern in the
United States; Hartford, with assets of $1.89 billion, ranked as
the 170th largest corporation.

Secondly, the acquisition was by one of the "top 200 manufacturing firms of . . . a leading producer in a concentrated industry." Hartford Fire Insurance Co., the complaint stated,
ranked "sixth among the Nation's property and liability insurance companies. . . ."

Assistant Attorney General McLaren, referring to the ITT-
Hartford suit, expressed confidence to the House Judiciary Committee on May 13, 1970 that those guidelines were a correct
interpretation of the laws and that the courts would not permit
their transgression:

> I think that the present act is a very flexible instrument, and I
> think that were there discernible, actual or potential anticompeti-
> tive effects resulting from two of the top 200 merging that we
> could proceed against that. And I would be very confident that
> we would prevail.[22]

The Justice Department filed four other suits through which
it expected to restrain the conglomerate acquisition process by

securing court rulings that antitrust laws apply not only to mergers between competitors (or between customers and suppliers)
but also to anticompetitive mergers of corporations not engaged
in the same industry. Those suits challenged the acquisitions by:

> Ling-Temco-Vought, Inc., of Jones and Laughlin Steel Corp.
> (complaint filed in April 1969);
> ITT of Canteen Corp., a food supplier and operator of vend-
> ing machines (complaint filed in April 1969);
> Northwest Industries of B. F. Goodrich Co. (complaint filed
> in May 1969); and
> ITT of Grinnell Corp., a manufacturer of fire protection
> equipment (complaint filed in August 1969).

The Justice Department had prepared a sixth suit to challenge
the combination of Chubb Corporation and First National City
Bank of New York. The would-be defendants, however, abandoned the merger upon learning of the impending litigation. The
anticompetitive effects from such a merger, had it succeeded,
Mr. McLaren stated, would have caused other banks to join in
similar combinations to gain the same advantage. Allowance of
one instance of industrial combinations, he explained, would
thus have resulted in a chain reaction of mergers:

> We were told after we announced to counsel that we were going
> to proceed against the Chubb-National City Bank merger, and
> they dropped it, . . . that many of the banks and insurance com-
> panies had dancing partners picked out and that had we not pro-
> ceeded against that particular merger, there undoubtedly would
> have been a regular group of mergers of this type.
>
>   So I think this is something that the legislation contemplates,
> that the Supreme Court has talked about. It is in the legislative
> history. If we are intervening in a merger trend that is going to
> trigger further mergers that is ultimately going to result in further
> economic concentration, I think the present law reaches that.[23]

So confident was the assistant attorney general that his challenges of acquisitions would prevail in the courts, that he did
not counsel Congress to enact new legislation to restrain conglomerate mergers. So strong was the government's case in those
five suits, Mr. McLaren informed the House Judiciary Committee, that the judicial precedent resulting from their adjudication

alone should prove that the Clayton Act without new amendment by Congress was adequate to stem the current trend of industrial concentration. He stated:

> I am inclined to defer recommending any new legislation at the present time. . . . We will of course continue our own enforce-ment efforts, and I am fully confident that we will be sustained by the courts.

Judicial interpretation of the Clayton Act, he continued, already supported the Justice Department's challenge of the mergers for their effect on market structure:

> our complaints, in every one of these cases, were based not only upon the clear legislative history of the Celler-Kefauver Amend-ment [to the Clayton Act] but upon well-established rules which had been announced by the Supreme Court in a series of cases in the last few years. Thus, our complaints in these five cases dealt with such matters as the elimination of potential competition; the creation of power to engage in systematic reciprocity on a large scale; the entrenchment of leading firms in concentrated mar-kets; and the contribution to, and proliferation of, a merger trend.[24]

Chairman Celler of the House Judiciary Committee asked whether, nevertheless, the present antitrust laws should be strengthened by legislation:

> very likely the success of the Celler-Kefauver Act, which pre-vented horizontal and vertical mergers because of reduction of competition, has probably encouraged conglomerates, where there isn't apparent competition between the acquirer and the acquired corporation. Do you think that some legislation . . . is still needed so that if a . . . conglomerate acquired a corporation that sells or manufactures an unrelated product, unrelated to the product made by the parent company . . . that there must be some sort of restraint imposed by law? Or do you feel the Celler-Kefauver Act is sufficient?
> Mr. McLAREN. I still think the Act is sufficient. I think that the present law is adequate to reach the major kinds of conglomerate mergers that we have proceeded against.[25]

The Judiciary Committee chairman congratulated Mr. McLaren for his vigorous assertion of Congress' design. An as-sumption that all forces were united behind the Antitrust Division chief's singleness of purpose of restraining industrial concentration, however, could be bound for disappointment. One particular indication that the government's traditional hesitancy over antitrust enforcement still persisted and that Mr. McLaren's course might not be completely free and open, was the Report of the Task Force on Productivity and Competition.

Prepared in late 1968, the document commonly known as the Stigler Report, advised the president of the United States to follow that same course recommended by Assistant Attorney General McLaren, except to move in reverse instead of forward: "substantial retrenchment . . . in the antitrust field is highly desirable," it observed.[26] Evidently, the report considered the Celler-Kefauver Amendment—which, as seen, generally proscribes merger of enterprises engaged in the same industry so as to prevent monopolies—a mistake. For the Federal Trade Commission study of 1948 on which the legislation was based and which indicated that the rate of industrial concentration was spiraling upward, the report stated, was "incompetent."[27]

Strict enforcement of consumer-protection laws generally, even of the Pure Food and Drug Act, was outside the Stigler Task Force's favor. The report concluded that such legislation can induce character flaws in consumers: "Overzealous enforcement of consumer-protection legislation can also have errant results . . . elaborate requirements relating to packaging, safety, etc. . . . can reduce the consumer's incentive to exercise care and—what is more serious—impose substantial costs on society."[28]

The merger guidelines announced by the attorney general in June 1969 (indicating that the Justice Department would challenge the merger of one of the 200 largest industrial corporations with a leading enterprise of another industry) should have appalled the Task Force. The much more lax guidelines of late 1968 it described as "embarrassing," "extraordinarily stringent," and "indefensible:"

> The Department of Justice Merger Guidelines are extraordinarily stringent and in some aspects indefensible. . . . [They are] so loose and . unprofessional as to be positively embarrassing.[29]

The Stigler Report found that consolidations of customers with suppliers, i.e., vertical combinations within the same industry (such as hypothetically, between General Motors and DuPont), which the legislation of 1950 seeks to prevent, pose no threat to competition and even help to combat monopolies:

> On the contrary, this form of [vertical] integration whether by merger or various forms of contractual arrangements, can and does enable the integrating firm to bypass or erode monopoly elsewhere, and equally important in achieving antitrust goals, to attain efficiencies in production and distribution.[30]

Not surprisingly, then, the report found no danger to competition from the possibility of reciprocal trading by conglomerates. A single sentence dismissed the idea:

> If this practice [reciprocity] leads to efficiency there is no reason to stop it; if it leads to inefficiency there is no reason why the conglomerate should adopt it (since it would reduce its overall profits).[31]

The nation's greatest wave of industrial concentration the Stigler Task Force took in its stride, cautioning against finding a "threat of sheer bigness to political or economic life." An anti-competitive conglomerate is a contradiction of terms, the report concluded: "Almost by definition such a firm poses at most a minor threat to competition."[32]

Rather than by enforcement of antitrust legislation, the Stigler Report recommended that competition be inspired by the words of the president of the United States urging that the nation be more competitive. The preferable form for such an exhortation, it advised, would be a nationwide address:

> We believe therefore, that the President should issue a general policy statement on competition and public regulation, to achieve at least three important purposes:
>
> . . .
>
> 3. To revive and strengthen public support for the policy of competition, and to establish the bonafides of the Administration as the protector of *both* consumer and businessman. . . . a major presidential address would be an appropriate vehicle for this declaration.[33]

The president's plea would be adequate to restrain the present era of economic concentration, the report assumed, while that era enjoyed yet another period of retrenchment of antitrust enforcement.

Industrial concentration was at an emergency level which did not permit the Justice Department to wait on the enactment of new laws. Thus, the government would proceed to halt the merger movement by implementing long-standing legislation which it deemed to be fully adequate, the Antitrust chief assured the committee on May 13, 1970.

As the members and the department witnesses filed from the hearing room that afternoon upon such optimistic assurance, the once irrepressible forces which the Stigler Report represented by all appearances lay prostrate at their feet. The staunchest adversaries of the department's aggressive antitrust action admitted its success.

That the Stigler Report philosophy not only would again raise its head but would in time prevail as never before was then the greatest possible absurdity. Hardly envisioned was the Justice Department's acceptance less than a year later of the argument that attainment of sufficiently gigantic size should exempt a corporate acquisitor from the laws of the United States.

PART II

How to Build a Conglomerate Corporation

Conglomerate corporations reputedly often pay debt securities, such as bonds, debentures with warrants, and, to a certain extent, preferred shares, for the companies they purchase. Such payment is derisively called "funny money" or "Chinese money" because it does not represent ownership in the acquiring company. The stockholders of the "target," i.e., the to-be-acquired company, surrender their outright ownership, usually represented by common stock, and receive in return, according to common conception, only evidence of the acquirer's indebtedness. In fact, however, conglomerates often pay generously in cash or equity securities for target company shares.

Four acquisitions illustrate not only such equitable methods of purchase but also methods which leave intact or even fill rather than deplenish the acquisitor's coffers. The first method is for the conglomerate to convince some bankers that its acquisition program for corporate concentration can benefit them. Show the bank what you can do for it and you will be surprised at what the bank can do for you. The conglomerate will transfer to the bank all the banking business of its to-be-acquired subsidiaries. Further, the acquisition program will enable the bank to secure millions of dollars of quick profits from various forms of stock market manipulation.

The underwriting of conglomeration will be so profitable to the bank that it will then conceive the idea of starting another acquisition program with another diversifying company. The bank will, for example, exchange large blocks of Pan American common stock held in its trust department for debt securities of a gambling casino to enable the casino to take over Pan American Airways.[1]

The conglomerate should not feel that it must choose a bank that conspicuously needs more business. Rather, it should choose from the biggest. It should choose a bank run by David Rockefeller.

Another method is for the acquiring conglomerate to pay the owners of the target company in cash and then transfer the debt from that cash outlay to the same company upon taking control. To take control, the acquirer need not go to the expense of buying all the stock; it needs only half of it. The owners of the other half may be startled by the sudden multimillion-dollar indebtedness. They may say that the debt has not increased the captive company's assets one cent but will diminish its earnings for the next quarter-century. If so, the conglomerate need only ask them why they did not sell out in time as did the other stockholders. Better, it will tell them in the annual report that the indebtedness is part of "new, imaginative debt structure."

A third method is to secure, perhaps with debt securities, a company rich in liquid reserves and use those reserves to purchase a second company. That way, without giving up any of its own capital, the conglomerate can make a $400 million purchase and afterward have $173 million more in liquid assets than it had before. It can then use those assets to purchase a second corporation from stockholders who insist on cash. In the end, the conglomerate will have spent none of its own capital and will have two new corporations and millions more in the bank than before.

The quickest acquisition method of all is to accept a call from the Pentagon some day, informing one that the army, by granting contract price increases, has in effect delivered an acquisition to the conglomerate.

CHAPTER 3

Make Friends with a Bank

Of those four methods, Gulf & Western Industries chose to convince a bank that profits were to be derived from helping conglomerates grow. On September 10, 1965, Chase Manhattan Bank of New York loaned Gulf & Western $84 million without security, solely for the purpose of acquiring New Jersey Zinc Co. New Jersey Zinc was Gulf & Western's first major acquisition outside the automobile-parts field. Its assets of $135 million exceeded Gulf & Western's assets by over $30 million. The profits of the acquired company more than doubled the profits of the acquirer.

Charles G. Bluhdorn, the founder and chief executive officer of Gulf & Western, came to the United States in 1943 at the age of 16, a refugee from Nazi-occupied Austria. By 1956 he had amassed a fortune from speculation over the price of coffee.

> Charles Bluhdorn, brash, excitable, and full of fire, is as he has always been, the dominant figure. The memories of his early hair-raising capers in the commodity market, which made him a millionaire in his mid-twenties, still live with him. . . .
>
> An outsider confronted with Bluhdorn for the first time has no difficulty imagining him as the *enfant terrible* of the commodity exchange. He delights in the scale of his dealings. His manner changes swiftly from persuasive explanation to table-thumping assertion, all enunciated in mile-a-minute Viennese-American. His single-mindedness about the rightness and logic of his mission in the business world can display itself in rudeness and irascibility as well as in sudden charm. And yet in many of his associates, including the heads of some of the companies that at first resisted Gulf & Western's advances, he inspires an admiration that borders on

love. Says Lindsay Johnson, president of New Jersey Zinc, which Gulf & Western acquired in 1966: "The more you are around Bluhdorn, the closer the moon is."[1]

In 1957 Bluhdorn purchased the Michigan Plating & Stamping Company. The small auto-parts manufacturer was the nucleus from which Gulf & Western Industries evolved. Exactly according to the original plan, the parts manufacturer served as the basis for acquiring other corporations.

At that time the Grand Rapids firm — Michigan Plating & Stamp- ing Company — had two hundred employees, one aging plant, $6.5 million in annual sales, a listing on the American Stock Ex- change — and, it turned out, more problems than its new young managers had realized. For a moment they had second thoughts and decided to dispose of the company and look for a better base on which to build. But as Charles G. Bluhdorn, chairman of the board of Gulf & Western, later recalled, "we couldn't sell that little bumper company, not even for $500,000 payable over five years, so we decided we had better get down to work."[2]

Fortune of March 1968 (p.125) states: "Two shrewd young financial officers have more recently signed on at Gulf & West- ern: Executive Vice President Don F. Gaston . . . and Roy T. Abbott, Jr., thirty-seven, who was a Vice President of Chase Manhattan Bank." A few months after Chase Manhattan Bank granted Gulf & Western the unsecured $84 million loan essen- tial to its acquisition process, Roy Abbott, the bank official who negotiated the transaction, became Gulf & Western's senior vice president. The "shrewd" former Chase Manhattan official could then oversee Gulf & Western's performance of its return favors to the bank for making conglomeration possible. He could also oversee securing from the bank more favors of the original kind. Gulf & Western's return favors, as will be seen and as Chase Manhattan admitted, were:

1. To enable the bank to acquire the business of competitor banks which choose not to use depositors' funds similarly for building conglomerates and accelerating the trend of concen- tration of American industry.

2. To enable the bank to profit from stock market manipula- tion. Gulf & Western secretly informed it of which stocks were

certain to rise in value as the result of Gulf & Western's take-over attempts. The bank itself financed those attempts, both real and feigned, resulting in artificial rises in the stock prices of the target companies.

The National Bank Act prohibits banks from acquiring control of other corporations.[3] The reason for the prohibition is to prevent those very favors which Chase Manhattan secured from its partnership with Gulf & Western. First, a bank could acquire its competitors' business from corporate customers sheerly by gaining control of those corporations with its depositors' money. Second, a bank could cause predictable fluctuations in market prices of companies it acquires or merely attempts to acquire.

Internal correspondence of Chase Manhattan and Gulf & Western (mainly involving the bank loan officer turned conglomerate vice president) shows that the two entities virtually formed a trust for the purpose, contrary to the law's intent, of securing unfair competitive and investment advantages through outright control of industrial enterprises. Through cooperation with Gulf & Western, Chase Manhattan Bank built a conglomerate as it could not have by itself.

1

Practically every trust created has destroyed the financial independence of some communities and of many properties; for it has centered the financing of a large part of whole lines of business in New York, and this usually with one of a few banking houses.

Louis. D. Brandeis, 1913[4]

Local banks must not be used. . . .

Gulf & Western *Executive Policy Manual*, 1967[5]

In February 1967 officers of Chase Manhattan Bank wrote about a luncheon conversation with Charles Bluhdorn, chief executive officer and chairman of the board of Gulf & Western Industries. He promised, they stated, that the bank would receive its due reward over its competitors throughout the country for having made the New Jersey Zinc acquisition possible:

Bluhdorn said that he and the Company had not forgotten that Chase's imaginative lending had put them into business with New Jersey Zinc. He said that some day Gulf & Western will be a billion dollar company, and that Chase will figure prominently in their banking position.[6]

"This is a red letter day," bank officer Roy Abbott wrote on negotiating an early acquisition loan.[7] He advised other officers on January 28, 1964: "We are right on the threshold of a big breakthrough. . . . Keep an eagle eye peeled for Mr. Bluhdorn." The loan officer continued: "I hope you will be on the lookout for him and roll out the red carpet when he arrives."[8]

From an appreciative bank president went a letter to an appreciative customer:[9]

FEBRUARY 3, 1964.

Mr. CHARLES BLUHDORN,
  Chairman of the Board, Gulf & Western Industries, Inc., Time & Life Building, Rockefeller Center, New York, N. Y.
DEAR MR. BLUHDORN: Tom Smith and Roy Abbott have told me the good news that Gulf & Western Industries became a customer of ours last Friday. This is wonderful news indeed because we have long hoped that we would have this additional relationship with John Duncan and yourself.
  I understand that you will be coming down for lunch soon. I hope I have the pleasure of seeing you then.
    Sincerely,

DAVID ROCKEFELLER.

"Charlie, I'm sure we can make this very attractive to you," Abbott wrote to Bluhdorn in reference to further acquisition financing. "I . . . would appreciate it if you could keep our friends in Newark out of the oil for the time being."[10] That meant to hold off taking out loans with Chase Manhattan's competitor Prudential Life Insurance Company.

The managers of Gulf & Western's acquired subsidiaries were not always cooperative. They had to be prodded to transfer their accounts to Chase Manhattan, as the bargain for the $84 million uncollateralized loan stipulated. Chase Manhattan complained of "malingerers," which curiously is a synonym for uncooperative subsidiaries. Gulf & Western drew up instructions to its

managers: "You are requested to see that the system is per-
petuated each month so that our good friends at the Chase will
not be constantly calling some malingerer to our attention."[11]
To the distant subsidiaries went the explicit directive: "It is in
our mutual interest for you to deposit your monthly withholding
taxes with the Chase Manhattan Bank . . . rather than using local
banks. It is considered as part of our required compensating
balance."[12]

The Bank of the Southwest, in Houston, "put up quite a howl"
when Gulf & Western transferred its accounts to Chase Manhattan. But since the Texas bank happened not to grant the conglomerate unsecured acquisition loans, it had little bargaining
power with which to retain that business. As a Chase Manhattan
officer wrote:

> Roy Abbott [while Chase Manhattan loan officer] was told today
> by Gulf & Western that everything still pointed to Chase Man-
> hattan as the prospective trustee for Gulf & Western's pension
> arrangements. However, . . . the Bank of the Southwest has put
> up quite a howl about the company's decision to give this business
> to us. The company has told the Bank of the Southwest that Chase
> Manhattan would be well-known to all of their scattered sub-
> sidiaries as a leader in this field whereas the Bank of the South-
> west would be completely unknown to them.[13]

That a factor other than familiarity with a bank's name entered
into the decision was not elaborated.

Abbott was attentive to Chase Manhattan's interests even after
his departure to Gulf & Western headquarters. Shortly before the
conglomerate's purchase of South Puerto Rico Sugar Co. in
March 1967, a Chase Manhattan official wrote:

> In response to the branch's interest, I contacted Roy T. Abbott,
> Jr., of the subject's proposed parent, Gulf & Western. Roy stated
> that as soon as the merger is finalized he will have the accounts
> moved to our Puerto Rico branch. In the meantime, he does not
> want to make any waves until they [P. R. Sugar] are in the fold
> [acquired].[14]

Chase Manhattan was only acquiring more business as Gulf
& Western was acquiring more companies — to acquire business
by fomenting the process of industrial concentration is only

natural, the bank explained. To rely "continually" on loans to generate more business "is true of any banking relation," the bank spokesmen told the House Antitrust Subcommittee in August 1969:

> Mr. HARKINS [Subcommittee counsel]. Did not Chase expect that its loan to Gulf & Western for the purchase of stock in New Jersey Zinc would result in a substantial increase in Chase's business?
> Mr. YOUNG [Chase Manhattan Bank vice president]. I think this is true of any banking relation. Every relationship we have we continually try to develop. When we make loans, this is improving our relationship and often with the improvement of relationship in the loan area there are also improvements in other parts of the relationship, too.[15]

Unanswered is whether Chase Manhattan turns down applications for loans unlikely to generate new business. Also unanswered is how a bank retains business, if it declines to make loans for industrial consolidation, against competitors who do.

2

> We are proud of our record as competitors in the American economic system. We believe that vigorous competition is essential for the preservation of that system. And the promotion of competition is what Gulf & Western Industries is about.
>
> David N. Judelson, President,
> Gulf & Western Industries, Inc.[16]

To acquire the business of Chase Manhattan's competitors at a faster rate, Roy Abbott (while at the bank) recommended acquisitions to Bluhdorn from confidential information obtained by the bank in its fiduciary capacities. An acquiring conglomerate's power to force suppliers of a target company to purchase from the conglomerate subsidiaries was a major recommendation calculation. The scheme, as seen, is called "reciprocity."

By that system, suppliers which sell goods to the target company are forced to reciprocate — i.e., to purchase their goods from the conglomerate—or else lose their conglomerate-acquired customer. Because reciprocal sales are not wrought by the competitive quality of the product, the scheme subverts freedom of enterprise and competition.

One recommended acquisition based on reciprocity calculations was the Chicago Railroad Equipment Co. With the fiduciary correspondence in hand, Abbott wrote Bluhdorn: "Having in mind your reciprocity with the automobile industry and, potentially, the railroads and also some overlap into the trucking industry, I thought you might be interested in seeing some information on the Chicago Railroad Equipment Division of AMK."[17] Subsequent recommendations also hinged on reciprocity. He did not mean that word in its literal sense, Abbott explained later: "It was a casual letter."[18]

Whether Gulf & Western's statement of policy against reciprocity is also "casual" he did not say. It provides:

> Reciprocity is that practice whereby one company seeks to obtain sales of its products by agreeing to buy from a supplier provided that the supplier in turn agrees to buy from it. Reciprocity embraces every form of agreement or arrangement to that end, whether expressed or implied, direct or indirect.
>
> It is the policy of this Company that our purchases shall not be used as a means of effecting sales of our products. All products should be sold upon their own merits, using as inducement to the customer our own superiority in such items as price, quality, delivery, service, design, etc. In the same way, our purchases should be made with the same factors in mind, so that our needs are serviced by suppliers on the competitive merits of their own products and services.[19]

David N. Judelson, president of Gulf & Western, emphasized that no exceptions to that policy are tolerated:

> In Gulf & Western we have a very firm policy against reciprocity. It is in our policy manual. It says the company will not indulge in reciprocity of any kind. We are very familiar with the fact that reciprocity is against the law, and we have never ever, at any time in our history, nor would we ever, have made any acquisition from the standpoint of building up economic power in order to practice reciprocity.[20]

But in disregard of the policy's clear purpose, Gulf & Western does plot acquisitions in order to secure sales independently of its products' "competitive merits." According to plan, the thousands of Gulf & Western employees would purchase insurance from to-be-acquired Associates Investment Co., not because their independent judgment of a competitive service so dictated but because their employer conglomerate so willed. E. W. Bliss Co. would deliver its "finance business" to Associates, not because of impartial choice of a superior service but because both concerns would be members of the same conglomerate syndicate. Thus assured of "tremendous potential" for noncompetitive sales, both the acquired and the acquirer would gain an advantage over competitors which had yet to join such a syndicate:

Why is Gulf & Western interested in Associates?
. . . Gulf & Western has a net worth of $420,000,000 with sales of $1,200,000,000. They have about 100,000 employees. And they have other transactions pending which will increase these figures. I am sure you immediately begin to see the tremendous potential for the sale of casualty and life insurance.
In the finance area, let's look at E. W. Bliss. They make and sell a lot of machines—and we do a lot of financing of machines in our Commercial Finance area. Luckily, the machines made by Bliss are the kind we can finance; so we have access to this finance business.
Gulf & Western has made an offer for a portion of the stock of Allis-Chalmers. It is one of the largest manufacturers of farm implements, farm equipment and other types of heavy duty equipment. As you know, we presently do quite a volume of business in farm equipment financing.[21]

Associates Investment Co., "the nice people with money to lend you,"[22] with assets of $213.3 million, is Gulf & Western's largest acquisition to date.

Illegal "block programming" similarly would free Paramount Pictures from having to rely for sales on its consumers' free selection. By such a plan, which the Supreme Court declared violative of the Sherman Antitrust Act,[23] Paramount Pictures would sell a distributor a good film only if he also agreed to pay for a bad one. According to a Chase Manhattan memorandum of early 1967 which records a conversation between Roy Abbott (while Gulf & Western vice president) and the vice president of Paramount Pictures, the distributor would have to pay for "B" pictures if he wanted any "A" pictures:

> While block programing is not legally allowed (block programing is where the movie studio will make the film exhibitor take some "B" pictures otherwise he can't get the "A" pictures) it is nevertheless a factor in getting a company's pictures shown.[24]

Gulf & Western Chief Executive Bluhdorn devised the contract for delivering to television viewers the otherwise unsalable "freight cars." He described the plan while at lunch in February 1967 with Roy Abbott and Chase Manhattan officials, whose notes record:

> Bluhdorn discussed the purchase of Paramount which he felt was equivalent to buying a "bank". . . . In his most recent lease package negotiations, he worked out a deal where the network had to take "locomotives" (that commanded record box office performances), "freight cars" (so-called "B" films) and reruns. . . . As he puts it, this market of network leasing is definitely a seller's market. . . .[25]

With that intelligence, Chase Manhattan officials at the luncheon table confidently contributed $10 million of the $30 million loan for the conglomerate's purchase of Paramount Pictures.

On August 7, 1969, at the moment the "block programming" memorandums were being placed in the record of the House Antitrust Subcommittee investigation, former White House assistant and counsel for Gulf & Western, Joseph A. Califano, entered the hearing room to deny that the conglomerate had put the "freight car" scheme into practice.[26] As evidence he asked that the subcommittee accept for the record a copy of a contract clause and statements of policy against "block programming" — policy similar to the conglomerate's formal expression against reciprocity. It was not denied, however, that the anticompetitive programming scheme was a factor, as the memorandums indicate, of the Paramount Pictures acquisition.

That "block programming" would deny television viewers a selection of programs determined by their preferences did not inhibit Gulf & Western from announcing that its "emphasis on customer satisfaction is in the oldest tradition of American business."[27]

3

Public knowledge of a proposed acquisition usually causes the market price of the target company to rise. The acquirer must pay more than the market price to induce the owners to sell. Investors thus raise their bid for the target company stock to the limit they believe the acquirer will pay. Investors with "inside" or confidential information of a proposed merger, therefore, may purchase shares of the target company with the accurate expectation of a quick rise in market value as soon as the acquirer makes a public announcement of the merger plan.

The House Antitrust Subcommittee counsel asked Mr. Bluhdorn whether, as to be expected, stocks of target companies rose after Gulf & Western merger agreements became known to the public:

> Mr. HARKINS. In the course of your acquisition program, Mr. Bluhdorn, have you observed that when the public became aware that Gulf & Western was considering an acquisition of a company, the stock in that company rose?
>
> Mr. BLUHDORN. I would say that whenever possible, we went to great lengths to keep these things of such confidential nature for that very reason. However, sometimes in the situations that we are dealing with, we must go to our attorneys continuously, as we had to do, for instance, with Simpson, Thacher. At times we were obligated to make announcements, but we only did so when [we] were required to under legal procedures.
>
> Mr. HARKINS. But my question was: When the announcement was made, or when it became public information that you were considering acquiring a particular company, did the price of the stock in that company rise?
>
> Mr. BLUHDORN. I couldn't say. For instance, in Paramount, I would recollect when it was reported the stock went down.
>
> The CHAIRMAN. It is a general question, Mr. Bluhdorn.
>
> Mr. BLUHDORN. Sometimes; yes.
>
> The CHAIRMAN. You don't have to give an explanation. Did the stock of the acquired companies usually rise?

Mr. BLUHDORN. More often than not, Mr. Chairman. I cannot give a "yes" or "no" answer. More often than not.[28]

The stock prices of all thirteen Gulf & Western acquisitions which cost over $7 million (90% of the conglomerate's acquired assets) rose considerably during the period of confidential merger negotiations. The stock prices of eight of those companies rose over 25% during the period of a month (at most) before public announcement of merger. With that period extended to the date of consummation of the merger, the price of eight of the thirteen largest target companies rose over 50%.

Column one in Table 5 shows the lowest price investors with "inside" information of pending merger could have paid for the stock of Gulf & Western target companies during the month before that information was made public. Column 3 shows the height to which the stock had risen by the date of merger (after public announcement). Column 6 shows the percentage of the appreciation, i.e., the profit to be gained from having purchased the stock a month (at most) before public disclosure of each merger plan.

The fact that the stock of all thirteen largest target companies sharply and consistently rose before the merger plans became public knowledge is strong indication that investors with that knowledge were purchasing the stock (in anticipation of its increased value) and thus raising the market prices. The holders from whom the investors purchased before the price rose would have of course retained the stock and the appreciated value had they likewise possessed confidential information of the pending acquisition.

Gulf & Western disagreed, contending that Tables 5 and 6 cannot indicate that certain investors purchased stock on the basis of confidential information from the conglomerate, and thereby deprived the former holders of the foreseeable gain, because they "abound" with errors and because "stock prices constantly fluctuate":

Gulf & Western believes that it is impossible to draw any valid conclusions on the basis of [Tables 5 and 6] because:

1. No consideration is given to the fundamental fact that stock prices constantly fluctuate as a result of a myriad of factors,

TABLE 5
Common Stock Prices of Major Gulf & Western Acquisitions

	Price range during period from date of press release to same date of previous month (1)	*Price on date of 1st press release* (2)	*Price on date of merger* (3)	*Percent change from the lower price in col. 1 to col. 2* (4)	*Percent change from col. 2 to col. 3* (5)	*Percent change from the lower price in col. 1 to col. 3* (6)
Crampton Manufacturing Co.	$3 7/8 to $4	$ 4 7/8	$ 6	25.8	23.1	54.8
Miller Manufacturing Co.	$10 to $10 5/8	13	14 3/8	30.0	10.5	43.7
New Jersey Zinc Co.	$32 3/4 to $38 1/2	38 1/2	51 1/4	17.6	33.1	56.5
Paramount Pictures Corp.	$65 5/8 to $81 3/4	81	75 1/4	23.4	(7.1)	14.7
North & Judd Manufacturing Co.	$33 to $35	35	38	6.1	8.6	15.1
Collyer Insulated Wire Co.	$32 1/2 to $44 1/2	43	53	32.3	23.3	63.3
Desilu Productions, Inc.	$9 to $11 5/8	15	14 5/8	66.7	(2.5)	62.5
South Puerto Rico Sugar Co.	$23 1/2 to $33	33	50	40.4	51.5	127.6
E. W. Bliss Co.	$23 3/4 to $28 1/4	27 1/4	34 1/8	14.7	25.2	43.7
Consolidated Cigar Corp.	$20 5/8 to $25 3/8	23 5/8	32	14.5	35.4	55.2
Universal American Corp.	$18 to $24	24	31 1/8	33.3	29.7	72.9
Brown Co.	$18 7/8 to $25 7/8	25 7/8	19 5/8	37.1	(24.2)	4.0
Associates Investment Co.	$25 1/4 to $33 3/8	33 3/8	38 1/2	32.2	15.4	52.5

SOURCE: *Hearings on Conglomerate Corporations*, Part 1, p.105.

TABLE 6

Common Stock Prices of Gulf & Western's Major Abandoned Transactions[1]

	Price range during period from date of press release to same date of previous month (1)	Price on date of 1st press release (2)	Price at which G.&W. sold upon abandon-ment of acquisi-tion at-tempt (3)	Percent change from —			Announce-ment date[3] (7)	Abandon-ment date[3] (8)
				Lower price in col. 1 to col. 2 (4)	Col. 2 to col. 3[2] (5)	Lower price in col. 1 to col. 3 (6)		
Universal American Corp.	$11 3/4–$17 1/2	$17 3/4	$ 12 3/4	47.9	(26.6)	8.5	Apr. 14, 1966	June 1, 1966
Armour & Co.	34 1/2– 44 1/2	44 1/2	36 3/8	29.0	(18.3)	5.4	Jan. 16, 1968	Feb. 5, 1968
Allis-Chalmers Manufacturing Co.	29 5/8– 33 5/8	33 1/4	32	13.2	(3.8)	8.0	May 7, 1968	Dec. 6, 1968
Pan American World Airways	20 5/8– 23 7/8	23 7/8	29 7/8	15.8	25.1	44.8	Sept. 16, 1968	Jan. 9, 1969
Sinclair Oil Corp.	76 1/2– 90 5/8	90 5/8	130	18.5	43.4	69.9	Oct. 24, 1968	Dec. 31, 1968

1. From the Investment Statistics Laboratory Daily Price Index for the New York Stock Exchange.
2. Parentheses indicate percentage decrease.
3. From Gulf & Western documents.
SOURCE: *Conglomerate Investigation Report*, p.197.

only one of which is the public announcement of a possible
merger;

2. No consideration is given to the special circumstances
surrounding certain of the enumerated transactions; and

3. Clerical errors with resulting inaccurate computations
abound in the charts.[29]

The prices shown in Tables 5 and 6, however, can hardly be
described as fluctuating; they consistently rise. Also, after submitting suggestions for minor changes reflected in the tables as
here shown, Gulf & Western withdrew its charge of inaccuracy.[30]

An investor which regularly received confidential disclosures
of Gulf & Western's proposed target companies was Chase Manhattan Bank—the very financier of the acquisition program which
would cause the predictable rise in the price of those merger
targets.

A Chase Manhattan memorandum of May 9, 1966 describes
the duty of the former bank loan officer, Roy Abbott, now Bluhdorn's vice president, to inform the bank of which companies
Gulf & Western proposed to acquire before the public knew. By
"notifying us [Chase Manhattan] prior to [merger] announcement in the newspapers," Abbott would enable his former employer bank to purchase stock of the target companies before it
rose upon public announcement of merger.

From Chase Manhattan Bank files comes this memo:

MAY 9, 1966.

CONFIDENTIAL
CREDIT FILES, GULF & WESTERN INDUSTRIES, INC.,
HOUSTON, TEX.
NEW JERSEY ZINC CO., NEW YORK, N. Y.

Roy Abbott stopped in late this afternoon to discuss various
aspects of both Gulf & Western and New Jersey Zinc, with Tom
Hill, Harold Young and myself. . . .

Incidentally, Roy also agreed to keep us better informed concerning proposed mergers and acquisitions and important investments, i.e. notifying us prior to announcements in the newspapers.[31]

Roy Abbott was asked directly whether he did in fact, as the
memorandum indicates, inform his former employer of pending
Gulf & Western acquisitions before the predictable rise in value:

Mr. HARKINS. Mr. Abbott, as an official of Gulf & Western, was it your duty to keep Chase informed of proposed mergers and acquisitions?

Mr. ABBOTT. It was, to the extent that they either were going to affect the company significantly as far as its financial situation or projections were concerned, or to the extent it may have affected any loan agreements or any written legal arrangements we had with them.

Mr. HARKINS. Did you notify Chase prior to the announcement of an acquisition in the newspapers?

Mr. ABBOTT. Occasionally, yes. It would have been much the same as if I had gone to a neighbor and said, "Look, I am going to extend my house, and [it's] going to cost about $5,000, can you lend me $6,000 to be on the safe side," and 3 or 4 days later he would look out the window and see a new car.

Mr. HARKINS. How is it like that?

Mr. ABBOTT. If he would look out the window subsequently and see I had a new car, my neighbor would be very upset. Very much in the same light we keep our banks informed of what we are doing as it will relate to our financial condition; obviously, we have loans, we have lending arrangements, and they are conditioned on what we have said we are going to be doing.

If our plans change, obviously these are important facts which the bank has to know.

Mr. HARKINS. Have you finished your explanation, Mr. Abbott?

Mr. ABBOTT. I have.

Mr. HARKINS. Did you agree to notify Chase prior to the announcement in the newspapers?

Mr. ABBOTT. I am sorry?

Mr. HARKINS. Did you agree to notify Chase of proposed mergers of Gulf & Western, prior to their announcement in the newspapers?

Mr. ABBOTT. If they would significantly affect the areas I just had mentioned.[32]

Chase Manhattan officials responded more directly:

Mr. HARKINS. After Mr. Abbott went to Gulf & Western, he supplied information to Chase about Gulf & Western's acquisitions; did he not?

Mr. YOUNG. Yes, sir.

Mr. HARKINS. Was this information he supplied given to Chase officials prior to public announcement of the mergers?

Mr. YOUNG. In most cases I would say yes, sir.

Mr. HARKINS. And as members of the credit department of Chase, did you expect Mr. Abbott to provide this type of information to you?

Mr. YOUNG. Yes, sir; we did.[33]

Gulf & Western, according to those admissions, had passed to Chase Manhattan confidential information of which stocks its own acquisition loans would cause to rise. The bank was enabled, then, to manipulate the stock market in its favor through its power to lend other people's money.

Further internal correspondence attests to Chase Manhattan's persistence in regularly securing the conglomerate's confidential plans of merger. A memorandum written by a Chase Manhattan vice president on April 22, 1966 recorded a recent disclosure:

Roy Abbott called to let us know that another proposed acquisition will be announced probably on Monday, April 25th. The company's name is Muntz Stereo Pak, Inc., which is in the cartridge tape business. This is the same company our Credit Department checked on recently for G. & W. The acquisition, if consummated, will be for stock.[34]

Gulf & Western Vice President Roy Abbott, in full appreciation of a loan of $15 million, would make sure that the Gulf & Western financial officer "discreetly" apprised the bank of the conglomerate's "acquisition plans," the writer concluded. Abbott wanted "us to let him know if we" needed more information.

Also had a general conversation on the advisability of Gulf & Western keeping all of its banks up to date on acquisition plans. Roy, of course, fully appreciates the problems from our side of the desk at the bank and said this is certainly their objective. However, he feels this function is one which belongs to Herb Neyland and will discreetly cover the area with him at an early opportunity. Roy also fully appreciates the position we have taken on the proposed $15,000,000 line of credit and wants us to let him know if we do not get everything we want from Herb.[35]

The same Gulf & Western financial official, a Chase Manhattan memorandum of February 23, 1967 recorded, "confidentially" apprised the Bank of subsequent acquisition plans.

6. Acquisitions . . .

He said that they would probably back out of the E. W. Bliss situation. Bliss' management has not been receptive at all to the possibility of a merger.

He mentioned that they had a merger and acquisition team which was constantly screening possibilities. At present he said they had three which are, *confidentially*, Panavision, Gulf Forge, and Gulf American Land Development Company.[36]

Actual acquisition is by no means essential to causing a rise in the stock price of a reputed target company. All that is necessary is to create the appearance of a take-over attempt by purchasing large blocks of a company's stock and issuing a press release announcing intent to acquire. Public investors expect the reputed acquirer to pay a premium over the market price for more stock. Consequently, they bid higher and higher. The reputed acquirer can then capitalize on public credulity by selling while its merger rumors persist and the price is still high. The decline comes after the supposed acquirer has safely liquidated its holdings.

From one such apparent acquisition attempt or "abandoned transaction"—the sale of stock of Armour & Co.—Gulf & Western gained $16 million in less than a year. The conglomerate sold before the public learned that Gulf & Western managers had abandoned plans for merger. From four such transactions, Gulf & Western gained over $51 million (see Table 7).

As it had financed purchases of real acquisition targets, Chase Manhattan financed Gulf & Western's profitable purchases of shares of the "abandoned targets."

The bank also learned from its former loan officer, before disclosure to the public, of the imminency of reports of rapidly increased Gulf & Western earnings. The reports resulted from nothing more than changes in the acquired companies' methods of accounting. New Jersey Zinc, for instance, Mr. Abbott reported to Chase Manhattan on September 28, 1966, would enjoy a $3.65 million profit increase (to be reported later) resulting entirely from a change in accounting for depreciation.[37] From that not-yet-public information of nonrecurring artificial gain any "insider" could expect an increase in market price and, hence, buy before it occurred.

TABLE 7
Gulf & Western Abandoned Transactions and Profits

	Cost of stock to G.&W. before it announced intent to merge	Proceeds received by G.&W. from sale of stock before announcing abandonment of merger plans and while public investors thought merger would occur	Profit	Date of transaction
Armour & Co.	$ 28,149,915	$ 44,400,000	$16,250,085	Jan. 16, 1968 to Oct. 15, 1968.
Allis-Chalmers Manufacturing Co.	117,074,000	122,080,000	5,006,000	May 7, 1968 to Dec. 6, 1968.
Sinclair Oil Corp.	88,774,283	112,953,620	24,179,337	Oct. 24, 1968 to Mar. 4, 1969.
Pan American World Airways, Inc.	10,802,844	17,250,000	6,447,156	January 1968 to Apr. 17, 1969.
Total profit			$51,882,578	

SOURCE: *Hearings on Conglomerate Corporations*, Part 1, p.110.

A similar accounting change, which likewise provided figures that indicated improved performance of an acquired company under Gulf & Western management, resulted in a showing of $641,000 nonrecurring increased earnings for Consolidated Cigar Corp. in 1967.[38] Still another change of depreciation accounting after merger enabled the Gulf & Western managers to report a $120,000 profit increase for Universal American Corporation.[39]

Gulf & Western's automobile-parts division, a company vice president informed Bluhdorn on June 6, 1964, would report earnings of $1.230 million. One million of that, he continued, would come not from "true earnings" but rather from Gulf & Western's changes of inventory accounting methods of the acquired Beard & Stone Electric Co. and from the sale of real estate. The real earnings of the parts companies are "virtually nil" he continued, "and I am extremely fearful of any detailed disclosures . . .":

> The consolidated statement of earnings for the nine months ended April 30, shows that the automotive parts subsidiaries have made $1,123,000 before taxes. Of this amount more than a million dollars represents "special items" such as inventory bargain, taking Beard & Stone off LIFO [last in, first out], gain on sale of real estate at Reading, etc.; thus the true earnings of the parts companies are virtually at nil for this year and I am extremely fearful of any detailed disclosures we might have to make in a registration statement.[40]

Chase Manhattan officials denied that the bank profited from the receipt of "inside" information by purchasing the stock which its acquisition loans later caused to rise. As Gulf & Western pointed to company policy statements as indication that it refrained from reciprocal trading, so Chase Manhattan resorted to policy declarations in asserting that it did not use confidential "inside" information in determining which publicly traded securities to purchase. The declaration of May 21, 1965 instructed all Chase Manhattan officers not to use confidential information for the bank's or for their own advantage:

> The lessons to be learned from the *Texas Gulf* case must not be forgotten. Inside information gained by the Bank or any employee

should not be used by the Bank or any employee to obtain an investment advantage. It is equally clear that such inside information should not be disclosed to persons outside the Bank since they might make improper use of the information or might disclose it to other persons who might make improper use of the information. It follows from these principles that inside information obtained from a corporation or its directors, officers, employees or other insiders is not to be used by the Bank or employees in purchasing or selling securities, or recommending to others the purchase or sale of securities.[41]

A subsequent declaration of November 4, 1968, again referring to the Texas Gulf Sulphur case, decided two months earlier, stated that the bank must not use information which it does not make public. To purchase securities on the basis of such "inside" information, the bank warned its employees, amounts to fraud:

The Court of Appeals has indicated that the anti-fraud provisions (Section 10 (b) of the Securities Exchange Act and SEC rule 10b-5) are applicable to any person in possession of material inside information even though such person may not be an insider. The court said ". . . *anyone* in possession of material inside information must either disclose it or . . . must abstain from *trading in* or *recommending* the securities concerned while such inside information remains undisclosed."[42]

"Inside" information must not flow between bank departments, the declaration continued:

To insure the proper use and control of information received by the Bank in its several capacities there is to be *no* flow, or incidental communication, of inside information regarding other companies from the commercial departments or divisions of the Bank to the Fiduciary Investment Department or to the Pension or Personal Trust Divisions of the Trust Department. Similarly, there is to be *no* flow, or incidental communication, of inside information regarding other companies from the Fiduciary Investment Department or the Pension or Personal Trust Divisions of the Trust Department to other departments and divisions of the Bank.[43]

To implement that policy, "we have very definitely . . . established a wall between the commercial department and other departments of the Bank," Chase Manhattan's counsel assured the House Antitrust Committee.[44]

The bank, however, gave no indication that the figurative wall existed other than by saying that it did and by referring to the policy statements. The cited office memorandums written over a period of years show that disclosure of acquisition targets was disseminated, as the bank admitted, to many of its employees. "No mechanism for control [i.e., prevention of access to the data by Bank divisions which purchase securities]," the House Antitrust Subcommittee report states, "was demonstrated."[45]

Chase Manhattan's regular insistence on confidential disclosure of Gulf & Western's target companies, its admonishments to the conglomerate whenever that information was not suitably forthcoming, and the careful recording of the disclosures do not add credibility to the professions of self-discipline.

One unheeded item of the policy declarations instructed bank employees that:

> In addition, trust and fiduciary investment personnel, when interviewing corporate officers or representatives of brokerage houses, should make it clear that they are not seeking [for investment purpose] inside information.[46]

The eagerness (revealed by the documents) with which the officers secured knowledge of Gulf & Western's next acquisition moves does little to dispel any assumption that they sought the information for purposes of profit.

Gulf & Western's annual reports to the public during the last decade show rocketing increases in resources and earnings. During the ten-year period 1960 through 1969 those reports indicate that total assets have increased by 18,743%, total revenues by 6,608%, net income by 1,674%, common stock equity by 9,057%, and net worth by 9,847% (see Table 8).

TABLE 8

Gulf & Western Industries, Inc., and Subsidiaries, Selected Financial Statistics[1]

(Dollar amounts in thousands)

	1960	1965	1966	1967	1968	1969	Percent increase, 1965-69	Percent increase, 1960-69
(1) Total revenues	24,047	182,079	322,089	656,621	1,336,462	1,613,204	786	6,608
(2) Net income	433	5,514	20,117	46,199	69,842	50,982[2]	825	1,674
(3) Total assets	11,527	104,096	294,239	749,439	2,055,334	2,172,027	1,987	18,743
(4) Long-term debt	1,799	29,940	102,367	267,988	917,892	962,400	3,114	53,396
(5) Preferred stock			1,657	44,140	47,545	46,890		
(6) Total (4) and (5)	1,799	29,940	104,024	312,128	965,437	1,009,290	3,271	56,003
(7) Common stock equity	5,932	37,251	105,919	185,105	490,329	543,176	1,358	9,057
(8) Net worth	5,932	37,251	107,576	229,245	537,874	590,066	1,484	9,847

1. Gulf & Western Industries, Inc., and subsidiaries annual reports. Prepared by the House Antitrust Subcommittee staff.
2. Excludes $32,000,000 gains on sales of securities.
SOURCE: Conglomerate Investigation Report, p.188.

TABLE 9

Gulf & Western Industries, Inc., Internal and External Growth, 1964–68[1]

Year	External growth[2]		Internal growth		Total G. & W. increase from previous year	
	Amount	Percent	Amount	Percent	Amount	Percent
Sales increase:						
1964	$13,593,000	55.0	$11,116,000	45.0	$24,709,000	100
1965	16,293,000	25.1	48,540,000	74.9	64,833,000	100
1966	94,957,000	70.1	40,497,000	29.9	135,454,000	100
1967	288,550,000	91.2	28,838,000	8.8	317,388,000	100
1968	557,615,000	83.4	111,403,000	16.6	669,018,000	100
Net income increase:						
1964	465,000	56.4	360,000	43.6	825,000	100
1965	807,000	39.3	1,249,000	60.7	2,056,000	100
1966	13,881,000[3]	94.9	722,000	5.1	14,603,000	100
1967	22,564,000	86.5	3,518,000	13.5	26,082,000	100
1968	19,345,000[3]	81.8	4,298,000	18.2	23,643,000	100

1. Information submitted by G. & W.
2. External growth is measured by G. & W. major domestic acquisition, i.e., acquisitions with total assets of $7,000,000 or more. Such acquisitions represent approximately 90 percent of G. & W.'s total acquisitions.
3. Net income less estimated C. & W. interest expense on debt incurred to make certain acquisitions.
SOURCE: *Conglomerate Investigation Report*, p.190.

The drastic increases, however, are overwhelmingly the result of simply adding each year the assets and revenues of acquired companies to Gulf & Western assets and revenues. In 1968 "external" sales and profits, i.e., amounts contributed by companies acquired that year, comprise 83.4% and 81.8%, respectively, of Gulf & Western's annual increase of sales and profits. Hence, had Gulf & Western acquired no companies in 1968, i.e., had the conglomerate's growth been entirely "internal," the figures for growth of sales and profits would have been but 16.6% and 18.2%, respectively, of the figures reported (see Table 9).

A consequence of such purchase of growth is the debt wrought by loans by which the assets and revenues are acquired. For every dollar of its net worth, Gulf & Western owed 30¢ in 1960 but owed $1.50 in 1969. In 1960, Gulf & Western could pay interest charges on its indebtedness seven times over from its earnings (see Table 10). By 1969, however, more than one half the conglomerate's earnings were spent on the payment of interest.

TABLE 10

Gulf & Western Industries, Inc., and Subsidiaries,
Selected Financial Stability Ratios

	1960	1965	1966	1967	1968	1969
Long-term debt/net worth[1]	0.30	0.80	0.95	1.1	1.5	1.5
Interest coverage	7.0	6.4	5.1	7.2	4.9	1.9
Interest and preferred dividend coverage	7.0	6.4	3.1	3.6	3.3	1.5

1. Includes minority interest.
SOURCE: *Conglomerate Investigation Report*, p.189; prepared by the House Antitrust Subcommittee staff from annual reports of Gulf & Western Industries, Inc., and its subsidiaries.

Writing in *Fortune* of March 1968 (p.204), W. S. Rukeyser asserted that justification for conglomerate industrial concentration should be the conglomerate management's improvement of the acquired companies. "To justify itself economically," he stated, "a conglomerate must demonstrate ability to improve the

TABLE 11
Gulf & Western Industries, Inc., and
Subsidiaries Capitalization Ratios
(*Amount in percent*)

	1960	1965	1966	1967	1968	1969
Long-term debt	23.3	44.6	48.8	51.8	60.7	59.9
Minority interest				3.8	3.7	3.4
Preferred stocks			.8	8.6	3.2	2.9
Common stock equity	76.7	55.4	50.4	35.8	32.4	33.8
Total capital	100.0	100.0	100.0	100.0	100.0	100.0

SOURCE: *Conglomerate Investigation Report*, p.188; prepared by the House Antitrust Subcommittee staff from annual reports of Gulf & Western Industries, Inc. and its subsidiaries.

performance of the companies it acquires." Charles Bluhdorn seemingly agreed, for he expressed (in the same article) the same obligation: "Our job is to motorize the driftwood." "Driftwood" is his word for the companies Gulf & Western acquires.

A comparison of pre-merger performance with post-merger performance should indicate whether the purchased companies were in fact driftwood before merger and whether the conglomerate management has succeeded in "motorizing" them, thus providing justification for concentrating formerly autonomous companies under its control. Profitability figures secured by the House Antitrust Subcommittee through the year 1969 for eleven of the thirteen major Gulf & Western acquired corporations—90% of G&W's total acquired assets—for the first time provided data for such a scrutiny. Comparison of performance after merger with independent performance indicates that eight of the eleven companies earned considerably less in proportion to their assets under Gulf & Western control than under independent management (see Table 12).

Profitability figures indicating Gulf & Western management ability during 1970 and after—information for which Congress did not exercise its subpoena power—the conglomerate did not disclose.

TABLE 12

Profitability Ratios of Major Gulf & Western Subsidiaries Acquired in the Period 1964–69 for the Last Fiscal Year before Acquisition, Compared with Post-Acquisition Fiscal Years[1]

(in percent)

Year subsidiary acquired	Before acquisition				Postacquisition				
	1964	1965	1966	1967	1965	1966	1967	1968	1969
1964									
Crampton Manufacturing:									
Net income to assets	5.4				7.7	8.9	4.0	(2)	0.6
Net income to sales	2.8				3.6	3.8	2.0	(2)	0.5
Sales to assets	195.0				210.0	237.0	199.0	203.0	116.0
Miller Manufacturing:									
Net income to assets	10.4				8.5	13.6	17.7	8.6	6.9
Net income to sales	5.9				6.4	8.8	11.8	6.3	5.4
Sales to assets	177.0				132.0	154.0	150.0	135.0	128.0
1966									
New Jersey Zinc:[3]									
Net income to assets		7.9				10.7	6.2	4.2	3.8
Net income to sales		12.6				16.1	12.4	7.0	5.0
Sales to assets		63.0				66.0	50.0	60.0	76.0
1967									
Taylor Forge & Pipe Works:									
Net income to assets			8.2				7.7	3.9	4.0
Net income to sales			4.5				3.9	2.2	3.1
Sales to assets			181.0				199.0	175.0	129.0
South Puerto Rico Sugar:									
Net income to assets			4.1				(4)	3.4	6.7
Net income to sales			8.1				(4)	7.1	13.7
Sales to assets			50.0				(4)	49.0	49.0

	1968		
North & Judd Manufacturing Co.:			
Net income to assets	11.2	8.5	7.3
Net income to sales	6.8	5.4	4.7
Sales to assets	163.0	157.0	157.0
Collyer Insulated Wire:			
Net income to assets	20.0	20.6	5.0
Net income to sales	7.6	9.6	3.1
Sales to assets	263.0	216.0	160.0
Consolidated Cigar:			
Net income to assets	4.6	5.4	4.3
Net income to sales	3.9	4.8	4.2
Sales to assets	117.0	113.0	130.0
Brown:			
Net income to assets	(2)	(2)	1.1
Net income to sales	(2)	(2)	0.9
Sales to assets	110.0	106.0	128.0
E. W. Bliss Manufacturing Co.:			
Net income to assets	2.5	3.2	0.3
Net income to sales	1.8	2.4	0.4
Sales to assets	137.0	132.0	78.0
Universal American:			
Net income to assets	6.4	6.5	4.6
Net income to sales	3.9	3.8	2.7
Sales to assets	164.0	170.0	168.0

1. Excludes finance subsidiaries and subsidiaries which did not maintain a postacquisition financial identity.
2. Loss.
3. Ratios do not include gain on sales of real estate and securities.
4. Not available.
SOURCE: *Conglomerate Investigation Report*, p.194; prepared by the House Antitrust Subcommittee staff from financial statements submitted by Gulf & Western.

CHAPTER 4

Shift the Purchase Debt to the Purchased Company

To the victor belong the spoils, and to the acquired belongs the acquisition debt.

James J. Ling attended the Naval Electrical School, saved $2,000 of his service pay, and at the end of World War II set out as an electrical contractor in Dallas. In 1961 Ling Electrical Co. acquired the aircraft manufacturer Chance Vought Corp. and changed its name to Ling-Temco-Vought, Inc. By 1964 LTV was 186th on *Fortune*'s list of the largest U. S. industrial corporations. By 1969 it was the 25th largest, producing in the fields of aerospace (aircraft, missiles, space maneuvering units), meat and foods, military electronics (reconnaissance and intelligence systems), wire and cable, floor covering, commercial electronics, traffic control systems, recreation and athletics, pharmaceuticals and chemicals, passenger and freight air transportation, and steel. During the five years ending in 1969 consolidated sales increased 800 percent, and consolidated assets, almost entirely acquired, increased 2,300 percent.[1]

In mid-1966, when LTV produced mainly in the fields of aerospace, wire and cable, and electronics, it began consideration of its greatest acquisition ambition (soon to be dwarfed) — Wilson & Co., one of the nation's most profitable meat packagers. With assets of over $195 million, it surpassed in size and revenue all the companies on which LTV had previously set its sights. Wilson & Co. operated eleven meat-packing plants in Iowa, Minnesota, Kansas, Nebraska, Massachusetts, California, Oklahoma, Utah, Maryland, and Colorado. One division, Wilson Athletic Goods Mfg. Co., was the largest producer of athletic goods in the U. S. In fourteen factories the division produced golf, tennis, baseball, football, and basketball equipment. Sales branches and warehouses were located in 31 cities. Wilson Chemical Industries, a second division, produced pharmaceutical supplies from animal sources, mainly in Illinois and Pennsylvania. The total revenue of Wilson & Co. surpassed $990 million.

Typical of acquiring conglomerates, LTV considered not what it could contribute to the target company, but rather what Wilson and its "excellent" management could contribute to LTV. LTV had no inclination to enter a field of industry which bore a relation to its capability—nor did it look for a field in which it might heighten competition. Rather, it looked for a well-functioning company which could increase LTV profits and be had for a good price.

"We make no claim to understand the industry," LTV stated unabashedly. To "diversify with companies that have above average management" was the objective avowed to LTV directors in December 1966. "Wilson's management is doing an excellent job. We believe management is the key to any successful diversification effort and our investment in Wilson is a vote of confidence in the people who make up this company."[2]

The presentation to the LTV directors did not explain the need an enterprise more than a hundred years old suddenly had for a

FIGURE 3
LING-TEMCO-VOUGHT, INC.
Organization Chart, January 1, 1969
Subsidiaries or affiliates in which LTV had 50% or more of the voting stock. Principal products or operations of subsidiaries or affiliates.

JONES & LAUGHLIN STEEL CORPORATION. LTV equity: 63%. *Products:* carbon, alloy, and stainless steels. *Divisions:* Stainless and Strip, Conduit Products, Container, Electricweld Tube, Steel Service Center, Wire Rope, Supply. *Subsidiaries:* Aliquippa and Southern Railroad Company, The Cuyahoga Valley Railway Company, Gateway Coal Company, Jalore Mining Company, Ltd., Jones & Laughlin Mining Company, Ltd., Magdalena Mining Company, The Monongahela Connecting Railroad Company, Normanville Mining Company, Union Dock Company.

LTV AEROSPACE CORPORATION. LTV equity: 70%. *Principal products:* aircraft; missiles; ground vehicles; management, technical, and administrative services; electronic installations. *Divisions:* Vought Aeronautics, Missiles & Space. *Subsidiaries:* Kentron, Hawaii, Ltd.; Computer Technology Inc.; Service Technology Corporation.

THE OKONITE COMPANY. LTV equity: 86%. *Principal products:* power cable, signal cable, telephone cable, control cable, wire products, carpeting and carpet padding. *Divisions:* Wire and Cable Division. *Subsidiaries:* Jefferson Wire & Cable Corporation, General Felt Industries, Inc., Ken-Tel Equipment Company.

BRANIFF AIRWAYS, INCORPORATED. LTV equity: 66%. *Services:* civilian and military passenger service, cargo transport.

WILSON & CO., INC. LTV equity: 81%. *Principal products:* fresh meats/processed foods, dairy products, grocery products, freeze-dried meats, poultry.

WILSON SPORTING GOODS CO. LTV equity: 75%. *Principal products:* sports and athletic equipment, athletic clothing, plastic products, spring "hobby" horses.

LTV ELECTROSYSTEMS, INC. LTV equity: 70%. *Principal products:* advanced electronic systems, command and control systems, guidance systems, super-power radio/radar, reconnaissance/surveillance systems, navigation equipment, tactical radio equipment. *Divisions:* Greenville, Garland, Memcor. *Subsidiaries:* Continental Electronics Companies.

LTV LING ALTEC, INC. LTV equity: 74%. *Principal products:* commercial/hi-fi sound systems, intercom systems, telephone transmission equipment, environmental test systems, high energy power supplies, test instruments, traffic control systems, RFI (radio frequency interference) measurement instruments, marine seismic equipment, capacitors, crystals, miniature switches, transformers, electrical education equipment. *Divisions:* Altec Lansing • Ling Electronics, University Sound. *Subsidiaries:* Altec Service Corporation, Allied Radio Corporation, LTV Ling Altec, Ltd., Staco, Inc., Tamar Electronics Industries, Inc., Whitehall Electronics Corp.

WILSON PHARMACEUTICAL & CHEMICAL CORPORATION. LTV equity: 77%. *Principal products:* pharmaceuticals, organic chemical specialities, polyester resins, cosmetic ingredients, food additives, vegetable hard butters, edible gelatin, sulfuric acid, edible fats.

Other Assets

INVESTMENT BANKERS, INC. Real Estate
LINGCO REALTY CORP. Inactive
LTV INTERNATIONAL N.V. International financial transactions
INMOBILIARIA NUEVA ICACOS S.A. de C.V. Hotel operation
CONSTRUCTORA INTERTRANSATLANTICA S.A. de C.V. Construction

SOURCE: *Hearings on Conglomerate Corporations*, Part 6, p.24.

parent management. Nor did it explain the logic by which the acquirer, making no claim to understand the industry, much less to perform and compete in it, expected Wilson & Co. to improve under LTV control. Those questions were beside the point. In the first place, there was very little room for improvement, according to LTV's "Reasons for Interest" in Wilson & Co., also presented to the board:[3]

QUALITY COMPANY
Established 1853 – third largest in industry
GROWTH IN SALES AND EARNINGS
Sales: 10-year annual growth rate of 4.5 per cent
Earnings: 10-year annual growth rate of 4.0 per cent
EXCELLENT FINANCIAL POSITION
Current Ratio 2.6/1
Working Capital $64.6 million
Total Debt only $27.2 million
Long term debt to equity ratio only 0.16/1
GOOD RELATION BETWEEN BOOK VALUE
AND TENDER PRICE
Book Value $44

Coupled with LTV's high regard for Wilson & Co. was its calculation – based on observation of fluctuating hog prices – that the time was ripe for a short-term rise in meat-packing profits. There would be a good chance, then, for showing an earnings increase right after acquisition. Hogs were in "long supply," James Ling was informed, and probably would be for two more years. And investors would be all the more pleased when those expected profit increases were accentuated by certain inventory accounting techniques.[4]

No less a consideration than the quality of the company and the market condition of the inventory was that LTV could pay more than the market price for Wilson shares and still report increased earnings per share after combination or "pooling" of the earnings of the two companies. The price of Wilson shares was low in comparison to earnings. Consequently those shares represented greater earnings in proportion to market price than did LTV shares. Thus, Wilson shareholders who took LTV stock in exchange (rather than cash, as did those who accepted the tender offer) received a security earning less profit than the one they had surrendered.[5]

One source of funds for LTV's purchase of Wilson shares was the retirement fund for LTV employees. The fund bought $5 million of LTV notes. The proceeds went to purchase the Wilson stock. The trustee, Republic National Bank of Dallas, objected to the use of employee funds for company acquisitions. Ling was informed of the "problem with Republic National" and that "the incidents . . . have had a serious effect on the operating relationships between the LTV Investment Committee and the Republic Bank as trustee. . . ." Nevertheless, the committee did approve the purchase of $5 million of those notes. In December of that year, LTV replaced the uncooperative Republic National Bank as retirement fund trustee.[6]

Curiously, later, when James Ling was asked during congressional hearings whether he thought LTV could properly use LTV employee trust funds for LTV acquisitions, he replied, "Not whatsoever."[7]

The bulk of the acquisition funds, according to Ling's first plan, would come from Bank of America.[8] With that loan LTV would purchase over half the amount of stock needed for control of Wilson from mutual funds and other institutional investors. But Bank of America did not share Chase Manhattan Bank's enthusiasm for helping conglomerates grow. The bank would not grant even a secured loan for acquisition – if "secured" is the adjective for a loan (as envisioned) collateralized by the very same stock it is used to purchase. Interest rates were soaring and the Federal Reserve Board's policy in late 1966 was to restrict credit.

Ling then devised the plan to borrow at a lower rate U. S. dollars held in Europe, or Eurodollars. It would work in reverse to the balance of payments crisis, resulting in the largest sum ever then to be repatriated. The U. S. Secretary of the Treasury, perhaps forgetting that the dollars would have to be paid back to the Europeans, was delighted.[9]

On December 7, 1966 the president of LTV wrote to LTV director W. H. Osborn, who also is an official of the investment banking firm Lehman Brothers:

the banks are extremely interested in our Eurodollar program and the uniqueness of this approach. They indicated a hundred percent support for it; in fact, I believe they were enthusiastic, particularly for bankers. I did not mention the name of the company involved, although there was a substantial interest in this; in fact, many implications could have been taken that they wanted to know the specific name.[10]

Rothschild's and Lehman Brothers then began selling the plan to European bankers who they hoped could locate 60 million expatriated dollars.

The banks would take as security for the loan the same Wilson stock which LTV purchased with the loan proceeds. Although the stock would then be out of LTV's possession, LTV would nevertheless still enjoy the voting rights. The conglomerate would gain a controlling interest in Wilson & Co. just as if it owned the Wilson stock outright.

By the theory of the plan, a stock purchaser with a sum of money infinitely smaller than a corporation's total value might acquire that corporation by successively purchasing shares with proceeds from successive loans secured by each stock purchase. By putting that theory into practice, LTV purchased Wilson & Co.

Through use of funds borrowed by LTV, in turn borrowed by the banks from the public, LTV acquired over $196 million in assets from that single acquisition without issuing one new share of common stock. Reported earnings per share were then determined by dividing conglomerate earnings only by the number of common — not preferred — shares. However, upon assuming control of the meat packager, LTV canceled the common shares of Wilson holders who had not accepted the tender offer to sell for cash. In payment for cancellation, the conglomerate issued them LTV preferred shares. Thus, the earnings of the two companies as combined after merger were divided by a smaller divisor (number of common shares) than those earnings had been before merger. The result was an astronomical increase in the reported LTV earnings per share and, consequently, in the market evaluation of LTV shares. The conglomerate's earnings rose from $13.683 million in 1966 to $34.003 million in 1967 after the merger (see Table 13). Sixteen million dollars of that $21 million earnings increase (resulting from other acquisitions as well) came from Wilson's addition.[11]

LTV attributed the rising earnings to its allegedly superior

TABLE 13
Ling-Temco-Vought, Inc., and Consolidated Subsidiaries – Selected Financial Statistics
(Dollar amounts are in thousands)

	1960[1]	1964	1965	1966	1967	1968	1969	Percent change 1960-69	Percent change 1964-69
Total revenues	$148,447	$324,184	$338,223	$469,072	$1,841,052	$2,780,500	$3,767,772	2,438.1	1,062.2
Net income[2]	3,051	4,904	5,984	13,683	34,003	27,712	2,336[3]	(23.4)	(52.4)
Total assets	93,460	126,968	202,384	298,418	845,113	2,648,150	2,944,336	3,050.4	2,219.0
Long-term debt	14,639	37,012	40,274	95,773	202,586	1,236,693	1,500,792	10,152.0	3,954.9
Preferred stock	5,694	4,796	2,641	434	4,792	2,560	2,522	(55.7)	(47.4)
Total	20,333	41,808	42,915	96,207	207,378	1,239,253	1,503,314	7,293.5	3,495.8
Common stock equity	22,839	23,766	27,893	58,472	240,257	172,893	265,652	1,063.1	1,017.8
Net assets	28,534	28,562	30,534	58,906	245,049	175,453	268,174	839.8	838.9

1. Ling-Temco Electronics, Inc.
2. Before extraordinary items.
3. $38,294 loss after various extraordinary items.
SOURCE: Hearings on Conglomerate Corporations, Part 6, p.66; prepared by the House Antitrust Subcommittee staff from Ling-Temco-Vought annual reports.

management ability. The increase demonstrated, its management asserted, that with the perfection of conglomerated concentration of corporate assets there had dawned a new era of corporate profitability.[12]

After the reporting of greater earnings per share, LTV common stock rose from a high of 52 in the fourth quarter of 1966 to a high of 166 less than a year later (see Table 14). A rising market price assures successful negotiation for more loans for more industrial combinations.

The only possible complication in the cycle is any failure of the new assets under conglomerate control to generate sufficient earnings. If those assets should provide less income than necessary to stimulate a rise in the parent company's stock, the acquisition process breaks down. Worse, if the acquired company's operations do not generate proceeds adequate even to pay the astronomical acquisition debt and interest, or — more unmentionable — result in a loss, havoc ensues.

But the mood was that of elation when in the third week of

TABLE 14

Quarterly Common Stock Prices of Ling-Temco-Vought, Inc., 1964–1969

Year and quarter	High	Low	Year and quarter	High	Low
1964:			1967:		
1st	13	$10^{1}/_{4}$	1st	$91^{1}/_{2}$	$50^{1}/_{4}$
2d	$12^{1}/_{2}$	$9^{5}/_{8}$	2d	$102^{7}/_{8}$	$80^{5}/_{8}$
3d	$12^{5}/_{8}$	$10^{1}/_{2}$	3d	$166^{1}/_{2}$	$97^{7}/_{8}$
4th	$12^{1}/_{4}$	$10^{5}/_{8}$	4th	$145^{3}/_{8}$	$110^{5}/_{8}$
1965:			1968:		
1st	$17^{1}/_{2}$	$11^{1}/_{2}$	1st	$128^{5}/_{8}$	$89^{3}/_{4}$
2d	$17^{3}/_{8}$	$13^{3}/_{8}$	2d	$132^{1}/_{4}$	106
3d	$19^{3}/_{8}$	$14^{3}/_{8}$	3d	$110^{7}/_{8}$	$82^{1}/_{2}$
4th	$37^{3}/_{8}$	$18^{1}/_{8}$	4th	$109^{7}/_{8}$	$87^{1}/_{8}$
1966:			1969:		
1st	$46^{5}/_{8}$	$32^{5}/_{8}$	1st	$95^{1}/_{2}$	$57^{1}/_{4}$
2d	49	32	2d	$56^{3}/_{4}$	$39^{3}/_{4}$
3d	42	$29^{1}/_{2}$	3d	$44^{3}/_{8}$	$30^{1}/_{2}$
4th	52	$26^{1}/_{2}$	4th	$44^{3}/_{8}$	$24^{1}/_{2}$

(Note: Prices adjusted for 3 to 2 stock split on Aug. 1, 1967).

SOURCE: *Hearings on Conglomerate Corporations*, Part 6, p.86; prepared by the House Antitrust Subcommittee staff.

December 1966, word came from across the Atlantic to the LTV
Tower in Dallas that commitments of Eurodollars lenders had
surpassed $42 million (see Table 15).

The moment to strike was at hand. On Tuesday morning,
December 21, Wilson shareholders across the nation unfolded
their newspapers and learned the splendid news. Almost overnight their investment had increased $15 a share above the mar-
ket price. LTV was offering to pay, they read, $62.50 for each of
their common shares selling shortly before for $47.00.

In turn, the European bankers soon learned that the shareholders were accepting the offer (of a little less than 33% cash
profit on the basis of pre-merger market price). Nothing suc-
ceeds like success. The banks immediately consented to increase
the loan limit by $20 million, to discard various security provi-
sions, and to send over 8 million more Eurodollars immediately.

TABLE 15

Ling-Temco-Vought, Inc.: $42,000,000 7⅞ Percent Notes
Due Jan. 6, 1969 (Issued Jan. 6, 1967)

Note No.	Lender and payee	Principal amount of notes
1	The American Express Company, Inc.	$ 2,000,000
2	Banque de Paris et des Pays-Bas Limited, London	1,000,000
3	Singer & Friedlander Ltd.	500,000
4	Lloyds Bank Europe Limited	1,000,000
5	Guinness Mahon & Co. Ltd.	500,000
6	Same	500,000
7	Same	500,000
8	Same	500,000
9	Kleinwort, Benson Ltd.	1,000,000
10	Anglo-Israel Bank Limited	1,000,000
11	N. M. Rothschild & Sons	2,000,000
12	Westminster Foreign Bank Limited	2,000,000
13	Bank of America, National Trust & Savings Association	10,000,000
14	Samuel Montagu & Co. Limited	1,000,000
15	National Provincial & Rothschild (London) Limited	500,000
16	J. Henry Schroder Wagg & Co. Limited	1,000,000
17	Banca Della Svizzera Italiana, Lugano (Switzerland)	2,000,000
18	Marine Midland Grace Trust Company of New York	5,000,000
19	First National City Bank	10,000,000
	Total issued and outstanding on January 6, 1967	42,000,000

SOURCE: *Hearings on Conglomerate Corporations*, Part 6, p.560.

LTV President Clyde Skeen wrote the vice president for finance, on January 11, 1967:

> With respect to the final word on the consents . . . in Europe—he [Osborne, the Lehman partner and LTV director] had just heard from Phillip Shelbourne and all banks had consented with the exception of Schroeders in London and BCI in Italy—and they anticipated these consents before the day is out, thereby making the consents unanimous. Both Bill and Shelbourne were elated by this state of events.[13]

Thirty million more dollars came from the "private placement" subscribed to by domestic lenders, including the LTV Employee Retirement Trust. With the $80 million borrowing, LTV had purchased 53% of Wilson voting stock, paying a premium of $19.5 million over the market price.

The acquirer, purchasing direct from the target company shareholders, never negotiated with the management. As the takeover became imminent, however, LTV Treasurer B. L. Brown perfunctorily sent the Wilson directors some literature about the conglomerate which in a matter of days would remove them from office. Director Thomas B. Freeman replied on Christmas Day that he had already apprised himself of LTV.[14]

DECEMBER 22, 1966.

Mr. THOMAS B. FREEMAN,
Tucson, Ariz.

DEAR MR. FREEMAN: At the request of Mr. James J. Ling, the enclosed material on Ling-Temco-Vought, Inc. is being forwarded to you. Similar material was given to some of the directors of Wilson & Co., Inc. but regrettably it was not possible to contact each of you personally in order to acquaint you with our company.

Sincerely,

B. L. BROWN.

THOMAS B. FREEMAN,
Tuscon, Ariz., December 25, 1966.

Mr. B. L. BROWN,
Treasurer, Ling-Temco-Vought, Inc.,
Dallas, Tex.

DEAR SIR: This is to acknowledge receipt of the LTV Material you sent me. However, it was a bit late as I naturally had immediately obtained adequate information about sales, operation results and balance sheets of your company and its affiliates, after learning from the press your company's announced intentions earlier this week.

It is apparent and fully recognized by me that you and your associates hold some, if not all of Wilson and Company's Directors in contempt and that you thought them beneath your consideration in laying your plans. It is also apparent that you and they intend to obtain control of Wilson and Company, Inc., if you can and for the purposes unknown to me.

From many past experiences with operators and operations such as you and yours seem to be, my opinion is that Wilson's competent and enthusiastic management we have been developing for the last thirteen years will quickly be demoralized and will lose much of its effectiveness in any event.

The fine line between profit and loss in the meat end of the business is such that a sizable profit can easily become a serious loss. We have ample evidence of that when we look at what has just happened to the meat operations of Rath, Cudahy, Hygrade and others. If you want to go into the meat business, you can acquire any or all of these at bargain prices.

A very large percentage of Wilson's sales are to consumers in the meat category. They benefit little from long profit, war inspired sales to the Army, the Navy, the Air Force or from other governmental projects.

Yours truly,

THOMAS B. FREEMAN.

Roscoe G. Haynie, president of Wilson & Co., Inc., received notification from President Skeen on January 12:

You are hereby advised that as of January 5, 1967, Ling-Temco-Vought, Inc., owned beneficially 1,295,597 shares of common stock of Wilson & Co., Inc. Suggest you amend proxy statement accordingly.[15]

LTV then had control of Wilson. So the conglomerate cancelled the Wilson shares (47% of the total) of the stockholders who did not accept the offer, and sent them the LTV preferred stock in its place.

On Sunday morning, January 8, 1967, the *London Financial Times* reported:

This is the first time that a Eurodollar loan has been made in Europe specifically for use in America. The loan, put together by M. C. Rothschild of London and Lehman Brothers of New York will be for the unusually short period of two years.

The period of indebtedness for LTV was to be even shorter. But Wilson & Co.'s expense for its surrender to LTV control is not so short. That debt has only begun. In order to pay LTV $50 million so LTV could quickly repay the European bankers, Wilson & Co. (as an LTV subsidiary) sold stock and subordinated debentures for which the meat-packer became obligated to pay principal and interest for a quarter-century.[16]

Wilson & Co.'s net worth before merger was $125 million. Transference to it of $50 million of the acquisition debt diminished the company's net worth by 40%. It will be restored only by the prices consumers pay for Wilson products.

But in the words of James Ling, it is "only proper" that the acquired company bear the acquirer's purchase debt.[17] Propriety does not come cheaply to Wilson & Co. — nor to the public consumers.

LTV management announced to all shareholders that it had "strengthened" Wilson & Co. by "financially innovative actions."[18] If to reduce shareholders' earnings by transferring to them equity and debt obligations amounting to more than a third of a company's net assets without adding one cent to those assets is to strengthen a company, then that statement is plausible.

As it had with stock of other major acquired companies, LTV placed the weakened Wilson shares on the public market while retaining majority control. That policy, denominated "redeployment," envisioned (as Ling stated in 1965) that the "earning power of these LTV assets will be translated into substantially greater values as measured by the market."[19]

But carrying "redeployment" a step further, for the first time the parent company divided the assets of the acquired company itself into publicly traded entities. Wilson Sporting Goods and Wilson Pharmaceutical Co. were severed from the meat-packing enterprise. Each appeared independently on the American Stock Exchange along with Wilson Meat Packing Co.

By the fall of 1969, however, the market was no longer "translating" LTV-controlled assets into greater values. The earnings of the three Wilson companies combined had fallen more than 40% since the surrender of independent management.[20] But even though LTV initiated no new acquisitions in 1969 (the first year in five it failed to do so), "redeployment" continued—the market would have another chance to reflect the greater value of the assets' earning power. Through the exercise of majority control, LTV took assets from Wilson Meat Packing Co. and divided them into four more publicly traded companies: Wilson Certified Foods Co. (beef, veal, lamb, and pork), Wilson Beef and Lamb Co. (fresh beef and lamb), Wilson-Sinclair Co., and Wilson Laurel Farms (poultry).

The next year LTV sold all its holdings, not just majority control, in the two most profitable Wilson companies—the sporting goods manufacturer and the pharmaceutical company. Ling succinctly explained that the sale was necessitated by "bank debt which carried with it heavy interest burden owing to prevailing high interest rates."[21]

The extremity of having to pay old acquisition debts not with income from the acquired assets, but rather with proceeds from their sale, came after, in Ling's description, the "single most devastating incident in LTV history."

By late 1968 the conglomerate had successfully completed the acquisition of Great America Holding Co. By the standard of asset value, it was double the size of Wilson & Co. Eighty percent ownership of Braniff Airlines constituted only a quarter of the holding company's total value.

Public recognition of the value of LTV's marketed assets was at its zenith during the transaction. Great America shareholders gave up their ownership rights not for ownership of LTV but, surprisingly, for LTV debt securities and warrants to purchase LTV common shares at a price of $115. Thus, the former Great America shareholders had for each share exchanged, besides the debentures, the right to purchase for $115 a stock which in late 1972 sold at around $12.

Flushed with the success of having gained $225 million worth of assets, again without having to give up even one share of its ownership (by issuing common stock), LTV set the stage for its most colossal acquisition—Jones & Laughlin Steel Corp. with assets in excess of a billion dollars. But the strategy of acquisition hinged not on the issuance of debt securities as in the Great America purchase. Rather, the take-over of Jones & Laughlin, like the take-over of Wilson & Co., was by outright cash payment.

First, LTV would purchase 63% of the steel producer's stock with $428.5 million largely from bank loans collateralized with securities of earlier LTV acquisitions (Braniff, National Car Rental, and Computer Technology). The Jones & Laughlin shares thus purchased would serve as collateral for further purchase of the same stock.

Second, LTV would create a shell corporation—the J & L Corp.—to hold the purchased Jones & Laughlin stock. Debentures, warrants, and common shares of that holding company would be issued in exchange for 18% more Jones & Laughlin stock. Most important was LTV's plan for further issuance of J & L Corp. debentures in order to retire the multimillion-dollar purchase loan from the banks.

The first step went splendidly. The banks were cooperative enough to enable LTV to pay Jones & Laughlin stockholders 70% above the market price, i.e., $85 for shares then selling on the New York Stock Exchange for $50.

The second step failed. It was the beginning of the reversal of the tide. LTV could not transfer to the J & L Corp. the huge bank debt incurred by the generous exchange offer. Ling attributed the failure to that "single most devastating incident"—the Justice Department's filing of an antitrust suit against LTV to prevent the merger. Because LTV's right to acquire Jones & Laughlin was then challenged, the public would not accept J & L Corp.'s security issuance.

LTV then had to shoulder the debt itself—just at the time when the earnings of all its subsidiaries were declining. Soon earnings were to disappear completely. Worse, operations in 1969 produced a loss of $80 million. Gone was any chance that the acquisitions could pay for themselves. The debt could be met only by the sale of the acquired divisions—only by dismantling an astronomically costly conglomeration for which the acquired companies and their customers will have to pay for decades.

CHAPTER 5

Acquire One Company with the Treasury of Another

Distinction for perfecting the acquisition method whereby the purchaser gains cash rather than spends it belongs to National General Corp. and Leasco Data Processing Co. Leasco purchased Reliance Insurance Co. for a value of approximately $400 million in Leasco preferred stock and afterward had $80 million of liquid reserves it did not have before. National General purchased Great American Insurance Co. with paper evidencing over $400 million of debt and after the purchase possessed $173 million more in negotiable securities.

Both insurance companies, because of longevity and good management, had accumulated millions of dollars in redundant capital. Redundant, because it was far in excess of the capital resources required by law for the protection of policyholders.

Each acquiring conglomerate, using the reverse of the LTV technique of transferring debt to the acquired company, accomplished the same ends of self-enrichment by transferring that excess capital from the acquisition to itself. Leasco used $38 million of Reliance Insurance Company's capital to finance Leasco operations. National General took $172 million of Great American Insurance Co.'s capital and used $13 million to purchase yet another insurance company.

On the basis of earnings of the last year of independent operations, Great American Insurance Co. was more than three times as large as its acquirer, National General. Reliance Insurance Co. was more than three times as large as Leasco. Ironically, therefore, neither acquirer could pay the purchase debt to the former insurance company owners without the assets which those former owners gave in exchange for securities evidencing that same purchase debt. Thus, the former owners could have retained their insurance companies and directly voted themselves the same type of securities which they took indirectly from the acquirers. The insurance company owners could have given themselves everything they got from National General and Leasco without going through the sale transaction.

Why, then, did they sell? Eugene V. Klein himself, president and chief executive of National General, in reference to "proxy statements" or literature which corporate managements send to shareholders to explain a merger and solicit their approval, stated:

> I believe that the shareholders are not in a position to understand the information because it is so highly legal and technical. Financial information is so complex that I believe it is beyond the capacity of a small shareholder to understand it. . . . I believe that a better way should be found of informing the shareholders of exactly what is going on.[1]

That is another way of saying that the conglomeration phenomenon is not the product of corporate owners' independent, considered judgment. Shareholders, according to Klein's statement, tend to accept unquestioningly management's recommendations of merger.

The proxy statements informed each insurance company's shareholders that they would take in exchange securities of a company strengthened by diversification. More specifically, however, the acquisition schemes were a design for obtaining the insurance companies' capital resources and circumventing laws enacted for the public's protection.

National General Corp. admitted to being a product of diversification from desperation. In 1961, it was an operator of motion picture theaters on the West Coast. To acquire other companies was the only way to avoid bankruptcy. Klein explained to the House Antitrust Subcommittee:

> we would have liked to acquire anything that showed cash flow and profit, be it any kind of business, because we were sort of

drowning and we were looking for companies to help us get well
financially. It was a day to day fight for survival.[2]

The company functions as an investment institution, without
a planned acquisition program. It does not hire management and
does not know in advance for how long it will retain a controlling interest or any interest at all in its purchased enterprises. After two or three years it may decide to acquire complete ownership or to divest completely.[3]

The owners of the first target companies, Designed Facilities
Corp., a mobile home manufacturer, and Mission Pak, Inc., a
fruit retailer, accepted National General common stock in exchange. They agreed to merge even though theirs were profitable companies while their acquirer could not exist without
them.

"When we got the wrinkles out of our belly," Klein explained,
"and we saw that we had a thriving company . . . we organized
our leisure time and financial services concept." National
General sold Designed Facilities and Mission Pak "for the most
advantageous price."[4]

So well did National General sell its concept of diversification to Columbia Savings & Loan shareholders that in August
1964 they (as did Great America Holding Co. shareholders selling to LTV) sold their ownership interest for National General
securities that were devoid of ownership rights—i.e., they accepted debentures and warrants allowing them to purchase
National General stock at $15 per share. The value of the war-
rants, however, increased as National General continued to acquire the earnings of its acquired companies and as its stock
consequently rose.

Pre-merger arrangements by four of the eleven National
General directors who owned substantial holdings of Columbia
facilitated the transaction. With other Columbia Savings & Loan
stockholders, the four National General directors, two of whom
were also on the Columbia board, and one of whom, Klein, was
president of the acquirer and chairman of the board of the
about-to-be-acquired company, put together a block of 39% of
Columbia stock for assured sale to National General. By the
time both boards and both sets of shareholders entered into

merger deliberations, therefore, National General needed only 11% more to achieve outright control (50%). The shareholders needed no convincing of which way to vote to be on the winning side.[5]

In April 1968 Klein received a call from Arthur Carter of the brokerage firm of Carter, Berlind & Weill (now reorganized and operating as Cogan, Berlind, Weill, Levitt-Hayden Stone, Inc.). Carter said he wanted to talk over some investment opportunities, specifically, possible further acquisitions for National General. He had more detailed information in a report, "The Financial Service Holding Company," just prepared by the firm. About three hundred copies were being sent out that week. Send one over, Klein said.[6]

The Netter Report, named after its author, Edward Netter, a vice president of the firm, while purporting to recommend methods for strengthening the insurance industry, explains devices by which debt-saddled companies can acquire the resources of successful insurance companies. The brokerage firm mailed 2,000 of the reports to prospective corporate acquirers.

Laws of various states restrict insurance companies from using their resources to control other businesses. Many states, for example, prohibit an insurance company from investing more than 5% of its resources in another company and from purchasing more than 49% of another company's stock.[7] The objective is to prevent an insurance company from overly concentrating its investment resources, necessary for public policyholders' protection, in so few enterprises as to control them.

But an insurance company may create the shell of another company (called a "holding" company, which the insurer owns or which theoretically owns the insurer), transfer assets to that shell, and in the shell's name begin functioning in other enterprises. The Netter Report merely explored departures from that principle, or loophole. An acquiring company (rather than a shell of the insurer's creation), Netter reasoned, could take over or "hold" an insurance company and then transfer the insurer's surplus capital to itself for its own operations. Or better, according to the report, for more acquisitions.

For instance, the Netter Report to Trans World Airlines suggested that the airline acquire an insurance company and then transfer to it the airline's growing debt. TWA summarized the report on December 12, 1967:

> Our analysis led us to the conclusion that acquisition of a fire and casualty insurance company would be an outstanding diversification vehicle for TWA's financing requirement:
>
> It would provide TWA with an immediate source of readily liquid marketable securities that could be converted to cash and utilized in satisfying TWA's financing requirement. . . . an insurance subsidiary would be permitted to purchase the debt of TWA . . . and therefore could be used to supplement TWA's other sources of debt capital.[8]

As might be expected, the word for the scheme of a company in distress to appropriate the assets of a healthy enterprise was "diversification." Unlike the report itself, the TWA summary did not bother with the pretense that the acquisition reward to the acquired insurance company would be anything other than the acquirer's free access to the insurance treasury.

The prime recommendations of Carter, Berlind & Weill (CBWL) were, naturally, insurance companies which had, through virtue of long and constructive operation, the greatest quantities of surplus capital. Listed as the choicest fruit were Great American Insurance Co., Insurance Company of North America, Hartford Fire Insurance Co., and Reliance Insurance Co. "Computation of Insurance Company of North America's capital redundancy," read the report, was $495.5 million as of December 31, 1966.

The Netter Report went mainly to corporations in need of cash. Secure funds of the insurers would be risked to aid sick investments. The brokerage industry's "finest example of creative research,"[9] then, sought not only circumvention of laws, but violation of that fundamental investment rule which warns against jeopardizing secure funds to rescue money in distress.

Though it might describe the scheme as a godsend to the insurance industry, CBWL could not deceive itself. The brokers anticipated well the reaction of any insurance management to a plan for taking over its treasury. The Netter Report stops short of advice on procedure for merger negotiations. In fact, it actually advises against conversations or confrontations with the prime

candidates' managements. The TWA summary of its considerations of the report concluded:

> In our discussions with Carter, Berlind & Weill they indicated that
> in their opinion it would not be advisable to attempt to discuss
> merger with any of the aforementioned fire and casualty com-
> panies. Management for the most part, does not appear to be in-
> clined toward the merger route.

But the conspicuous void in the otherwise fully prepared plan
really did not matter. An insurance company's stockholders
could just as well be dealt with directly:

> Therefore, it would appear that the most feasible course to pur-
> sue would be some sort of a tender offer for at least 51% if we so
> desire.[10]

There would be no need to purchase more stock than necessary
to get control of the treasury.

However, Netter did have discussions with the management of
one candidate. A. Addison Roberts, president of Reliance Insurance Co., responded with a lawsuit charging that CBWL and
others were conspiring to manipulate the price of Reliance
stock.[11] But the suit made no impression on Reliance stockholders. Apparently they saw no reason to think beyond the
description of the benefits of "diversification" set forth in the
exchange-offer literature. The acquisition of Reliance Insurance
Co. was the initial outstanding success of the Netter plan.

The CBWL brokerage firm denied that the scheme of the
Netter Report was to use insurance capital to build conglomerate
corporations.[12] CBWL must then resort to its own interpretation
of the word "conglomerate," for the report under the section
entitled "leverage" states:

> The degree of insurance premium volume written as a percentage
> of adjusted capital and surplus will determine the potential avail-
> ability of capital for immediate diversification.

The report does not describe other uses for the surplus capital of
successful insurance companies: instead of augmenting the trend
of corporate concentration by corporate acquisitions, those funds
can be used to reduce policyholders' premium payments or to

improve and extend their protection. Policyholders' premium payments, after all, are the original source of the surplus capital. While pondering whether to allow the largest insurance company acquisition in history, the Justice Department learned that acquisitors' take-over of insurance assets had resulted in marked deterioration of insurers' capacity to serve the public (see chapter 13).

Eugene Klein read his copy of the Netter Report and decided it had possibilities for National General. He called up Arthur Carter and Alan Alan, members of CBWL, and suggested they meet on May 9, 1968 for dinner at Club Twenty-One. He in turn could give them information on National General. The corporation had just finished acquiring Grosset & Dunlap, and Klein saw no reason to stop there. Four days after the dinner, Klein called Alan and said he was ready to decide on a definite insurance company target. The two agreed to aim for Great American Insurance Co. CBWL had carefully kept Klein informed of Great American's stock holdings.[13]

On May 28 National General's executive committee authorized the purchase of 500,000 shares of Great American at not more than $55 per share. CBWL said it knew where to locate block holdings. By instigating a merger with its Netter Report, the brokerage firm sought not only a million-dollar finder's fee but also commissions from the transfer of stock—based on the firm's buying and selling transactions—and, later, fees for acting as agent during the tender offer.[14]

Suddenly a cloud appeared on the horizon. One day in early June, Klein studied the board tape from the New York Stock Exchange. To his consternation he read that another suitor was bidding for Great American. AMK Corporation was negotiating directly with the management.

Immediately a crisis session assembled. It was essential for the success of the offer to purchase shares direct from the stockholders that National General first hold a block of the stock outright. National General could purchase that block only with the proceeds from the sale of its Designed Facilities subsidiary. But it would not receive that money until July 1. AMK Corporation could complete its transaction within that time.

CBWL knew where to purchase 266,300 Great American shares. But try as it might, National General could not come up with the cash. The plan was falling apart just because of a lapse of three weeks.

For CBWL to transact the purchase without possessing the money would amount to a violation of the principal rules of the Federal Reserve Board. Regulation T requires, understandably enough, that a purchaser must pay for the shares he orders within seven days.[15]

But the brokerage firm which stood to gain millions in finder's, transfer, and exchange fees through implementation of its plan to take advantage of a loophole in the law was not to be cowed by a Federal Reserve Board regulation which the board itself does not bother to enforce. With the same logic of entrusting chickens to the protection of a fox, the board entrusts enforcement of its regulations to the New York Stock Exchange.

On the morning of June 11 a CBWL broker called Klein and asked, "Will you purchase the 266,300 shares if you cannot get twenty-one day delivery?" Meaning, will you purchase if you have to pay within seven days as required by law?

"No," replied Klein. "I cannot purchase and will not purchase unless I can get twenty-one day delivery [wait twenty-one days to pay]. Now check with your people and see if it can be done."

He had done it many times before, Klein told the broker.

A few minutes later, the CBWL broker called again and said, "confirmed."

Klein: "O. K. We have a transaction."[16]

The inadequacy of funds to support stock exchange transactions led to the 1929 stock market crash. Regulation T, which requires adequate payment, thus is among the most important reform features of the Securities Exchange Act of 1934.

The New York Stock Exchange determined on June 14, 1968 that CBWL had violated Regulation T by arranging for 21-day delivery. The exchange, however, did not require that the purchase of Great American shares be rescinded as the regulation prescribes. Rather, it decided that "liquidation of the purchase would unreasonably upset the markets in both National General Corporation and Great American stock. . . ." The exchange thus reasoned, in an opinion of August 15, 1968, that "exceptional" circumstances warranted its granting an extension of time for CBWL to complete the transaction:

> It was decided, therefore, that while "exceptional circumstances," justifying an extension of time, did not exist at the time the transaction was executed, the results of the execution had created such "exceptional circumstances." The Exchange then granted an extension.[17]

By that reasoning, the greater the violation of Regulation T and the greater the possibility of harm to the investing public the greater are the chances that the New York Stock Exchange will permit the violation.

The excuse CBWL gave the New York Stock Exchange was that Regulation T is too complicated to be understood. The firm produced "one of the finest examples of creative research ever seen in the [brokerage] business" (its own words). Yet CBWL did not know, its managers explained to the New York Stock Exchange on September 3, 1968, that its delayed payment for the purchase of Great American Insurance Co. shares for National General amounted to a violation of Regulation T:

> As we have previously stated to the Exchange, neither Carter, Berlind & Weill, Inc., nor persons associated with Carter, Berlind & Weill, Inc. were aware that the contract at the time it was made was not in conformity with the requirements of Regulation T. On the contrary, it was believed that the form of contract— seller's option—as an NYSE-approved form of contract (the other approved forms being Cash, Next Day, Regular Way, etc.) satisfied all appropriate regulatory requirements.[18]

The New York Stock Exchange actually took that excuse at face value. Ignorance of the law, it replied, is no justification. "In very simple terms," the exchange told CBWL, "a firm that places its services before the entire investment community must be absolutely certain it knows and understands every rule application." On October 15, 1968, the firm's managers read from their teletype that though they received a fine of $5,000, the transaction would stand.[19]

From that unlawful transaction, in spite of the $5,000 fine,

CBWL received $425,975.[20] Evidently the exchange's acqui-
escence to a Federal Reserve Board regulatory violation hinges
on the profitability as well as on the magnitude of the unlawful
transaction.

Under the present system of relegation to the New York Stock
Exchange of enforcement of Federal Reserve Board regulations,
the exchange need not report to any government authority or
make public disclosure of violations. Compliance with the
government regulations it enforces is thus a private matter between the exchange and its members:

> Mr. HARKINS [House Antitrust Subcommittee counsel]. What
> are the S.E.C.'s normal procedures for review of the stock ex-
> change disciplinary procedures?
>
> Mr. BUDGE [Securities and Exchange Commission Chairman].
> Under the decision of Congress the New York Stock Exchange is
> a self-regulatory body charged with being responsible for the
> conduct of its membership. The Commission has an oversight
> responsibility over the New York Stock Exchange. Normally,
> there would not be a disciplinary action taken by both against a
> member firm.
>
> Mr. HARKINS. Are the procedures applicable to this relation-
> ship spelled out in a regulation?
>
> Mr. BUDGE. I think not. As a matter of fact, I am not sure that
> until very recently the Commission was even aware of the dis-
> ciplinary actions taken by the New York Stock Exchange against
> member firms. I think historically we have not been advised of
> that.
>
> Is that correct, Mr. Loomis?
>
> Mr. LOOMIS. We were not as well advised as we are now, al-
> though we did get a certain amount of information, I think, all
> along.
>
> Mr. HARKINS. How well are you advised now?
>
> Mr. LOOMIS. I think quite well.
>
> Mr. HARKINS. When was this change put into effect?
>
> Mr. LOOMIS. It has been a gradual thing over the year since, let's
> say, 1963 or 1964.
>
> Mr. HARKINS. Are there specific regulations requiring submis-
> sion of anything concerning disciplinary action?
>
> Mr. LOOMIS. There are no specific regulations requiring it. We
> just get it.

Mr. BUDGE. The person against whom the disciplinary action is
taken, of course, has the right to appeal to the Commission. No, I
guess that is with the NASD. We would get it if it came through
the National Association of Securities Dealers.[21]

Thus, if the New York Stock Exchange does happen to notify
the Securities and Exchange Commission of a member's violation of provisions for investor's security, according to the SEC
chairman, the exchange so reports because it so condescends.

Now the battle was joined. Of the two suitors, Great American
saw rival AMK as the lesser evil. On July 15 the insurance company advised its shareholders against accepting National General's offer of debentures (IOUs) for their common stock. On
July 18 it announced, "The management . . . is giving favorable
consideration to a proposal by AMK Corporation. . . ."[22]

National General countered on July 29 with its own advice to
the same (target insurance company) shareholders: "If the AMK
proposal is presented to the stockholders of Great American, as
substantial holders of shares we intend to vote against it, and
will urge our fellow shareholders also to reject it."[23]

In the end, National General won. For the company which
possessed approximately $300 million in surplus capital alone
(including that required by law), the acquirer paid approximately $500 million in debt securities. By January 1970, the time
of the hearings at which Klein testified, the value of all the
securities the former Great American shareholders took in exchange did not even equal the amount they would have secured
had they liquidated that surplus capital rather than selling
to National General.[24]

The conglomerate's purchase debt, paradoxically, as already
seen, could not be paid to the former Great American owners
without the total wealth and earnings which they gave National
General in the act of becoming its creditors.

Great American Insurance Co. had never paid a dividend of
more than $2.50 per share. On January 14, 1969, during the first
year of control by National General (owner of 98% of Great
American stock), the insurer paid a dividend to National General
of $55 per share. In all, $173 million. The majority shareholder
thus shaved the reserves down to the very limit required by law

as minimum protection for policyholders. On April 2, 1969 the superintendent of insurance of the State of New York received from his staff an opinion that the extraordinary dividend declaration was contrary to the interests of the insuring public:

> However, the loss of 57% of policyholders' surplus may inhibit the Great American's ability to continue to underwrite its historical proportion of the total demand for insurance coverages and to maintain its competitive position and status in the industry. In such respects, aside from any questions of legality, the dividend action instituted at the first Board meeting after the change in ownership cannot be considered to have been in the best interests of the insurer and the insuring public.[25]

Before acquisition, the insurer had the freedom to greatly expand its underwriting. After National General's declaration to itself of $173 million dividend from its policyholders' reserves, Great American was bound to its current level of business and could not rise above it. The company had lost "potential for substantial growth," the superintendent's opinion continued:

> It is apparent that the payment of the special dividend of over $170,000,000 not only represents a loss of more than $5,000,000 annually in investment income but sharply reduces the possibility of material future capital gains, since the securities transferred were the equivalent of one-half of the common stock portfolio. Thus the Company has lost an important potential for substantial growth in the future—to maintain and increase its ability to respond to the growing demand for insurance and still increase its surplus.

The Insurance Department of New York pondered not only whether Great American's operations would be permanently curtailed by the surrender of its capital reserves, but whether that most successful of companies in its field had "commenced voluntary liquidation or dissolution."[26]

"We asked management what was a safe dividend to declare. They came up with a recommendation and figure and we accepted their recommendation and subsequently declared a dividend," the president of National General explained during congressional hearings.[27] National General, of course, controlled that management.

A few days after the declaration of the dividend, the Securities and Exchange Commission reminded National General that it had promised as a condition of its offer for the insurer's stock that "No change is now contemplated in the identity, business . . ." of the insurance company. The commission asked how it reconciled that statement with appropriation to itself of half the insurer's treasury.[28]

The extraordinary dividend declaration amounted to no change in operations because the management while still independent had contemplated the very same distribution, National General replied.

Secondly, the commission inquired, what would the acquirer do with its $173 million dividend?

"We are unable to reply definitely at the present time," National General answered on February 11, 1969. It assured that, in any event, possible acquisitions were "not yet even conceived."[29]

One week and one day after that reply, National General announced its offer of $15 cash for each share of stock of a second insurer, Republic Indemnity Co. The $13 million cash paid for 97% of Republic's stock came entirely from the Great American cash dividend. National General's management had entered into an agreement to purchase Republic on January 16, two days after the declaration of the Great American dividend.[30]

Five owners of substantial holdings of Republic stock were officers or directors of the acquirer. Symmetrically, the National General board chairman and president, Eugene Klein, was a Republic director; the Republic board chairman, Marvin Finell, was a National General director. Together, the two board chairmen owned over a third of Republic's voting stock. Finell was also chairman of the Great American operating committee. Several days before the declaration of the $173 million dividend he had received a fee from National General for his legal advice on "whether to go forward on Great American . . . and other items involving that corporation."[31]

National General's management maintained that $15 per Republic share was a price reasonable to the purchaser, that the amount would have been lower if the purchaser had not been bidding against another contender. Nevertheless, those five

officials, while deciding the amount of National General's offer, were in effect determining the portion of the Great American
dividend that would be paid to themselves. Together they received for their personal accounts over half the amount paid
for Republic Insurance Company.[32]

By January 1970 the fate which the Netter Report recommended for the ten wealthy (and, therefore, specifically selected) insurance companies had befallen eight of them. Klein
explained to the House Antitrust Subcommittee that the wealth
of those companies was indicative of poor management and, for
that reason, of their need to be taken over by conglomerates.
Chairman Celler of the subcommittee was skeptical. He questioned the Netter Report objectives:

> In other words, this document prepared by the firm Carter,
> Berlind is sort of an inducement for companies like your own to
> make an acquisition of an insurance company because it has in its
> portfolio a great many stocks and bonds the total value of which
> is beyond that which is required by the authorities. A so-called
> surplus is required to take care of contingencies by floods, hur-
> ricanes, what-have-you, whatever you may call it. Surplus-surplus
> is the excess over that amount. This Carter, Berlind document
> encouraged you, and others like you, to take over such a company;
> and when you take over that company you just syphon off for your
> own purposes this so-called surplus surplus.
>
> Now, don't you think that when an insurance company has been
> in existence for many years, and acquires a portfolio of various
> types of investments — in your case they were blue-chip stocks, I
> understand — that that fund cannot be looked upon as an ordinary
> surplus, and isn't it in the nature of a trust fund for the policy-
> holders?
>
> Do you think that you, as a principal stockholder, or your col-
> leagues as principal stockholders, have an inherent right to shave
> off that surplus surplus and use it for your own purposes?
>
> Mr. KLEIN. Yes, sir.
>
> The CHAIRMAN. Isn't an insurance company different from an
> ordinary business? If you acquired an ordinary business operation
> that had a tremendous book value, a tremendous portfolio of finer
> stocks the cash value of which wasn't needed in the operation of
> the business, I would say, "All right, take those blue-chip stocks
> and divide them among the stockholders."

But here you have an insurance company built with blood, sweat, and tears over the years. It is an old company you took over, and it had this surplus. You come along, and I can use the word "ruthlessly" take over this surplus surplus—even if you had the consent of the superintendent of insurance of the State of New York—and I think it was a New York corporation. I think there is something amiss here, something that is unusual, and should have given pause. . . .

Mr. KLEIN. . . . I disagree with the contention that we did anything wrong: I mean specifically that we were ruthless. That is a tough word, Mr. Chairman.

The CHAIRMAN. I am meaning to be tough.

Mr. KLEIN. I understand that, sir. I understand that. That is why I paraphrased it as "a tough statement."

. . .

No. 1, at no time and under no circumstances did the declaration of that dividend do any harm to the reserves of the policyholders of the insurance company. The remaining reserves were totally adequate, more than adequate to meet any contingency, any emergency, any disaster, any flood, as proven by the fact that 1969 was one of the worst years the insurance company ever had in all its existence, and incorporated into 1969 were such disasters as Hurricane Camille, which cost the company in excess of $6 million.

. . .

So, in the worst year, or approximately the worst year of the company's history, with untold disasters and catastrophes, unlooked for, such as Hurricane Camille, the company met its obligations with no strain whatsoever.

. . . This company . . . is over a hundred years old. These securities have appreciated greatly. This is true of many insurance companies, and it is also true that, because of that very strength, that strength that was not needed, it had more than twice as much financial strength than was needed by any stretch of any imagination; it had, in my opinion, and our opinion due to a great deal of laxity on the part of management of insurance companies.

The CHAIRMAN. Will you yield a moment?

Mr. KLEIN. Yes, sir.

The CHAIRMAN. Why couldn't you have, in the public spirit and in the interest of that company and public relations, spread the good gospel of your company by taking that huge surplus and, by the use of it, reduce the rates to your policyholders? Why didn't you do that?

Mr. KLEIN. Well, that is a different question, sir, and I will come to that.

The CHAIRMAN. It is quite relevant.

Mr. KLEIN. No. 1, I believe that an insurance company, like any other business enterprise in the American system of business, seeks to operate at a profit.

The CHAIRMAN. Are you an expert in the insurance business?

Mr. KLEIN. No, sir.

The CHAIRMAN. How long have you been in the insurance business?

Mr. KLEIN. I was a director of an insurance company for approximately 5 years before.

The CHAIRMAN. Only 5 years and you have been in an operating position now for a year, is that right?

Mr. KLEIN. Correct.

The CHAIRMAN. Or rather a year and a half. Do you deem yourself an expert on insurance?

Mr. KLEIN. No, sir.[33]

In the fall of 1967 the Netter Report fell on the desk of Saul Steinberg, 28-year-old chief executive of Leasco Data Processing Co. Leasco had been incorporated in 1965, and in two years its income, mainly from leasing computers, had risen from $196,-000 to $1,389,000. The investment community regarded the company highly, awarding it a price of thirty times earnings, or $62 per share.

Of the report's prime candidates, Steinberg chose Reliance Indemnity Co. The redundant surplus capital—the amount of capital reserves in excess of that required by law for policyholders' protection—by the most conservative estimate surpassed $80 million.

In "A Confidential Analysis of a Fire and Casualty Company" of January 11, 1968, Leasco listed attainment of that capital as its primary objective. Secondly, a merger with Reliance would automatically increase Leasco's per-share earnings because Reliance's shares sold at a lower price in comparison to earnings.[34]

Steinberg and three other Leasco officials met Netter and other CBWL members at the brokerage firm's office, also on January 11, 1968. One Leasco representative was five minutes late and thereby missed the entire meeting.

"We were annoyed and we got up and walked out," Steinberg

stated. As soon as the Leasco officials walked in the door, CBWL
handed them a memorandum. Listed were three demands. First,
"Carter, Berlind & Weill will be given one seat on the Leasco
Board immediately and acquired company board subsequently."
Second, "All purchases of stock in the acquired company on
board [the New York Stock Exchange] or off board will be made
exclusively through Carter, Berlind & Weill." Also, the firm "will
have a joint managerial position . . . on future public offerings
and private placements." Third, the firm demanded a $750,000
finder's fee.

That list "really jolted us," Steinberg said.

> We left. We laughed. We were weak. . . . It really jolted us, and
> we didn't expect that our future would be edicted to us. . . . we
> showed him [Leasco's investment banker] the list of demands
> and he said in his 40 years or 30 years of Wall Street he had not
> encountered such a thing.[35]

But in spite of that awkward beginning, by spring bygones
were bygones. CBWL modified its demands somewhat, Steinberg met Netter, Cogan, and Carter at Club Harmonie for lunch,
and both parties agreed to cooperate for the common goal.

The value and importance of the firm's cooperation with
Leasco was that the brokers knew where to locate the large
blocks of Reliance stock. With particular savvy and "connections" the firm knew which mutual funds and other institutions to approach.

As the season wore on, however, Carter, Berlind & Weill grew
impatient. Leasco, the firm thought, was dragging its heels, and
worse, was not laying all its cards on the table. On June 11, 1968,
CBWL brokers urged Steinberg to announce a tender offer for
Reliance stock the very next day. "How can I talk with the
Funds," Cogan asked, "if you don't give me any information?
You are not keeping me informed."[36] Cogan then urged Stein-
berg to offer $120 per Reliance share.

"We [Leasco] expressed surprise and astonishment and said
that with that view he could not possibly have analyzed the
economic consequences of such a transaction." On second
thought, the CBWL brokers suggested the price of $85 per share.
Cogan argued on behalf of his firm's customers — which group

included the firm's members — stating that they would have to receive substantially more than they had paid for Reliance stock.[37]

Six months earlier, in December 1967, Carter, Berlind & Weill had urged Reliance Insurance Co. to sell out for $45 (in paper, not cash) per Reliance share — approximately half the price it was now urging Leasco to pay.

The brokers' impatience with Steinberg was nothing compared to their exasperation with A. Addison Roberts, president of Reliance. To the firm's chagrin, Roberts was content to manage the insurance company. Obviously, he represented the competent management which turns a company into a broker's target.

The discontent worked both ways. CBWL's circulation of rumors of an imminent take-over of Reliance did not sit well with Roberts. Netter was attempting to drive up the price of Reliance stock by stating that Carter, Berlind & Weill were the managers of the merger when as yet there was not even a merger partner. According to Roberts:

> For a long time we knew that Carter, Berlind [CBWL] were stating to people that they were definitely going to involve us in a deal. But . . . [said those people] they [CBWL] wouldn't tell us who it [the would-be acquirer] is. So . . . it was a misstatement to buy this stock. This is a good opportunity to make a profit.[38]

Netter urged the president of Reliance at least to show a little interest in the merger, so as to give some substance to CBWL's rumors. "Won't you say to me that you are going to make a deal?" Netter pleaded with Roberts.[39]

"He also, as you might know," Roberts recounted, "called my secretary and asked her once what my reaction had been to the Eaton, Yale & Towne suggestion and that time was running out on me if I didn't do more."[40] Netter had in mind the forklift manufacturer Eaton, Yale & Towne and Gulf & Western, besides Leasco, as possible Reliance merger partners.

If only Roberts would cooperate, CBWL told him in February 1968, the firm would put Reliance stock at $40 or $50 per share — the stock for which in June it would ask $85–$125.[41]

But CBWL's efforts were succeeding without Roberts' co-

operation. By May Reliance stock had risen to the point that the
insurer's board of directors feared that the shareholders could
easily be tempted to sell. The directors thought, the president
recounted, "we were going to be forced into a deal and I was
authorized to find any company that I thought would be acceptable for us. . . ."[42]

Did he then discuss merger with many other companies in an
effort to supplant Leasco with an acquirer of Reliance's own
choice? Yes. With "half of America, it seemed like."

Leasco purchased $4,400,000 worth of Reliance stock in
March for prices between $30 and $40 per share. In April the
stock rose above $50, causing Steinberg to consider changing the
target to the lower-priced Hartford Fire & Casualty Co. (then not
yet acquired by International Telephone & Telegraph Co.).

But on June 22, 1968, to CBWL's delight, Leasco at last issued
a press release announcing its intent to tender an offer to the
shareholders.[43] A month later, on July 23, Leasco offered Reliance owners $72 in Leasco securities for each share.

Reliance management, in its own words, was "totally un-
receptive." On the same date it informed its shareholders by
letter that Leasco's entire earnings for the past five years equaled
little more than *half* the $9 million to be paid CBWL for ex-
change transaction expenses alone.[44]

Reliance management advised its shareholders that those
brokerage expenses were exorbitant: "We caution you that
brokers' opinions favoring merger may be influenced by the
generous fees to be paid them by Leasco." CBWL received almost a quarter-million dollars just from transfer of the shares in
its possession. During the first half of 1968, CBWL was encourag-
ing its customers to buy those shares from which purchase it
would receive a commission; at the same time it was arranging
their sale to Leasco, from whom it would receive another transaction fee. In effect, then, it was arranging buy and sell transactions
of the same securities at the same time. Inexplicably, CBWL
stated to Senate investigators that it had no significant part in
the plan for resale of those shares to any acquiring company.[45]

At the congressional hearings, A. Addison Roberts, still president of one-hundred-year-old Reliance, sat beside his new guard-
ian superior, Saul P. Steinberg, chief executive of Leasco. "As

head of Reliance, as chief executive officer for Reliance," he
stated, "I thought it was better for Reliance to stay independent."
He would still be resisting the takeover by suing Leasco and
CBWL, he continued, were there any chance:

> Chairman CELLER. What happened to the lawsuit, Mr. Roberts?
> Mr. ROBERTS. On the advice of our lawyers we withdrew the
> lawsuit because they felt that we could not prove the conspiracy.
> Chairman CELLER. Or was it due to the fact that a better offer
> was made subsequently?
> Mr. ROBERTS. No, sir. Let me say this: If we had thought this
> could have been won, I think we still would have been fighting.[46]

As a result of the $400 million acquisition of the enterprise
that surpassed Leasco's earnings ten times over, the acquirer's
net worth increased 1,361 percent, from $16 million to $236
million. Net income increased 1,834 percent, from $1.4 million
to $27 million.[47]

CHAPTER 6

Accept Delivery from the Pentagon

In the late spring of 1966, George Manis, chairman and principal stockholder of Memcor, Inc., called Chief Executive James Ling to ask if Ling-Temco-Vought, Inc. would be interested in merger. Manis said he was in poor health and could no longer manage the company. Memcor produced electronic equipment, principally the PRC-25 walkie-talkies used by the U. S. Army in Vietnam and by foreign military services.

Memcor's drawing card, Ling's subsequent investigation report ironically disclosed, was the very factor which revealed serious organizational disorder. The company could not fill large backlogs of walkie-talkie orders. To obtain those orders, it had underbid RCA by more than $200 per instrument. The undated report read:

PROGRAM STATUS

1. Behind on all deliveries . . . , has delivered about 7,000 units and is about 10,000 units behind.

2. Ruffin [president of Memcor] was able to con Philadelphia into a 95% progress payment under (1) above. They have used up 90% of the 95% to date.

3. RCA's present price on the PRC-25 is $820 per unit; MEMCOR's bid was $615 per unit at one time. Looks as if MEMCOR bought into program with hopes of recouping by the ECP route, which did not happen.

4. Even though MEMCOR is very late in delivery . . . the Army will not press for liquidated damages since the equipment is urgently needed for Southeast Asia.

5. U. S. Army indicates they will bail them out of any financial

98

bind if they are unable to find a way. However if the Army has
to do this, MEMCOR's future with the Army is dead.[1]

To have "bought into the program in the hopes of recouping by
the ECP route" means that Memcor had recklessly but purposely
submitted a lower-than-possible bid to remove other producers
from the competition. The only hope of salvation after that des-
perate gamble would be the Pentagon's granting of an Engineering Change Proposal—a euphemism for an agreement to pay
Memcor more than the price arrived at by competitive bidding
for which Memcor promised to perform the contract.

The gift of that envisioned price increase from the Pentagon
would mean that the system of competitive bidding—by which
only the most competent producer should win the contract—
would be thrown to the winds. Although LTV considered that
Memcor was "'in' with the Army," the conglomerate concluded
that there was no chance that the Pentagon would free Memcor
from its own trap. It could not envision such a gratuity as a Pentagon price increase which would reward a contractor for scheming
to eliminate competition. A memorandum of June 29, 1966 to
LTV Vice President J. W. Dixon based on confidential information from the Army Electronics Command stated:

> Memcor equipment is definitely good, but it is late. The company
> is losing money on each one because their costs are too high and
> their costs have gone up since they bid the job. They are trying
> to get contract modifications to bail them out, but they are not
> going to get them through.[2]

LTV guessed wrong. The Pentagon did grant Memcor's requested increase.

LTV Vice President Dixon concluded, after an inspection trip
of Memcor facilities in Huntington, Indiana, and Salt Lake
City that various competitors stood ready to produce the product
which Memcor could not "deliver." He wrote to Ling and LTV
President Clyde Skeen on July 15, 1966:

> Customer Relations and Competition: Because of inability to
> deliver, resulting from financial problems, customer relations are
> anything but good. The army has done everything possible to help
> Memcor, including increasing progress payments on PRC-25s to

95% but will not give them more business unless they demonstrate performance. Additional PRC-25 spares business is currently going to RCA and other companies on a component basis. It is conceivable that Memcor could get more of this business if they solved their problems. The Army has indicated they do not think highly of Memcor's present operating management.[3]

Dixon's report specified the other companies capable of producing the PRC-25:

In the components area, Memcor said the following companies were their prime competitors in an annual market of $75 to $100 million. These are: Ohmite, Ward-Lenard, Sprague, Mallory, and International Resistance Corporation. The latter three of these companies are growing and profitable organizations.

Memcor required 50 man-hours to produce each PRC-25 unit. LTV's information was, however: "Attainable man-hours—30, RCA is doing it in 32."

Another company apparently capable of PRC-25 production was Magnavox, the sales agent for all Memcor products in Europe. As LTV inspectors reported to Ling on July 14:

the Swedes came to Magnavox and insisted they [Magnavox] be the export agent for their order of the PRC-25's to Memcor. The Swedes have released $2.5 million to a United States bank, but the bank has to guarantee that this money will not be spent on anything but the Swedish order. If Memcor cannot deliver the PRC-25's to the Swedes, they are going to turn all drawings, inventory, work-in-progress, etc. over to Magnavox, and Magnavox is to complete the order.[4]

As with the Wilson merger, a major consideration was the effect that the "pooling" or mingling of Memcor revenue from defense contracts with LTV's revenues would have on the latter's earnings reports. For again, the plan was to give in exchange conglomerate securities earning less profit (in proportion to their market price) than were the securities to be acquired. This time, pooling of revenues would produce results more spectacular. On July 18 LTV finance manager George Griffin wrote to Ling and Skeen:

Assuming 600,000 shares LTV Electrosystems Inc. [the acquiring LTV subsidiary] common are exchanged for Memcor shares

> Memcor would increase LTE's [Electrosystem's] 1966 earnings by about 10–15% (including 9 months of earnings – last quarter FY 1966 at breakeven).

But if LTV Electrosystems preferred stock were given for Memcor stock, through pooling-of-interest accounting the LTV subsidiary's earnings could increase by as much as 25%. And if debentures, by 50%.

> Assuming a 5½% convertible preferred at $9 million Memcor would increase LTE's 1966 earnings by 20–25% on the same basis. If a convertible debenture were used, there would be an increase of twice this rate, because of the deductibility of the interest. However, the use of debentures would make the transaction taxable and therefore, less desirable to Memcor stockholders.[5]

Such a sharp rise in earnings normally would result in an increase in market value of LTV stock and, thus, in greater wealth to the conglomerate for further corporate acquisitions.

When asked whether the possibility of increasing LTV earnings was the primary purpose of the acquisition, Skeen replied during the House Antitrust Subcommittee hearings that there were two main objectives: "The first was to get into an area of electronic products that none of the LTV companies was in, and secondly, obviously, to increase the earnings of the Company if we can make it profitable."[6]

On July 21, 1966 Ling recommended to the Board of Directors that LTV purchase Memcor:

> Incidentally, Memcor is not shopping for a merger or to be acquired but because of Mr. Manis' serious illness for over a year, coupled with his feeling that Memcor's long-term outlook would be better teamed with LTV Electrosystems, he approached us to explore the feasibility or possibility of merging with Electrosystems.[7]

The boards of directors of both companies voted for merger. On July 25, 1966 a joint press release announced agreement in principle to merge. But the agreement was short-lived. Further LTV investigations indicated more strongly that Memcor could not produce its backlog of orders. Without that production, Memcor's revenue could not heighten LTV's earnings as the finance director had calculated.

"It was the unanimous conclusion," Clyde Skeen explained to the subcommittee," that Memcor was in substantially worse shape than we had anticipated, primarily because their backlog of PRC-25 radios, which was one of their great assets in our view, had a built-in loss of several millions of dollars. . . . Merger negotiations were called off finally and formally."[8]

On July 29, 1966 Ling wired all LTV directors and credit line banks: "Negotiations for the merger of Memcor into LTV Electrosystems were terminated upon mutual agreement of both companies."[9]

That a third party might intervene to render Memcor's operations so profitable that mingling its revenues with LTV revenue would result in realization of the conglomerate's original calculated earnings increase was not envisioned by the strongest imaginations. On September 2, 1966, however, Treasurer B. L. Brown returned to the LTV Tower to find on his desk a note from R. L. Thomas, an LTV corporate counsel:

> George Bergland (First National Bank in Chicago) called for you today and in your absence, informed me as to the following:
> 1. The Army wanted us to know that it had increased its quantity order on the three PRC-25 contracts by $3\frac{1}{2}$ million dollars; that it had granted and settled a claim in the amount of $167,000 in Memcor's favor; and that it had removed the liquidated damage clause from the three PRC-25 contracts.
> 2. The bank wanted us to know that its credit agreement with Memcor had been amended to eliminate any default prior to March 31, 1966, and increased the amount to 3.5 million; that it had extended the equity date to November 30; and that Alexander Grant is now in a position to issue a "clean" audit.
> All the above, just in case we are still interested.
>   R. L. T.[10]

LTV finance officer George Griffin immediately called the First National Bank to learn more. "Most significant," he wrote to Ling on September 9, 1966, "is the Army's specific request that LTV be informed of the remedial action being taken by them."

He explained, "In short, the Army appears to have done all that might be possible to make Memcor marketable by funding its past sins and anticipated underpricing on the PRC-25."[11]

Not only was the army increasing the walkie-talkie contracts by 25%. It was suddenly recognizing an old Memcor claim — the validity of which not even Memcor's auditor discerned. Griffin's memorandum continued:

> Tyler Port, Under Secretary of the Army, specifically wanted LTV to know that the Army had increased the price on the PRC-2J contracts by $100 per unit for the express purpose of making Memcor more attractive to LTV or other parties who could come in and give Memcor the management it needs.
>
> . . .
>
> The Army also wanted LTV to know that it had agreed to a settlement in full in Memcor's favor of a pending ASBCA claim in the amount of $170,000. (This also significant to Alexander Grant's opinion, as they questioned the carrying value of this claim.) In addition, the Army has eliminated the liquidated damages clause from the PRC-25 contracts.
>
> (In short, the Army appears to have done all that might be possible to make Memcor marketable by funding its past sins and anticipated underpricing on PRC-25. . . .)

The Army Contract Adjustment Board asserted, in an attempt to justify the price increase and claim recognition, that Memcor's walkie-talkie production was needed in Vietnam and that without those financial gratuities Memcor could not survive. But the army's decision made no mention of the other companies which, according to LTV's earlier investigations, were clearly capable of the same production.

By transferring the order to those companies, the army could have obtained the PRC-25 production without rewarding Memcor's scheme to "buy into the contract." According to that scheme as already seen, the company purposely submitted impossibly low bids to eliminate competitors from consideration. Thus, Memcor accurately anticipated that the Pentagon would increase the contract price even though that price surpassed the bids of the eliminated competitors.

If Memcor's "past sins and anticipated underpricing on the PRC-25" walkie-talkie contracts to eliminate competition — with bids so low that Memcor had to have "additional incentive" even to complete the contracts — was obvious to LTV, a safe assumption should be that the practice was obvious also to the Pentagon.

LTV President Clyde Skeen was asked whether the Pentagon, by raising the contract prices sought to enhance Memcor's profit-ability so that it would be an attractive acquisition target. "Yes, undoubtedly," he replied.

> Mr. HARKINS [House Antitrust Subcommittee Counsel]. Was the purpose of the Army's contractual actions which have been discussed to assist Memcor in a merger?
> Mr. SKEEN. Yes undoubtedly. This followed a formal action of the Army Contract Adjustment Board from which I quote: "It is hoped that the action will also enhance the possibility of a merger with a financially sound company, and the Army fully expects Memcor to follow through on its announced intent to seek such a merger."[12]

Thus, the army's justification for instigating the LTV-Memcor merger by rewarding Memcor's spurious contract bid was that the conglomerate would in some way inject financial strength into its acquisition. Two years after the merger, however, LTV did not have the revenue to pay the interest on its acquisition loans much less to help acquired subsidiaries. With the excep-tion of the first full calendar year after merger, 1968, LTV oper-ated at a deficit. The government's rejection of the competitive bidding process, therefore, produced no sure method for strength-ening government contractors.

The Pentagon's $3.5 million, 25% price increase for future Memcor production, the Pentagon's grant of theretofore unrec-ognized Memcor claims against itself, and the elimination of grounds for its claims against Memcor amounted to delivery of the company to LTV. For then the conglomerate was assured that the profit from the walkie-talkie production would more than offset the amount paid for Memcor and produce the calculated good results on LTV earnings.

To receive delivery without asking causes a person to ponder what he might get if he asks. LTV officials decided to try to pro-cure two million more dollars from the Pentagon by bringing "pressure" on the army to bring "pressure" on the navy to award a Memcor claim which—according to the judgment of LTV officials themselves—"does not appear to be valid."

LTV also planned for the Pentagon to bring "pressure" on Memcor itself to accept a purchase offer favorable to LTV.

Assistant comptroller of LTV Electrosystems, B. B. Pettigrew, advised the acquisition managers on November 11, 1966:

Action needed
1. Develop an offer.
2. Discuss with the Army (General Latta and Tyler Port) the offer before discussions with Memcor.

I believe the Army will put up to $2 million more in Memcor in order to get out of the management problem that they now have. Memcor should not be a party to this, and it should be agreed to before the negotiations are complete with Memcor but finalized after. There appears to be several ways that this money could be made available to Memcor. These will be discussed below.

Make the offer to Memcor. Let the banks, insurance company and the Army know that negotiations are being held. These people will apply pressure on Mr. Manis if any is necessary. I believe that the Army would insist that he take an offer of $6 per share for his stock. However, they have been approached by several companies; specifically, Chrysler, Laboratory For Electronics, Ecuadorian Corporation (they have business in the Bahamas and in Ecuador and are reputed to have considerable cash), Allied Research of Boston (they have MacNamara's [*sic*] representative to NATO, Lawrence Levi, on their Board of Directors), and others.

The Army wants out in the worst way and will pay to get out and will force Mr. Manis to accept a reasonable offer.[13]

Four days later that same LTV official further advised:

It is believed that the Army will pay $1 to $2 million to eliminate their financial risk in Memcor and management responsibility for Memcor. This could be accomplished through use of one or more of the following items:
(1) Pressure Navy into paying part or all of the $800,000 85–804 claim on the URN-20. The claim does not appear to be valid (but it may be a good vehicle), and the Army might have to furnish the funds for its payment (by MIPR).[14]

The fact that after the merger Memcor profits increased in spite of declining sales indicates the thoroughness of the govern-

ment price increases. Memcor stands alone as the LTV subsidiary which experienced increased earnings under LTV control through 1969.

The Memcor stockholders received $7 in LTV Electrosystems
common shares for each Memcor share. As a result of "buying
into the contract" Memcor thus secured for itself a much greater
exchange value than it otherwise could have hoped for.

The Purpose of the Conglomerate Headquarters

Diversified corporate acquirers rarely, if at all, reveal facts which disclose whether their management benefits or impairs their acquired corporations. Figures for comparing post-merger performance with pre-merger performance of the formerly independent companies are the conglomeration process's most tightly guarded secrets. Acquiring managers, though seldom at a loss for words asserting that they improve the acquired companies, do not divulge statistics for proving the point. Describing that reticence of conglomerate managers, Dr. Willard F. Mueller, director of the Federal Trade Commission's Economic Report on Corporate Mergers, stated to the Senate Judiciary Committee:

> So I am fearful that many people that are doing research on this subject today, who are interviewing leading conglomerators and others who are all charming, articulate people, are going to have a very difficult time cutting through all the jargon and rhetoric to find out what the facts really are.[1]

For want of more revealing disclosure, the profitability of entire conglomerates is often compared with industrial averages. Such comparison, however, offers only vague insight into the question of whether acquired companies secure advantage from the substitution of conglomerate control for their independence.

Forbes of January 1, 1973 (p.156) lists the return on total capital (assets owned outright plus borrowed assets) of 46 conglomerate corporations. That group's median annual earnings during the five years ending January 1, 1973 were 7.8% of total capital (see Table 16). *Forbes's* 29 industrial groups – among which the conglomerate group ranked 20th – returned median earnings of 8.5% of total capital. Thus, the conglomerates' return from assets under their control was less than that of the companies of other classifications. Further comparisons of conglomerate averages with representative industrial averages show very similar ratios of return on total capital.

TABLE 16
Conglomerates: Yardsticks of Management Performance

Company	5-Year return on total capital			Latest 12-month return on total capital Percent
		Rank		
	Percent	In this industry	Among all companies	
National Serv Inds	16.8[1]	3	49	16.9
U S Industries	16.8	1	47	12.4
Alco Standard	16.8	2	48	6.9
Chromalloy American	11.8	6	167	8.6
AMF	9.9	11	268	14.5
Indian Head	9.1	16	328	8.1
Textron	13.2	4	103	12.4
TRW	11.9	5	166	9.3
Gulf & Western Inds	6.3	30	530	6.3
White Consolidated	6.5	27	515	6.9
Dayco	8.1	20	383	5.5
Fuqua Industries	8.6	17	357	8.6
Tenneco	6.7	25	496	6.8
Studebaker-Worthington	8.3	18	368	5.9
City Investing	10.9	7	216	6.5
Teledyne	10.8	8	227	6.9
Dart Industries	10.0	10	265	8.3
Intl Utilities	6.2	32	539	6.8
Intl Tel & Tel	9.8	12	274	8.3
Lear Siegler	10.4	9	246	6.2
Sybron	9.8[2]	13	275	9.8
Singer	9.2	14	317	9.1
Martin Marietta	8.0	21	387	6.0
Whittaker Corp	9.2	15	319	3.8
Brunswick	7.6	23	423	10.7
Northwest Industries	6.0[2]	33	560	8.1
Amfac	7.9	22	391	7.5
FMC	7.5	24	429	4.0
Avco	6.2[2]	31	538	5.4
Ogden	6.5	28	518	5.9
Walter Kidde	8.1	19	381	8.0
Litton Industries	6.6	26	502	def
Transamerica	6.3	29	529	4.4
Allied Products	5.7	35	585	5.6

TABLE 16 *(continued)*

| Company | 5-Year return on total capital | | | Latest 12-month return on total capital Percent |
	Percent	In this industry	Among all companies	
A-T-O	5.8	34	574	5.8
W R Grace	4.9	36	642	5.5
Signal Companies	4.1	37	677	5.1
SCM	3.7	38	691	1.8
Illinois Central Inds	3.5	39	699	3.0
Universal Oil Prods	2.0	42	732	6.7
National Industries	3.2	40	710	6.6
Bangor Punta	1.1²	43	740	1.3
American Standard	def	44	752	def
LTV	3.1	41	712	def
Omega-Alpha	(3)			def
National Kinney	(3)			14.0
Industry Medians	7.8			6.7

1. Three-year average.
2. Four-year average.
3. Not available; not ranked.
   def = Deficit.
SOURCE: *Forbes*, January 1, 1973, p.156.

By congressional demand, the House Antitrust Subcommittee obtained pre-merger and post-merger performance statistics of companies acquired by the four largest subjects of its investigation: International Telephone & Telegraph, Litton Industries, Ling-Temco-Vought, and Gulf & Western Industries.[2] Conglomerates had never before disclosed such direct means for evaluating their ability to operate the companies they acquire.

Data for estimating efficiency of the acquiring managements are presented in terms of three ratios: net income as a percentage of sales, net income as a percentage of assets, and sales as a percentage of assets. In most instances, the last full year of independent management is compared with the subsequent years of conglomerate management through 1969.

The data for Fitchburg Paper Company, the earliest acquisition shown for Litton Industries, for example, indicate that the

TABLE 17
Profitability Ratios of Major Litton Subsidiaries
Acquired in the Years 1964 Through 1969[1]
(in percent)

Company and date acquired	Fiscal years ended—						
	1963	1964	1965	1966	1967	1968	1969
Fitchburg Paper Co. Apr. 1, 1964:							
Net income/sales	3.4	2.4	3.6	4.0	7.4	2.2	3.9
Net income/assets	5.5	2.6	4.7	5.3	8.3	2.0	4.0
Sales/assets	159.6	105.6	127.8	131.9	112.3	91.0	103.9
Hewitt-Robins, Inc. Feb. 24, 1965:							
Net income/sales		2.9	2.2	2.4	2.7	1.4	1.0
Net income/assets		3.9	3.2	3.6	4.3	2.3	1.5
Sales/assets		132.7	146.5	148.9	158.5	169.3	148.6
Louis Allis Co. Feb. 16, 1967:							
Net income/sales				3.8	2.8	2.2	[2]
Net income/assets				6.5	5.0	2.7	[2]
Sales/assets				167.6	177.0	123.0	116.9
Jefferson Electric Co. Feb. 23, 1967:							
Net income/sales				[2]	[2]	[2]	2.9
Net income/assets				[2]	[2]	[2]	5.0
Sales/assets				204.4	159.1	170.1	173.1
American Book Co. Mar. 31, 1967:							
Net income/sales			8.9	9.1	4.8	8.7	4.5
Net income/assets			8.6	9.3	5.3	7.9	3.9
Sales/assets			96.9	101.2	109.5	90.1	86.9
The Rust Engineering Co. June 7, 1967:							
Net income/sales				1.1	1.9	.9	1.4
Net income/assets				5.7	7.2	3.3	4.5
Sales/assets				536.8	369.2	377.2	332.5

1. *Hearings on Conglomerate Corporations*, Part 5, p.85.
2. Net income showed a loss.
SOURCE: Prepared by the House Antitrust Subcommittee staff from financial statements submitted by Litton Industries.

TABLE 18
Profitability Ratios for ITT Subsidiaries Which Maintained
a Postacquisition Financial Identity[1]
(*in percent*)

	1964	1965	1966	1967	1968
Subsidiaries Acquired in 1964[2]					
Barton Instrument:					
Net income to assets	5.1	6.5	7.9	8.8	9.5
Net income to sales	6.7	7.1	8.1	9.1	9.5
Assets to sales	131.0	110.0	107.0	104.0	100.0
Terryphone:					
Net income to assets	4.3	5.3	3.4	5.1	6.3
Net income to sales	13.1	12.2	7.5	9.8	13.0
Assets to sales	304.0	229.0	222.0	193.0	207.0
Subsidiaries Acquired in 1965					
Avis:					
Net income to assets	4.0	3.0	3.1	2.8	2.6
Net income to sales	6.1	4.0	4.0	2.8	2.8
Assets to sales	150.0	130.0	129.0	100.0	107.0
Henze Valve & Instrument:					
Net income to assets	14.4	11.9	5.7	3.0	4.3
Net income to sales	9.2	8.2	5.6	2.9	3.6
Assets to sales	63.0	69.0	97.0	97.0	83.0
Subsidiaries Acquired in 1966[1]					
Airport Parking Co. of America:					
Net income to assets		1.1	5.9	5.2	5.4
Net income to sales		.5	2.3	2.4	2.1
Assets to sales		49.0	39.0	47.0	38.0
Electro Physics Laboratories:					
Net income to assets			11.4	13.9	7.2
Net income to sales			3.3	4.3	2.4
Assets to sales			29.0	31.0	33.0
Jabsco Pump:					
Net income to assets		13.7	5.1	10.6	6.4
Net income to sales		8.9	9.0	9.0	8.9
Assets to sales		65.0	175.0	85.0	139.0
Howard W. Sams:					
Net income to assets		6.5	2.9	4.0	5.4
Net income to sales		6.6	2.9	4.0	5.0
Assets to sales		102.0	100.0	102.0	92.0
Wakefield:					
Net income to assets			5.6	5.8	5.3
Net income to sales			4.3	4.1	3.6
Assets to sales			76.0	70.0	67.0

1. Excludes financial subsidiaries.
2. *Hearings on Conglomerate Corporations*, Part 3, p.191.
SOURCE: Prepared by the House Antitrust Subcommittee staff from financial
statements submitted by ITT.

TABLE 19
Profitability Ratios of Two Major Ling-Temco-Vought
Subsidiaries
(in Percent)

The Okonite Co. and Subsidiaries

	1965	1966	1967	1968
Net income to total revenues	3.7	8.5	8.7	3.5
Net income to assets	5.4	1.4	6.6	4.0
Total revenues to assets	144.2	171.4		116.3

Wilson Cos. Combined

	1966	1967	1968	1969
Net income to total revenues	1.5	1.5	1.4	0.9
Net income to assets	7.7	7.6	6.1	3.9
Total revenues to assets	499.9	509.6	441.0	426.6

SOURCE: *Hearings on Conglomerate Corporations*, Part 6, p.132; prepared by the House Antitrust Subcommittee staff from financial statements submitted by LTV.

rate of net income from sales, 3.4% during the last full year before acquisition, rose to higher percentages during four of the six post-merger years. Fitchburg's rate of net income from assets for all post-merger years except one, however, is lower than for the last year of independent management.

Data are available for 28 of the four conglomerates' acquired companies (see Tables 12 [p. 62], 17, 18, and 19). Twenty-one of those companies show declining performance as measured by at least two of the three efficiency ratios. Twenty-two of the 28 acquisitions show declining performance as measured by the amount of income generated by assets.

That other factors besides management efficiency bear on profitability need not be elaborated. However, the fact that at least three-fourths of the acquired companies for which statistics can be produced show declining performance after merger should not prove that conglomerates enhance the operations of their acquired parts. As the Antitrust Subcommittee Report more affirmatively states: "Inasmuch as these companies perform in many different industries, and in the light of the fact that until

1970 the trend of annual corporate profits was up, it would be reasonable to conclude that these ratios reflect ineffective management."[3]

The question arises, then, of the purpose of the conglomerate headquarters. The House Armed Services Committee pondered that point on April 17, 1972, as admirals appearing before it described "the organization structure we now have to deal with" after a conglomerate acquires a shipbuilding contractor. The deputy chief of Naval Materiel for Procurement and Production, Rear Admiral Rowland G. Freeman, explained that the corporate acquirer imposes over the shipbuilder a less accessible "absentee management," which is motivated more by cash than by efficiency. A diagram of the contractor's pre-merger independent management organization was then flashed on the screen of the hearing room.

PRIOR TO MERGER

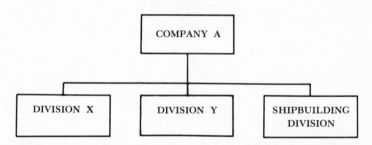

Admiral FREEMAN. One other area difficult for us — one in which we have a hard time managing. This is an illustration of a shipbuilding company we dealt with about 5 years ago. Very simply, we dealt with them day to day, and reached the president very easily. The project manager was pretty much in control, due to the contractor's operations and the philosophies followed.[4]

Then the diagram of the organization under conglomerate control was flashed on the screen.

SUBSEQUENT TO MERGER

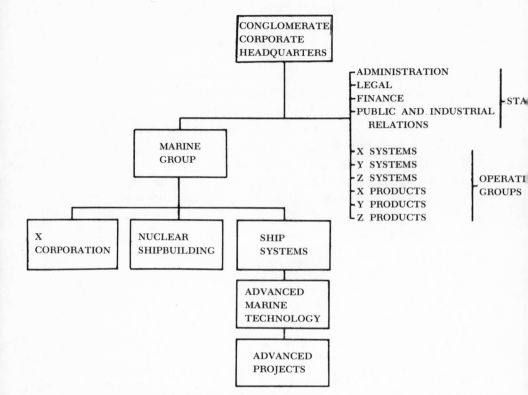

Admiral FREEMAN. Subsequently this company was bought and merged and this is the organizational structure we now have to deal with. It has high cash motivation, and it is very difficult to reach the people who actually have to make the corporate decision when you are talking dollar schedule performance. It can take months.

We can criticize our own bureaucracy, which is true. However there is the same fault in an organization like this and the ability to do business promptly and easily is impaired.

The congressional panel asked for elaboration. Admiral Freeman continued:

Actually, there are several problems involved with a large organization [conglomerate acquirer] which is primarily motivated through cash flow and profit, which is what they are in business for—to move money. They are almost an absentee management, or are a large heavily divisionalized management. It is very difficult to get the senior members of the corporation's attention in many cases. If it is an absentee management, the things we talk about, that is, performance and requirements—in some cases we believe do not get the attention we would like them to have.

It is a different environment to operate in when you are operating with an individual entrepreneur, such as a number of our companies used to be.[5]

When the hearing ended, the riddle of the purpose of the absentee management remained unanswered.

CHAPTER 7

The Purpose of
International Telephone & Telegraph

After World War II, International Telephone & Telegraph Corp. decided it had set off in the wrong direction when it was founded in 1920. It summarized its problems by concluding that the company was, after all, in the wrong business.

While other American industries busily prospered from the booming postwar economy, International Telephone & Telegraph reeled from the war damage to its overseas telephone systems. Almost all its stockholders were American citizens but almost all its assets were in foreign countries. Furthermore, the American Telephone & Telegraph monopoly, impregnable then as now, prevented transfer of operations to the United States. Harold S. Geneen, president and chairman of the corporation, explained to the House Antitrust Subcommittee in November 1969:

> During World War II, practically all of ITT's companies in Europe were overrun and seized. Currency conversion problems which persisted for many years after the War, and the necessity for rehabilitating and rebuilding our companies, were ITT's primary concerns and difficulties. I might point out that these serious losses and difficulties occurred at a time when most U. S. companies were rapidly expanding from the U. S. plants which had been developed for war time purposes and were quickly converted to peace time capacity usages, thus providing an uninterrupted flow of growth and earnings for their stockholders.
>
> ITT had no such advantages. In fact, many of our companies have not been recovered from the World War II expropriations. And even more recently, our Cuban telephone company was ex-

116

propriated without compensation by Mr. Castro. A short time later, our Brazilian telephone company was also expropriated. And only two weeks ago, we sold our Peruvian telephone company to the Government of Peru in recognition of their national aspirations.

Experiences of this kind, therefore, regarding the business risks involved in foreign operations convinced the management and Board of Directors of ITT of the necessity and of our obligation to diversify into the relatively secure and growing U. S. and Canadian economies. Our first point of entry into the domestic market might logically have appeared to be the telephone equipment manufacturing business, as this was our major field abroad. However, ITT's traditional areas of telecommunications were essentially foreclosed in the U. S. because of the captive market position and vertical integration of AT&T and its manufacturing subsidiary Western Electric Co., and General Telephone and Electronics and its manufacturing subsidiary Automatic Electric Company.[1]

ITT, like National General, is the product of diversification from desperation. Yet, if the conglomerate system has an authentic function, a benefit to provide acquired enterprises, ITT should be the company to demonstrate that function.

When conglomerate stock fell from dazzling heights in 1969 and 1970, ITT conspicuously maintained its equilibrium. By mid-1971, when the wildest imaginations could not envision the return of most conglomerate stock even to the low of 1968, ITT easily surpassed its high of that bull-market year.

Its return from acquired assets, however, is not as impressive as its stock market performance. The company ranks 12th among the 46 conglomerates which *Forbes* lists according to their rate of return from total capital for the five years ending January 1, 1973. Among the entire listing of 780 companies, ITT ranks 274th.

ITT shrewdly shuns that hackneyed argument that conglomeration provides financial resources for acquired subsidiaries. A conglomerate's income comes only from subsidiary operations. When an acquirer claims that it reverses that process and provides capital to its subsidiaries usually it is referring, at best, to its shifting of capital from one acquired company to another.

TABLE 20

Acquisitions of U. S. Corporations by ITT (Jan. 1, 1964, to Jan. 1, 1969)

Company	Date acquired	Accounting treatment	Total consideration	Type of consideration
Hayes Furnace Manufacturing & Supply Co.	June 29, 1964	Pooling of interest	$1,065,188	Common Stock (7.41).
Aetna Finance Co.	Aug. 31, 1964	Pooled with financial subsidiary, ITT Financial Services (separately reported).	34,812,664	Combination of common (0.2208) and series E preferred (0.05581).
Terryphone Corp.	Sept. 30, 1964	Pooling of interest	3,813,016	Common (0.087).
Barton Instrument Corp.	Nov. 30, 1964	do	12,270,053	Common (0.2922).
Semi-conductor Assets of Clevite Corp.	Jan. 29, 1965	Purchase	9,188,484	Cash.
Henze Valve & Instrument Co., Inc.	Apr. 30, 1965	Pooling of interest	1,242,000	Common.
Avis, Inc.	July 22, 1965	do	51,021,352	Common (0.1375) and series F preferred (0.1).
National Auto Renting Co.	do	do	3,013,725	Common and series F preferred.
Hamilton Management Corp.	Aug. 6, 1965	Purchase and pooling (part of finance subsidiary, ITT Financial Services).	17,245,536	Cash and common (.3494).
Kebby Microwave Corp.	Aug. 17, 1965	Pooling of interest	646,855	Common.
Documat, Inc.	Aug. 20, 1965	Pooling of interest	751,300	do
Press Wireless, Inc.	Sept. 7, 1965	Purchase	4,188,140	do
Electro Physics Laboratories, Inc.	Feb. 15, 1966	Pooling of interest	1,497,168	do

Company	Date	Method	Shares/Amount	Consideration
Wakefield Corp.	Feb. 24, 1966	Purchase	12,023,406	Cash.
Jabsco Pump Co.	Feb. 28, 1966	Pooling of interest	9,616,213	Common and series F preferred.
Brooks Equipment Co.	June 21, 1966	Purchase	125,000	Cash.
Consolidated Electric Lamp Co.	Oct. 28, 1966	Pooling of interest	7,720,584	Common.
Howard W. Sams & Co., Inc.	Oct. 31, 1966	do	29,257,869	Common (.423) and cumulative convertible participating preferred (.236).
Airport Parking Co. of America	Nov. 14, 1966	do	26,356,616	4.50 cumulative convertible preferred of ITT Consumer Services Corp. (.285).
Amplex/Lustra Corps.	Mar. 7, 1967	do	7,955,942	Common.
Cleveland Motel Corps.	May 18, 1967	do	9,490,437	do
Mears Motor Livery Corp.	June 16, 1967	do	2,120,261	Series F preferred.
Selected assets from National City Trucking Rental Co.	July 31, 1967	Purchase	892,000	Cash.
Bramwell Business College	Aug. 19, 1967	do	40,000	do
Texas Tool & Machine Co.	Sept. 28, 1967	do	150,000	do
Simonds–Worden–White Assets of H. K. Porter Co.	Nov. 15, 1967	do	750,000	do
Modern Life Insurance Co.	Dec. 15, 1967	Purchase (part of finance subsidiary, ITT Financial Services).	5,212,404	do
Jasper-Blackburn Co.	Jan. 2, 1968	Pooling of interest	19,067,784	Common (.67) and series H preferred (.05).
Levitt & Sons, Inc.	Feb. 1, 1968	do	93,445,976	Common (.57).

TABLE 20 *(continued)*

Company	Date acquired	Accounting treatment	Total con-sideration	Type of consideration
Massachusetts Trade Shops	Feb. 20, 1968	do	609,000	Common.
Sheraton Corp. of America	Feb. 28, 1968	do	293,514,613	Common (.5212) and series K preferred (.05).
Bailey Technical Schools, Inc.	Apr. 24, 1968	do	439,979	Common.
Rayonier, Inc.	Apr. 26, 1968	do	301,858,224	Common (.3950) and series I preferred (.2675).
Allied Institute of Technology	May 17, 1968	do	918,000	Common.
Pennsylvania Glass Sand Corp.	June 27, 1968	do	113,810,343	Common (.628) and series I preferred (.27).
Sterling Design Corp.	June 28, 1968	do	493,391	Common.
ETC Corp.	July 19, 1968	do	9,559,375	do
Speedwriting, Inc.	July 22, 1968	do	7,891,610	do
Continental Baking Co.	Sept. 13, 1968	do	275,744,066	Common (.72) series K preferred (.25) and series L preferred.
Transportation Displays, Inc.	Sept. 25, 1968	do	3,874,856	Common and series K preferred.
Peters & Russell, Inc.	Sept. 30, 1968	Purchase	4,000,000	Cash.
Gotham Lighting Co.	Oct. 4, 1968	Pooling of interest	2,125,701	Common.
Speedwriting of Canada, Ltd.	Oct. 11, 1968	do	786,200	do
State Auto Parks, Inc. & United Parking, Inc.	Oct. 31, 1968	do	624,149	do
Gremar, Inc.	Dec. 20, 1968	do	4,468,890	Common (.17).
Pennway Corp.	Dec. 30, 1968	do	3,336,080	Common.

SOURCE: *Hearings on Conglomerate Corporations*, Part 3, p.37.

TABLE XI

ITT Acquisitions of U. S. Corporations, Jan. 1, 1969 to Oct. 31, 1969
[50 percent or more of voting stock or substantially all of the assets]

Company name	Acquired	Purchase cost (stock/cash)	Product	Annual sales (in millions)
Thorp Finance Corp., Thorp, Wis.	Jan. 3, 1969	$46,485,000 (stock-K)	Consumer loans	$ 18.880
Temple School, Inc., Washington, D. C.	Feb. 6, 1969	$2,250,000 (stock-cmn)	Business school	1.800
Peterson School of Business, Inc., Seattle, Wash.	Mar. 6, 1969	$740,000 (cash)	do	.800
Hopkins Airport Hotel, Inc., Cleveland, Ohio.	Mar. 7, 1969	$3,500,000 (stock-K/cmn)	Hotel	1.300
United Homes Corp., Seattle, Wash.	Mar. 14, 1969	$13,600,000 (stock-cmn)	Builders	24.495
Liberty Investors Benefit Insurance Co., Greenville, S. C.	Mar. 25, 1969	$2,863,695 (stock-cmn)	Insurance	1.800
Marquis Who's Who, Chicago, Ill.	Mar. 28, 1969	$7,500,000 (stock-cmn)	Publishers	2.916
Decca Systems, Inc., Washington, D. C., Decca Radar, Inc. (50 percent), New York, N. Y.	Mar. 31, 1969	$7,000,000 (cash)	Navigational equipment.	8.600
Stautzenberger Business College, Inc., Toledo, Ohio.	Apr. 11, 1969	$680,000 (stock-cmn)	Business school	0.900
Hammell Business University, Inc., Akron, Ohio.	Apr. 15, 1969	$150,000 (cash)	do	.235
Joseph B. Giglio Enterprises, Inc., Tampa, Fla.	Apr. 17, 1969	$3,525,000 (stock-cmn)	Avis franchisee	2.630
Canteen Corp., Chicago, Ill.	Apr. 25, 1969	$244,966,840 (stock-K/cmn)	Food service	360.000
Electronics Institute of Technology, Inc., Detroit, Mich.	Apr. 28, 1969	$50,000 (cash)	School	.327
Avis Option Cities, Nebr., Miss., Calif., Fla.	May 2, 1969	$2,275,000 (stock-cmn)	Avis franchisees	2.500
Pascal Lease, Inc., San Jose, Calif.	May 19, 1969	$987,350 (stock-cmn)	Avis franchisee	1.200
Link's School of Business, Inc., Boise, Idaho.	May 21, 1969	$185,000 (cash)	Business school	.250
United Building Services, Inc., Columbus, Ohio.	May 23, 1969	$2,925,000 (stock-cmn)	Cleaning services	3.000

TABLE 21 (continued)

Company name	Acquired	Purchase cost (stock/cash)	Product	Annual sales (in millions)
The Office Training School Co., d.b.a. Columbus Business University, Columbus, Ohio.	May 29, 1969	$840,000 (stock-K)	Business school	.700
C & S Lighting Maintenance Co., Cleveland, Ohio.	June 24, 1969	$260,000 (stock-cmn)	Commerical lighting installation and service.	.500
Industrial Credit Co., St. Paul, Minn.	June 30, 1969	$12,888,451 (cash)	Finance company	60.000
Wadsworth Land Co., Fla.	July 15, 1969	$2,100,000 (stock-K)	Land holdings	3.430
Industrial Cafeterias, Inc., and Menumat, Boston, Mass.	July 25, 1969	$825,000 (cash)	Food service	
Nancy Taylor Secretarial Finishing School of Chicago, Inc., Chicago, Ill.	Aug. 25, 1969	$50,756 (cash)	Speedwriting franchisee.	.145
American Electric Manufacturing Corp., Southaven, Miss.	Aug. 28, 1969	$7,446,924 (stock-cmn)	Manufacturer of street lighting.	7.000
Minnesota School of Business, Inc., Minneapolis, Minn.	Sept. 9, 1969	$890,000 (stock-K)	Business school	.950
G. K. Hall Corp., Boston, Mass.	Sept. 23, 1969	$7,556,250 (stock-cmn)	Publishing	2.034
American Building Services, Inc., Kansas City, Mo.	Oct. 10, 1969	$3,475,000 (stock-K)	Building services	4.041
Southern Wood Preserving Co., Atlanta, Ga.	Oct. 30, 1969	$12,727,500 (stock-K/cmn)	Treated timber producer.	27.000
Grinnell Corp., Providence, R. I.	Oct. 31, 1969	$251,273,972 (stock-K/cmn)	Manufacturer fire protection sprinklers.	370.000

SOURCE: *Hearings on Conglomerate Corporations*, Part 3, p.32.

ITT's motives for purchasing Pennsylvania Glass Sand Corp. and Jasper-Blackburn Co. (an electronics equipment manufacturer) dispel any idea that the purpose of acquisition is to bestow financial resources on the acquired company. Just the reverse is true. ITT calculated before those mergers how much the largely debt-free companies would add to the parent company's borrowing capacity. It determined, in effect, the amount of financial resources the target companies could provide the conglomerate.

The Jasper-Blackburn Co. of St. Louis, an ITT finance officer informed President Geneen on June 13, 1967, could add $6.5 million to the conglomerate's cash borrowings:

> Blackburn has a strong balance sheet with a current ratio of 5.5 to 1 and over $9 million in equity. The acquisition of Blackburn would generate approximately $6½ million additional borrowing power for ITT.[2]

The Pennsylvania Glass Sand Corp., President Geneen told the ITT Board of Directors on February 14, 1968, could provide the conglomerate with $28 million borrowed cash:

> Over the past ten years, profit margins have exceeded 15% in every year and have recently increased to a current rate in excess of 20% of sales. The company has operated virtually debt-free during this period, and consolidation of Pennsylvania's balance sheet would add over $28 million to total ITT borrowing power.[3]

When asked whether it was usual to consider how the acquired assets would add to ITT's borrowing capacity, Geneen replied, "There is no question about the point."[4] Table 22 indicates the extent to which the conglomerate did in fact secure funds through increasing the debt of acquired companies after merger.

The ratio of long-term debt to net worth before and after acquisition of eleven major subsidiaries shows that the debt of four of the companies decreased after merger. The debt of three of those four, Airport Parking Corp., Levitt & Sons, and Sheraton Corp., however, varies according to real estate mortgage requirements. The other companies show substantial increases in debt after ITT's assumption of control.

The columns on interest coverage show that after acquisition

TABLE 22
Selected Financial Stability Ratios of ITT's Major Acquired Subsidiaries[1]
for the Last Audited Fiscal Year Ended Preceding Acquisition
Compared with ITT Ratios for the Next
Fiscal Year Ended after Acquisition

Subsidiary	Long-term debt plus preferred stock to common-stock equity		Long-term debt to net worth		Interest and preferred dividend coverage		Interest coverage	
	Before	After	Before	After	Before	After	Before	After
Avis, Inc.	0.52 to 1	0.84 to 1	0.52 to 1	0.58 to 1	10.0 to 1	3.2 to 1	10.0 to 1	3.7 to 1
Airport Parking Corp. of America	0.85 to 1	0.75 to 1	0.85 to 1	0.53 to 1	7.0 to 1	3.1 to 1	7.0 to 1	3.5 to 1
Barton Instrument Corp.	0.13 to 1	0.66 to 1	0.13 to 1	0.47 to 1	58.0 to 1	4.6 to 1	58.0 to 1	5.3 to 1
Continental Baking Co.	0.27 to 1	1.02 to 1	0.14 to 1	0.56 to 1	10.9 to 1	3.2 to 1	25.8 to 1	4.5 to 1
Howard W. Sams & Co., Inc.	0.40 to 1	1.17 to 1	0.40 to 1	0.65 to 1	14.8 to 1	3.0 to 1	14.8 to 1	3.4 to 1
Jasper-Blackburn Co.	0.02 to 1	1.0 to 1	0.02 to 1	0.56 to 1	74.6 to 1	3.2 to 1	74.6 to 1	4.5 to 1
Levitt & Sons, Inc.	1.5 to 1	1.0 to 1	1.5 to 1	0.56 to 1	1.5 to 1	3.2 to 1	1.5 to 1	4.5 to 1
Pennsylvania Glass Sand Corp.	0 to 1	1.0 to 1	0 to 1	0.56 to 1	71.7 to 1	3.2 to 1	71.7 to 1	4.5 to 1
Rayonier, Inc.	0.58 to 1	1.0 to 1	0.58 to 1	0.56 to 1	9.2 to 1	3.2 to 1	9.2 to 1	4.5 to 1
Sheraton Corp. of America	3.01 to 1	1.0 to 1	2.9 to 1	0.56 to 1	1.8 to 1	3.2 to 1	1.8 to 1	4.5 to 1
Wakefield Corp.	0.12 to 1	0.75 to 1	0 to 1	0.53 to 1	39.7 to 1	3.1 to 1	[2]	3.5 to 1

1. Excludes financial subsidiaries.
2. Interest expense immaterial.
SOURCE: Hearings on Conglomerate Corporations, Part 3, p.158; prepared by the House Antitrust Subcommittee staff.

ITT subsidiaries' debts rose more sharply than did their revenues. Three companies—Barton Instrument Corp., Jasper-
Blackburn Co., and Pennsylvania Glass Sand—had more than
ten times the resources for interest payment before merger than
after.

ITT World Headquarters, Geneen asserted, increases the debt
of acquired companies after merger to provide capital for the
conglomerate's aggressive growth policy.[5] However, that capital,
provided by the acquisitions themselves, comes from resources
available to them before merger, not from the coffers of the acquiring company.

Rather than the provision of capital, the purported contribution of World Headquarters to the 120 acquired companies is
management ability. As seen, however, of the nine major acquisitions for which ITT supplied pre-merger and post-merger
performance statistics, all but three have experienced decreasing
returns from assets after ITT management's assumption of control.

Nevertheless, President Geneen told shareholders in the 1971
Annual Report: "There is no question in my mind that the reason
for this continued ability to perform under adverse as well as
favorable conditions is primarily the result of our worldwide
management strength."

The 1971 Annual Report explained that management proficiency is the purpose of World Headquarters' control of the subsidiaries:

> From 1959 through 1971 we have steadily increased sales, net
> income and earnings per share because we have developed a
> management process which has given our Company a capability
> we believe to be unique in international industry. . . . More than
> 200 days a year are devoted to management meetings at various
> organizational levels throughout the world. . . . ITT long ago re-
> jected the "ivory tower" approach to management. . . . The test
> of how well any management performed is simply results. . . .
> Throughout this wide range of products and services, the common
> distinguishing element is management. . . .

However, testimony to the House Antitrust Subcommittee
does not make clear that the conglomerate headquarters does

manage its acquired subsidiaries. "We do not manage any of the
line operations from the headquarters in New York City," Geneen stated on November 20, 1969.[6]

"I wonder whether the Good Lord has given anybody the
prowess and the expertise, the ingenuity," Chairman Celler inquired, "to be able to control all those operations in these various
fields [under ITT control] that cover almost every conceivable
product, and we are a little concerned about that, naturally, sir."[7]

"I couldn't begin to run one hundredth of what we have, and
I don't," Geneen replied. "But I see that it is run."[8]

ITT subsidiaries function as independent "profit centers," he
explained. The purpose of the 1,000 officials in ITT World Headquarters in New York is to "aid and support" the acquired companies. That Headquarters, which had no role in the companies'
functions and usually no experience in their fields of endeavor,
somehow gives direction to the approximately 2,000 executives
who created and very successfully operated those companies
before merger. In Geneen's words:

> Each of these people [executives of acquired companies] lay out
> their own operations, lay out their own plans. We review them
> with them. We insist that they deal with facts and be not over-
> optimistic or, on the other hand unduly pessimistic. Their own
> plans are what they run against, their own performance is what
> we monitor with them and then we have this large central staff
> of about a thousand people which I have mentioned which are
> there to aid and support them when they get into any problems
> where they can't meet their own predictions. So each of these
> people are essentially running their own companies with the sup-
> port, the help, and monitoring, if you want to call it that, of the
> central staff, which is a large staff.[9]

Strangely, the parent corporation is able to exercise more effective discipline over the two thousand executives than the discipline formerly required of them for survival as independent
entrepreneurs. "Let me see if I can make clear what the control
is," Geneen continued:

> We will insist that they [acquired executives] get the facts and
> we will insist that they make sensible decisions based on the facts.
> I am in no position to countermand facts, no matter what my au-

thority is, so they run it. If we had somebody that was not running it well or was proceeding against the facts, let's say his market was disappearing and he was proceeding to build new plants, this is a combination of facts that doesn't make sense and I think we present these facts to him and ask him to make a proper decision.[10]

Executives who founded and operated the formerly independent subsidiaries need the nonmanaging New York office supervisors to tell them to "get the facts." How the acquired profit centers were able to come into being, compete, and prosper without ITT World Headquarters' insistence on "sensible decisions" remains a mystery.

"We can hold them [the subsidiary executives] responsible for performance," the president explained.[11] That is to say, successful operations before merger — when the executives had no parental "help, support and monitoring" to fall back upon — required a lesser degree of responsibility.

ITT acquires only prosperous enterprises. To qualify for ITT acquisition consideration, a company must have a pre-merger growth-rate capability of ten percent annually.

The conglomerate, then, does not agree with Thomas Jefferson in the belief that the best government is the least government. "We are always trying to look for a growing company because we can't manage them ourselves," Geneen stated.[12] Stockholders and public consumers assume the bill for a second, nonmanaging government superimposed over the original, and in all cases, successful, acquired corporate government.

With the invention of the "monitoring" concept perhaps ITT has added a new horizon to corporate functioning. But credit for the corporation's growth, claimed by the superimposed conglomerate headquarters which neither manages nor directs nor orders may be due to other factors. First of all, ITT subsidiaries were prospering on their own feet before acquisition.

Secondly, the conglomerate feeds from its own mass.

ITT acquired Avis Rent a Car in early 1965. Robert Townsend, president of Avis at that time, suggested to Geneen that not only the conglomerate's divisions and 30,000 employees, but also ITT suppliers (appreciative of ITT trade) and their employees, serve as assured, if not captive, Avis customers. "[W]e must set up a basis by which we can call IT&T," Townsend wrote, "when we are ready to go after the car leasing business of their divisions, suppliers, friends, etc. and we will get real help. . . . when we are ready to put charge cards into the hands of employees, suppliers' employees and friends' employees we can call and will get real help."[13]

Geneen was enthusiastic. His response was to carry the idea further. Avis should rely not merely on the consumer power of the 30,000 ITT employees, he wrote, but also on their power to win friends and influence people. All ITT employees should be ITT salesmen:

> in addition to working out a basis where you can proceed through ITT's people to develop business, it would be desirable to develop a simple basis whereby all of our employees, to the extent useful, could become salesmen for Avis.
> . . . We have over 30,000 employees in the country and if these could be brought in to use it should help. We are awaiting a program from you as to how and in what manner to switch all of our own use over to Avis.[14]

According to Geneen's and Townsend's plan, a car rental agency which is not a subsidiary of a conglomerate possessing assets of four billion dollars and employing the third greatest number of employees in the United States would just have 30,000 fewer possible customers, and 30,000 fewer possible salesmen serving without pay. Nor could an independent rental agency count on the suppliers of over 120 subsidiary companies, or those "suppliers' employees and friends' employees" as likely customers.

If a seller of goods or services can make sales from the personal needs of its employees and their friends and relatives and of its suppliers' employees, of course the competitor which employs the largest mass of consumers and purchases the largest amount from suppliers will be in a favored position. The process of survival of the fittest, or of the favored, then strengthens the apprehension (see p. 1) that the trend of corporate concentration will reduce the number of independent enterprises to two hundred before the end of the century.

For justification, Geneen cited the example of the nation's number one monolithic monopoly.

I don't see anything wrong with our employees believing in our company and being salesmen for it. I think the Telephone Company has people who speak well of them and try to sell telephones.[15]

American Telephone & Telegraph Co. uses its employees as unpaid salesmen, also, he stated.

The scheme of "going after the car leasing business of ITT . . . suppliers" is another example (as seen before in Chase Manhattan Bank's outline for Gulf & Western acquisitions) of an acquisitor's effort to gain reciprocal sales advantages from vastness of operations. Through reciprocity a company forces a supplier to be its customer, not through underbidding or outperforming competitors, but by threatening to curtail its purchases from that supplier. Sales secured by reciprocity, therefore, are not a reward for a manufacturer's high-quality performance in a freely competitive system, but rather a reward for the magnitude of his purchases.

In prepared testimony for congressional hearings, the ITT president could not have expressed his corporation's official abhorrence of reciprocity in stronger terms:

Efforts to purchase or sell goods or services on the basis of so-called "reciprocity" violate basic management principles of building a business soundly and permanently by being at all times capable of meeting open competition and having a trained business organization capable of meeting the challenges and problems created by competition. . . . The theory of "reciprocity" is therefore repugnant as a basic business philosophy.[16]

Geneen then read the "formal ITT Company Policy" against reciprocity, a directive disseminated to managers in 1966 to make sure that the long-standing formal abhorrence was "clearly understood throughout the system":

RECIPROCITY

The United States Supreme Court has held that reciprocal buying practices or "reciprocity," is "one of the congeries of anticompetitive practices" at which the antitrust laws of the United States are aimed. Reciprocity is also an unsound business practice, since it distorts the market process and the normal development of economic efficiencies and product improvements. Consequently,

for both legal and business reasons, it is the policy of ITT to purchase and sell products and services on the basis of the commercial criteria of superior quality, suitability, efficiency, service,
and price.

. . .

No attempt shall be made to develop sales of any service or
product through the use of, or threatened withdrawal of, any
existing or potential reciprocal buying leverage or "reciprocity."

In this connection, information concerning ITT System purchases from particular suppliers shall not be made available to
personnel who are concerned with developing sales and marketing.[17]

Thus ITT asserts that it does not try to make customers out of
suppliers.

But subsidiary managers who forget that policy directive and
lapse into reciprocal thinking, as did the Avis executive, apparently need not fear chastisement. President Geneen himself,
after reading that formal policy of 1966 at congressional hearings
on November 20, 1969, forgot the policy the next day. On November 21, at the same hearings, he stated: "Yes, reciprocity
effect is an awfully difficult one to define, and I gather a very
new term. As a matter of fact, I have never heard of it before the
last few months."[18]

The policy statement, however, is not without a most valuable
purpose. In 1965 the government sued to prevent the merger of
J. R. Reynolds Tobacco Co. with Penick & Ford, a producer of
starch used in the manufacture of paper. The government contended that Reynolds could secure sales for Penick & Ford from
the paper manufacturers from whom Reynolds purchased in
large quantities. In 1969, for the same reason—to prevent market
restructuring conducive to reciprocal sales—the government
sought to prevent the acquisition of B. F. Goodrich Co., a manufacturer of chemicals and other industrial products besides tires,
by Northwest Industries. Evidence was introduced that Northwest Industries and Goodrich's customers and suppliers traditionally traded on the basis of reciprocity. The government
claimed the merger would certainly serve to strengthen that
tradition. The U. S. district courts denied both government requests for preliminary injunctions against the mergers because both aspiring acquisitors, Reynolds and Northwest Indus-

tries, had expressed disdain for reciprocal trading in formal, written policy statements.[19] Those statements, the courts decided, overrode the evidence of practice of reciprocity.

Similarly, the U. S. District Court for Connecticut, also in 1969, denied the government's request for a preliminary injunction against ITT's acquisition of Hartford Fire Insurance Co. and Grinnell Corp., a manufacturer of water sprinklers. The very same self-serving antireciprocity statement which Geneen read to the House Antitrust Committee, the court decided, outweighed the evidence of ITT's inclination to practice reciprocity.[20]

However, designs to secure reciprocal sales, as well as other methods for reaping sales advantages from sheer mass of acquired operations—as distinguished from ability to compete—are apparent from random samples of ITT internal correspondence alone.

The manager of the Wakefield, Ltd. subsidiary, a manufacturer of lighting fixtures, asked ITT World Headquarters in April 1966 to use its influence to secure Wakefield sales:

> A sample special fixture has been submitted to Manufacturer's Life Insurance Company, Toronto. . . . Any ITT connections that could influence this purchase should be employed.[21]

He did not bother to specify the connections envisioned.

A major consideration for the acquisition of Hamilton Mutual Fund was that the fund would "tie-in" with and provide captive business for the previously acquired Aetna Finance Company. The Hamilton Fund, while independent, had developed the business of loaning over $10 million annually to its shareholders, taking fund certificates as security. Certain banks in Denver provided the cash. ITT acquisitions strategists reasoned that once acquired, the Hamilton Fund could take that business away from the local Denver banks and give it to ITT's Aetna Finance Co. They wrote Geneen in May 1965:

> Tony Tyrone of Hamilton Fund was in St. Louis recently, and in discussing the possibilities of cooperation between our two companies, it was discovered that many of Hamilton Fund customers borrow money from Denver banks, pledging their Hamilton Fund certificates as security. I suggested to him that possibly arrangements could be made whereby Aetna could make those loans.[22]

Again Geneen was enthusiastic. Although this was before the time (according to his testimony) he had heard the word "reciprocity," evidently he was familiar enough with "tie-ins." In a document entitled "Aetna Tie-In," Geneen urged ITT directors to approve the purchase of Hamilton Mutual Fund for that very "perfect tie-in" reason expounded by the strategists:

> Hamilton has increased the practice of loaning shareholders on the value of their fund holdings up to 60% of the equity. This is being done through local banks. . . . it is our estimate that the amount would substantially exceed $10 million per year and is growing annually. This would present a perfect tie-in with Aetna's 170 loan offices for loans on a very secure basis and as a basis of integrating loan revenues and profits from this source, particularly as the fund and the insurance in force doubles and triples in size.[23]

"I didn't write the document," Geneen told the congressmen. "I didn't write it, Mr. Chairman."[24]

ITT Rayonier produces wood pulp used for newspapers. In late 1968 it sought to procure sales reciprocal to ITT Continental Baking Co.'s purchase of Argentine beef. A single Argentine corporation, Transmundo, Inc., like ITT, was both vendor and purchaser. The South American conglomerate bought the wood which ITT sold and sold the beef which ITT bought. Rayonier advised ITT World Headquarters on November 19, 1968:

> A meeting with ITT Continental Baking Company has been scheduled during November to explore the possibilities of selling more paper pulp in Argentina, using leverage of Continental's large purchases of beef in Argentina.[25]

The term "leverage" meant a threat to curtail Continental's annual purchases of $5 million worth of Argentine beef from Transmundo, Inc., unless its newspaper, *Transmundo*, reciprocated by purchasing ITT Rayonier pulp wood.

The meeting was dutifully held. ITT Continental informed Geneen on December 23, 1968:

> A group from ITT headquarters and ITT Rayonier met with us on November 22 to discuss potential barter arrangements in Argentina. We purchase over five million dollars worth of Argentine

beef in a year. Rayonier is attempting to sell product in Argentina.[26]

A representative of the baking subsidiary met with the president of the beef supplier the following January. According to ITT Continental Baking Co.'s monthly report to Geneen of January 23, 1969, they discussed how Transmundo "could be helpful to ITT in Argentina":

> George Vail met on January 17 with George Senosian, President of Transmundo, Inc. through whom we purchase our cooked Argentinian beef. They discussed in general terms ways in which Transmundo could be helpful to ITT in Argentina. This matter will require further discussion with Transmundo before we can expect tangible assistance.[27]

Geneen contended during the House Antitrust Subcommittee hearings on November 21, 1969 that the discussions with Transmundo's president, George Senosian, were only an attempt to arrange barter transactions to avoid the use of inflated Argentinian currency. Further elaboration was not forthcoming:

> Mr. HARKINS [subcommittee counsel]. My question is: What did George Senosian do to help them [ITT]?
> Mr. GENEEN. I don't know. I don't know George Senosian and I don't know what he did.[28]

Attempts to turn the magnitude of operations to one's own advantage come in various dimensions. Some might involve a single piece of real estate in Paris—a "particular little problem which is very small," Geneen said. Other plans might involve securing or capturing multifarious markets upon which hinges a ninety-million dollar acquisition.

In 1967 Avis Rent a Car purchased more than $28 million worth of automobiles from Chrysler Corporation. Chrysler was ITT's largest supplier. In September 1968 Avis managers wrote ITT World Headquarters:

> Thanks to pressure on Chrysler we got the garage Dupleix in Paris. This garage is the most sensible proposition which we have encountered in more than two years of searching. It solves our critical fleet service problem for Paris.[29]

Geneen contended that "pressure" was an unfortunate choice of words. But whatever it was that ITT put on Chrysler, it worked. ITT, as the manager said, got the garage.

Levitt & Sons plans, develops, builds, and sells entire residential cities in the United States and abroad. Construction progresses in various geographical areas simultaneously. Levittowns in New York, New Jersey, and Pennsylvania are but the builder's better-known cities. Sales of $72 million in 1966 made Levitt the largest private builder in the world.

In March of that year the brokerage firm Lazard Frères described to ITT acquisition managers the captive market the conglomerate would acquire for myriad other products upon purchase of Levitt & Sons. Families could just as well spend 25% more when buying their Levitt houses, the broker wrote.[30] Through such an increase the acquirer would rope them in as purchasers of other ITT products.

That "ready-made virgin market for a complete range of consumer goods and services" would not just be for household products, such as furniture and electrical appliances. Rather, the captive market could encompass the whole range of needs of American family house dwellers—even "all lines of insurance, mutual funds, mortgage services, etc."[31]

The assured customers would not be the type that comes and goes. "Levitt creates not only new homes but new households that represent continuing purchasing power," Lazard Frères told Geneen.

Regardless of the Levitt customer's original intention, he would purchase much more than a house. Regardless of which insurance salesman he had been patronizing, he would get the bill from the conglomerate acquirer only, for "every single item to make a liveable home." "The list of items is limitless," Lazard Frères went on, "when one thinks of lawn sprinklers, swimming pools, radio and television, hi-fi equipment, . . . etc."[32]

Better yet, profit from family accessory needs would not only exceed, but might well double, profit from sale of the Levitt-built house. "The gross mark-up and profit margin on this type of business are so substantially higher than those for houses," the brokers' memorandum explained, "that the total net profit per unit could easily be double that of the house alone."[33]

Even nondiversified Levitt was already benefiting from some

of those easy markets. Think, then, the broker implored, what a real conglomerate operating in the various fields of homeowner consumption could do with such an array of markets:

> These sales will give the company a good retail profit margin as the sales facilities already exist at each site. The potential earnings from this program of selling auxiliary items for the home are major and could add measurably to current profits. The eventual scope of such a program is large.[34]

ITT purchased Levitt & Sons for $93,446,000 in February 1968. The housing developer was the largest of all its acquisitions. But not for long. In that same month ITT purchased the Sheraton hotel chain for $293,515,000; in April, Rayonier Corp. for $302,000,000; in June, Pennsylvania Glass Sand Corp. for $114,000,000; and in September, Continental Baking Co. for $276,000,000. Total acquisition prices for that year, not including the Levitt purchase, easily surpassed one billion dollars (see Table 21).

According to the Lazard Frères information upon which ITT acted, the purpose of the Levitt acquisition was to secure trade advantages that were unavailable to competitors who were not members of conglomerate syndicates. Levittown buyers would be manipulated into buying certain brands of goods and services irrespective of the brands' competitive quality. A competitor may well have no alternative but to seek the same advantage for himself by likewise acquiring captive customers through conglomerate membership. If the advantage works (as ITT claims its performance figures demonstrate), the stronger participants in particular industries will be conglomerate members. Again, that prediction of the drastic reduction in the number of independent enterprises brings Darwin to mind. The strength of the surviving fittest will come not from their ability to provide superior goods and services but from their manipulation of suppliers, suppliers' friends, suppliers' employees, subsidiaries, subsidiaries' friends, subsidiaries' employees, subsidiaries' employees' friends — and the ever-expanding citizenry of Levittowns.

The profit from the Levitt scheme flowed beyond the conglomerate. The benefit to Lazard Frères for locating those captive customers was a $250,000 acquisition finder's fee.

Excluding that amount, between January 1, 1966 and September 5, 1969, Lazard Frères received $2,075,000 for ITT merger services. For other brokerage services, Lazard Frères received an additional $1,792,790 from ITT. In 1968, 34.2% of the firm's acquisition-fee income involved ITT mergers.[35]

In public testimony and with impressive authority, Félix Rohatyn, a Lazard Frères partner and director who is also an ITT director and ITT executive committee member, described a system of interlocking directorships which keeps the acquisition process well greased. At least one of the brokerage firm's partners was on the boards of directors of 27 of the companies involved in the 68 mergers the firm arranged from 1964 through September 1969.[36] Rohatyn first conceded and then denied that such interlocking board service helped the firm get the business.[37] But with no equivocation he stated that any failure of Lazard Frères to secure the business of a company on whose board a Lazard Frères official served would be "to our chagrin."[38]

Interlocking directorships enabled Lazard Frères to perform better service, Rohatyn rationalized. "I would certainly hope that if one of our partners is a director of a company, that we would be . . . selected to perform the advisory service."[39]

Lazard Frères had no reason to be disappointed. The firm's income from mergers of companies with which it "locked" at least one directorship increased from $841,030 for the entire year 1964 to $2,217,802.50 for the first three quarters only of 1969.[40]

Nor should Rohatyn and his partners be concerned over getting their fair share of merger business. The system is unbeatable, works just as well in reverse, and feeds on itself. The firm acquires merger business through interlocking directorships and acquires interlocking directorships through merger business:

> generally corporate clients sooner or later will invite one of our partners on the board, because really this is the way it happens. . . . If we had dealings with a company and have performed services, by and large, at some point or another we will be invited on the board, and the relationship may become close.[41]

Lazard Frères has also benefited from arbitraging the stocks of the companies involved in the mergers it initiated. To arbitrage the stock of merging companies is to purchase that company's stock which is expected to rise and sell short that company's stock which is expected to decline, as a result of the merger. A broker who participates in an acquisition may lawfully arbitrage the stock of the two companies only after the announcement of the merger. Therefore the public had the same opportunity Lazard Frères had to profit from arbitraging stocks of the companies the brokerage firm helped merge.

To sell short is to attempt to profit from the decline of a company's stock, and hence from the deterioration of its performance. Lazard Frères states that it has therefore adopted a rule of self-restraint against arbitrage of mergers involving companies for which a Lazard Frères partner serves as director. The firm never places itself in a position, then, of hoping for a decline in the performance of a company with which it interlocks directorships – the firm says.[42]

Nevertheless, partners of Lazard Frères gained $236,321.09 from arbitraging the Rayonier-ITT merger by purchasing Rayonier stock and selling ITT short.[43] A Lazard Frères partner, Rohatyn, was a director and an executive of ITT at the same time.

The rule presented no obstacle, Rohatyn explained, because the firm's holding in the two stocks was distributed to all the partners individually, except to ITT director Rohatyn.[44] But the partners thereby benefited the same as if the firm had still held the stock. The rule designed to prevent selling short the stock of companies with which Lazard Frères interlocks directorships, obviously, then, can be circumvented at will. But by virtue of the rule, Rohatyn stated, "we have always managed to be absolutely purer than Caesar's wife."[45]

Another system which, like interlocking directorships, establishes rapport among parties to merger negotiations is the promise by acquiring officials to raise the salaries of the acquired managers. *Forbes* reported on May 1, 1968 (p.28):

> Geneen, incidentally, uses money to attract not only people, but companies as well. His favorite technique for making sure that managements will favor being acquired by ITT is offering management five-year contracts and huge increases. His recent

arrangement with Sheraton Corp. is typical. ITT has entered into
five-year contracts with Sheraton's top three officers. The trio will
be paid a total of $315,000 a year vs. their pre-ITT salaries of
$172,000. Small wonder so few managements object to being ac-
quired by ITT. Happiest of all are executives about to retire. For
they can stay on the ITT payroll at substantial increases, when
they would have had to live on some slender pensions otherwise.

Officials of Continental Baking Co. received salary increases
of 50% immediately after merger. Officials of Rayonier received
increases of almost 50%. Officials of Avis received increases of
100%. The three highest salaries paid by Sheraton Corp. were
increased upon merger as follows: $55,000 to $85,000, $56,000
to $105,000, and $61,000 to $125,000.[46]
In reply, Geneen contended that the shareholders, not the
managers, vote on merger, and that the increases could not,
therefore, have influenced the decision to consolidate with ITT:

> MR. GENEEN. . . . These mergers are voted on by the stock-
> holders. They make their own individual decisions as to whether
> they want to come with us or not.
> Chairman CELLER [of the House Antitrust Subcommittee]. I
> can't disagree with you more. If managements are given substan-
> tial increases, they undoubtedly can have their effect upon the
> objectivity of management's recommendations to the stockhold-
> ers. There is no doubt about it.[47]

Salaries of acquired company officials was public information
prior to the mergers. Geneen, however, asked that the subcommittee not disclose the list of salaries submitted to it:

> My own feeling is that this is personal information to the individ-
> uals and companies. Unless it serves some useful purpose, I
> would request the Committee to keep it confidential.[48]

"Why should this type of information be available [through the
SEC] when a company is an independent company," the subcommittee counsel asked, "but not available to the public after
it is acquired by a conglomerate?"[49]
There was no reply.

CHAPTER 8

The Purpose of LTV, Inc.

Not all corporate acquirers attempt to use the size of their operations to secure competitive advantages. Some conglomerate headquarters, in fact, appear to acquire with no operating purpose.

James Ling, the founder of Ling-Temco-Vought, Inc., was chief executive during the five years when that corporation acquired over $2.817 billion of other companies' assets. His relationship with management was severed in mid-1970 when the banks questioned the company's ability to repay its acquisition loans and interest. The stockholders have since changed the corporate name to LTV, Inc.

James Ling's memorandums written during the company's greatest acquisition period, however, describe the management philosophy which led to the intense concentration of assets of formerly independent companies. That concentration elevated LTV from the 285th largest U. S. industrial corporation in 1960 to the 25th largest in 1969.

Paradoxically, Ling's explanations of LTV's management purpose indicate that the primary benefit to the acquired company was that it would be permitted to operate as if acquisition had not occurred.

LTV consistently instructed its managers that the consolidated companies were to be left to function independently of the parent company. Of the services the conglomerate headquarters performed, the most definite was the direction of "external growth," i.e., acquisition of more companies. "Internal growth," i.e., growth by any means other than acquisition, was strictly the responsibility of subsidiary, not parent, management.

At the outset of the acquisition program, on June 18, 1964, Ling enunciated the "operating umbrella versatility" concept. Through it he sought to explain the advantage derived by the acquired company from membership in the conglomerate system. In a memorandum entitled "LTV Corporate Headquarters' Operating Philosophy" he wrote to division executives:

> A distinct advantage materializes to the benefit of the division in that the division has most of the fringe benefits of a small business and yet retains the operating umbrella versatility and strength of the LTV corporate structure.[1]

Those benefits, Ling elaborated in testimony to the House Antitrust Subcommittee in April 1970, were that LTV

> furnished corporate services to them [the subsidiaries] in industrial relations, public relations, and so forth. On the other hand, from their point of view, the fringe benefit was that they would have quick reaction capabilities to their customers, as opposed to going through the morass of the big bureaucratic corporate structure which undeniably exists at times. In other words, they had the advantage of being a small business by comparison but on the other hand, had the advantages of a parent company which could give full support to them by providing legal, accounting and planning functions for the benefits of the underlying subsidiaries.[2]

Why the parent company could perform legal, accounting, planning, and public relations functions for the subsidiary more adequately than the subsidiary itself was not explained.

Three years after the June 1964 explanation of operating philosophy, and after having acquired 175 million more dollars' worth of assets, Ling reiterated the same idea that subsidiary operations were, naturally, the subsidiary's concern. The parent was to be left free to negotiate more acquisitions. On October 16, 1967 he wrote to company officials:

> Within the area of internal growth . . . the primary responsibility for securing that growth belongs to each of the subsidiary presidents and his management. It is LTV's desire and expectation that *subsidiary management will concentrate its time and efforts* [Mr. Ling's emphasis] on the development of products, processes,

services, marketing and distribution, production and inventory control, and administrative and financial control to ensure the planned internal growth.[3]

That encompassing list of management responsibilities might leave for the conglomerate headquarters a function of "review" or "counsel." "Ultimate responsibility" for management goals, however, clearly lay with the subsidiary management, he continued:

> LTV corporate staff will review, counsel and assist within the scope of our particular expertise in the settling of operating plans, financing of expansion, solving operating problems and, in general, the attainment of internal growth goals, but the ultimate responsibility for attainment of these goals is that of subsidiary management.

The memorandum stated that the parent company's true purpose and real duty was to acquire more corporations:

> It is, and has been, a stated objective that LTV and its subsidiaries will grow externally to supplement planned internal growth. Growth in this context, as has been stated previously, is simply defined as an increase in earnings per share for all the shareholders of LTV and its subsidiaries which results in a higher intrinsic, or market, value for the shareholders' security.
> . . . within the area of external growth, the sole responsibility for planning, negotiating, consummating and integrating acquisitions and mergers for LTV and all its subsidiaries belongs to the LTV corporate staff. More specifically, the total responsibility within this area belongs to the office of the Chairman of the Board and Chief Executive Officer. This responsibility has been delegated to the Vice President — Corporate Financial Plans for implementation in all its phases, but its ultimate responsibility is mine.

Two years later, after having acquired 913.8 million more dollars' worth of assets, Ling told the chief executive officers of the subsidiaries that their divisions were to become even more "operationally self-sufficient," and, more emphatically, that they were not to bring their problems to him — *"the buck passing stops at the CEO level of each company!"* he insisted:

LING-TEMCO-VOUGHT CORPORATE
INTEROFFICE CORRESPONDENCE
OCTOBER 14, 1969

To: See Attached Distribution.

From: James J. Ling.

In my closing comments made during the recent planning session at the Ranch, I suggested that you submit any suggestions you might have concerning same. We here at Corporate are convinced that a change in format is in order, particularly in view of the new companies which will be coming on stream shortly. So send your suggestions directly to me—we can discuss as time permits.

Last year and again this year we stressed the goal that all the underlying subsidiaries should become operationally self-sufficient as soon as possible, and that in support of this goal, LTV would exercise its expertise and experience through the mechanics of the executive committees and boards of directors of the subsidiaries. Oversimplified, the Chief Executive Officers of each of the subsidiaries will have complete responsibility for operations and profit performance—*the buck passing stops at the CEO level of each company!* I am sure you understand, and I am equally sure that you will do everything you can to make this fundamental aspect of redeployment work.

I'm looking forward to an "on target" report from you at next year's off-site meeting.

JAMES J. LING[4]

Though the benefits to the acquisitions from conglomeration might at best be ambiguous, their duty to the conglomerate was clear. Loyalty of the acquired management was owed first to the parent company and only secondarily to the subsidiary. In the memorandum of June 18, 1964 Ling urged the managers of acquired companies who had been transferred to the "remote" LTV Tower headquarters to "completely eliminate prior feelings of allegiance" to their formerly independent companies:

LING-TEMCO-VOUGHT, INC.,
June 18, 1964.

To: LTV Corporate Staff Heads and
    Division Managing Executives.

Subject: LTV Corporate Headquarters Operating Philosophy.

We have completed a most significant step in establishing our

Corporate Headquarters in a separate location and as a compact
unit here at the LTV Tower. This move to a central location, remote from any major division, for the Corporate group reflects a
business strategy and an operational philosophy. We can more
clearly establish clear cut lines of authority and responsibilities
which rest with the divisions and subsidiaries and those that re-
side in the LTV Corporate group. We, at the LTV Corporate level,
must more completely eliminate prior feelings of allegiance or
emotional stimulus that could make us subjective as a result of
our background ties and experience with any particular division.
We must become completely unemotionally detached from our
heritage in this respect.

The rationale and vital necessity for doing so is quite clear. Our
responsibilities are clearly set forth. We must produce a profit
result for the Corporate owners which will provide increased
earnings per share and will build value per share on a long range
as well as a short range basis.[5]

Four days later, Ling issued a clarifying memorandum. An
executive's loyalty to the acquired subsidiary, though developed
and nourished over the years, is a liability rather than an asset.
A subsidiary, he said, is above all a saleable commodity. Too
much attachment for an acquired company might impede the
conglomerate's chances of selling it for the best price:

The rationale for pushing the point about becoming emotionally
detached from the prior heritage of a division is as follows: Chart-
ing the course of LTV over the next several years will call for
various and vigorous actions in organizing and reorganizing,
personnel placement, apportionment of R&D/BP&E funds and
favoring emphasis on some divisions more than on others. We
can play no favorites.
To illustrate: If it were to our best interest to sell off a division,
a program or product line and redeploy the assets in a more rewarding manner, then this we must do.[6]

Profit to the parent company resulting in increased earnings
per share was the ultimate objective. The memorandum continues:

The rationale and vital necessity for doing so [eliminating the
managing executive's "emotional stimulus"] for the division is
quite clear. Our responsibilities are clearly set forth. We must

produce a profit result for the Corporate owners which will provide increased earnings per share and will build value per share. . . .

To the House Antitrust Subcommittee Ling stated, nevertheless, that the sale and acquisition of a company can be deleterious and disruptive to its operations. LTV had recently announced plans to sell Okonite Cable Co. Okonite would thus be sold for the third time in 12 years; "apparently after the acquisition," he explained, "there is a deterioration of morale."

The following colloquy ensued:

> Mr. HARKINS [Subcommittee counsel]. Do you think that there has been a disruption of its [Okonite's] operation resulting from LTV's purchase of the company in 1966?
> Mr. LING. Well, did we disrupt the company?
> Mr. HARKINS. Yes.
> Mr. LING. I think from that point of view the record is quite clear there was a possible disruption.[7]

In spite of that admission, the LTV chief executive saw no reason why acquirers should not trade and deal their acquired companies as saleable, fungible commodities:

> CHAIRMAN [Emanuel] Celler [of the Antitrust Subcommittee]. Suppose you were a shareholder of Okonite and it was purchased by Kennecott [acquirer of Okonite in 1958] and then sold by Kennecott to LTV who subsequently sells it to somebody else. What would be your attitude as a shareholder?
> Mr. LING. My attitude would be, what price did they pay? They could not do all those things without buying up securities. If they offered enough money, I would be like the shareholders have been; I would probably sell it.
> Chairman CELLER. If I were a shareholder, I would kick like hell.[8]

LTV sold Okonite Cable Co. in 1971 to Omega-Alpha Company, a holding company which James Ling now manages. Also Braniff Airways was to be sold to comply with a judicial consent decree whereby LTV would be permitted to retain control of Jones & Laughlin Steel Co. In 1970 and 1971, in order to pay acquisition debts, LTV sold three of its most profitable acquisitions: Wilson Sporting Goods, Wilson Pharmaceutical Co., and Allied Radio. Previously the conglomerate sold its controlling interest in National Car Rental, Stonewall Insurance Corp., First Western Bank & Trust, and American Amicable Life Insurance Co. The banking and insurance interests amounted to over $100 million. Other companies in which LTV sold its controlling interest in 1969 are listed in Table 23.

LTV internal management reports indicate that a corporate acquisitor which leaves operations entirely to the acquired managements does not fare as well as one which controls its subsidiaries so as to gain competitive advantages through the size of the combined operations. A mere comparison of International Telephone & Telegraph Corp.'s income statement with LTV's statement, which shows deficits for 1969, 1970, and 1971, should be indication enough.

The U. S. Army arranged for LTV's acquisition of Memcor so that the conglomerate (according to the Army Contract Adjustment Board decision of September 12, 1966)[9] would correct Memcor's "lack of competent management." But LTV managers' reports leave doubt that the conglomerate headquarters which told its subsidiary officers *the buck passing stops at the CEO* [subsidiary chief executive officer] *level of each company!"* successfully attained that goal for its Memcor subsidiary. An early February 1967 managers' report to LTV headquarters states that Memcor profit was $8,000 above "target" only because of the army's gratuitous payment increases, and that sales were $6.3 million below target. A few weeks later, the reports continue, 30% of Memcor's PRC-25 production was rejected.

LTV informed its shareholders in its divisional Electrosystems 1967 Annual Report that the Memcor merger had resulted in the conglomerate's "continued strengthening of management and scientific staff" and "increase of high-level technical skills." However, managers' internal reports of that same year indicate that LTV itself was experiencing exactly the same problems which the army expected the conglomerate to correct in the acquired company. Because of manpower problems, according to managers' reports later in 1967, even under the acquisitor's management, Memcor still could not produce its backlog of orders.

TABLE 23

Name of company sold	Principal product lines	Date sold	Stock or assets disposed of (thousands)
Vought Industries, Inc.	Mobile homes	March 1962 (effective November 1961)	$ 3,938
Information Systems, Inc.	Computer control systems	April–June 1962	2,485
Crusader Finance Co.	Mobile homes financing	July 1962	10,950
United Electronics	Special purpose vacuum tubes	January 1963	840
Ed Friedrich, Inc.	Air conditioning units and freezers	January 1964	10,202
Spectral Dynamics, Inc.	Electronics	November 1967	100
Micromodular Components	do	May 1962	375
LTV Graphite Division	Graphite blocks	September 1964	81
Jet Steam Products, Inc.	Laundry equipment	November 1965	32
Dumont Laboratories, Mobile Communications Division	Mobile communications	December 1968	825
Columbia Industries Division	Bowling balls	September 1968	850
Gonset, Inc.	Radio communication equipment	1967	213

SOURCE: *Hearings on Conglomerate Corporations*, Part 6, p.62.

The internal report of March 25 explained that the major manufacturing problem—utilization of available manpower—had become "grim."

The report of April 24 stated that the problem had not abated and that Memcor, as before merger, could not produce the business it had contracted.

On May 30 the managers reported no improvement: "23 failures to date and all of them catastrophic."

On June 25 the Memcor managers sent word to the LTV Tower that electronic equipment being produced for the Italian Navy did not meet "specification." They urged that LTV try to persuade the Italians to sell the failing equipment to a NATO command.

The vaunted conglomerate ability to aid distressed subsidiaries was to no avail, or did not exist. On August 28 the managers related that although LTV president Clyde Skeen had advised Memcor to draw on the assistance of the other conglomerate subsidiaries, its deficiency in engineering talent persisted.

The managers' report of October 24 stated that not even available manpower was being utilized. Referring to "serious degradation of the application of senior engineering talent," it concluded: "The loss will grow, possibly double."

As distinguished from those confidential reports, LTV public earnings statements after the early 1967 Memcor merger revealed no sign of the management problems. The conglomerate's Annual Report of 1967 stated that the acquiring division's [Electrosystems'] profits were up 102%, from $2.6 million in 1966 to $5.3 million in 1967. LTV's calculation of the good bookkeeping effects obtainable from the pooling of revenues of the merging companies had come true. A footnote added, however, that Memcor profits had been added to the division's 1967 (post-merger) profit total but not to the 1966 (pre-merger) total. Thus, in announcing a 102% profit increase, LTV was comparing the combined profits of two companies with the profits of one company. In 1968, when combined profits had to be compared to combined profits of the previous year, the difference became a 32% decrease as opposed to the 102% increase in 1967.

By adding the income figures of its acquired companies to its total income figures, an acquiring company can thus ostensibly report rising income. By reporting rising income, it heightens the market value of its stock and, in turn, obtains greater power to continue acquiring other companies.

In December 1967 LTV purchased General Felt Industries, Inc., a manufacturer of floor covering. The acquisition's revenue and earnings were added to the figures of the previously acquired Okonite Cable Co. During the first year of LTV control, General Felt's sales rose dramatically. So much so, that Okonite's $8 million decline in sales in 1968 was reported to the public— after combination with General Felt sales—as an increase of 85%. LTV reported to shareholders in the 1968 Okonite Annual Report:

> The year 1968 was a mixed one for the Okonite Company. While certain of the year-end figures proved disappointing, there was progress. Much was accomplished. Much was begun. . . . Sales rose to $190,848,000, an increase of 85% over the prior year's mark of $103,238,000.

The disappointing figures were that Okonite's pretax earnings had decreased from $16.4 million in 1967 to $12.1 million in 1968 (even with the addition of General Felt's earnings). Again, the management's internal reports are not consistent with its public reports. In the 1968 Annual Report to shareholders, LTV said that the reasons for the profit decline were "lack of expansion in utilities and industries" and the copper strike during the first part of the year—reasons which absolve the conglomerate management from blame. Public acknowledgment by management of responsibility for the profit decrease, and thus of management deficiency, would likely cause a decline in the market value of Okonite stock.

The managers' internal reports, however, explicitly refute those public explanations. Further, they raise the question, not mentioned to public investors, of management's ability to compete:

> 24 June 1968: During the recent meeting, it was stated that the cable industry was way off. This seems reasonable in the case of construction, but for manufacturing, OEM and the utilities, it does not make sense.
>   . . . now that the copper strike is over and producers' copper is now available, it might have been expected that the Okonite situa-

tion would have improved substantially. However, such is not the case; rather their situation has worsened.

A managers' report of July 10, 1968 cited "severe competition" as the reason for sharply declining Okonite sales and profits.

Though amalgamation of income figures may result in higher earnings on paper, amalgamation of operations of industrially unrelated companies (the cable manufacturer and the floor covering manufacturer) does not result in added financial resources, the July managers' report indicated:

> There is a higher level of operating cash requirements for General Felt as ccmpared to what Okonite has been used to. As a result of their cash shortage, they have added $7 million short-term credit. Okonite has stopped commitments for any capital improvements or maintenance until the cash situation improves. The biggest factor concerning shortage of capital is the fact that the Santa Maria facility [an Okonite plant] has not been sold and leased back.

A distinctive feature of LTV's method of conglomeration is the sale to the public of the minority interest in acquired subsidiaries. LTV retains the majority or controlling interest (more than 50 percent of the voting stock) of several subsidiary companies while their minority interest is traded publicly on the American Stock Exchange. LTV has divided Wilson Meat Packing Co., which had been traded as one entity on the market before acquisition, into seven distinct and separate publicly traded companies. By that system, which Ling denominated "Project Redeployment," the conglomerate obtains control of the subsidiary without having to expend capital for more than 51% of its voting stock.

Such division of subsidiary ownership by a parent company exercising control of the publicly traded subsidiary raises issues of conflicting interest. For example, Wilson owners who chose not to accept LTV's generous cash tender for their stock suddenly found themselves minority shareholders of a company controlled by LTV. Their preferences and interests conflicted with the interests of the acquirer, which cancelled their Wilson common and issued them LTV preferred shares—an exchange those stockholders would not have made voluntarily.

The practice of public sale of minority interest in a subsidiary is gaining favor among other corporate acquirers. Thus the issue of collision of interests comes more into prominence. *Forbes* of January 1, 1972 (p. 125) reported:

Ling's specialty at L-T-V was not only acquiring companies, but also rearranging them and splitting them off into independent, partly publicly owned enterprises. "Redeployment" he called it in 1965 when he spun off LTV Aerospace, LTV Electrosystems and LTV Ling-Altec, and again in 1967 when he broke Wilson & Co. into three independent parts.

Curiously, few imitated Ling's strategy in L-T-V's days of glory, but now that L-T-V has collapsed, many more have adopted it. Brunswick Corp. has sold off 15% of its Sherwood Medical subsidiary, Studebaker-Worthington has opened to public ownership STP, Turbodyne, Clarke-Gravely, Wagner Electric and Massonelan International. Whittaker Corp. has done the same with Computing & Software. Walter Kidde sold off 15% of LCA Corp. and 30% of Globe Security Systems. Gulf & Western sold off 10% of APS, Inc., its original auto parts business, and ATO at least talked of selling off minority interests in both Rawlings and American La France.

For such companies, the advantages were considerable. In selling 30% of Globe Security Systems, for instance, Kidde generated some $11 million in much needed cash, converted an asset with a market value of about $30 million. The creation of a public market has its advantages, notably in easing the disposition of added shares in the future.

A policy designed to prevent conflict of interest between LTV and minority shareholders restricts parent company officials from owning shares of subsidiary companies.

The minutes of the LTV Board of Directors meeting of May 9, 1968 provided:

RESOLVED, That it shall be the policy of Ling-Temco-Vought, Inc. to prohibit its officers and directors from owning any securities issued by any of its subsidiary corporations, as well as the securities of any other companies in which LTV subsequently may acquire control; provided, however, that this policy shall not prohibit any person who may be both an officer of a subsidiary corporation and an officer or director of Ling-Temco-Vought, Inc. from owning any securities of the subsidiary of which he is an officer through the acquisition of stock by open market purchases or by exercise of stock options.[10]

"This is an old policy," Ling explained to the House Antitrust Subcommittee, "which was put into effect in 1965, in order to avoid conflict of interest."

> As an illustration, I do not own any securities in any of these under-lying LTV subsidiary companies, because the policy forbids it. It provides I can't do it. On the other hand, Mr. Lawrence [president of Braniff] is a director of LTV, and thus should have an interest in LTV. On the other hand, his principal endeavor is in the future of Braniff, so thus he would be entitled to have an equity position in each company. Thus, oversimplifying, the reason for the policy is to eliminate the possibility of conflict of interest.[11]

Ironically, LTV and the New York Stock Exchange, while guarding against conflict of interest so well that both disallow the remote power that a parent company official might hold over a subsidiary (of which he is not an official) through his trading of its stock, absolutely allow the parent company the power to name the entire boards of directors of all the publicly traded sub-sidiaries.

Voting rights of securities of the LTV subsidiaries, with a few exceptions, are noncumulative. LTV, therefore, if it chooses, can name their entire boards of directors, filling them with its own directors or other representatives, by virtue of its ownership of at least 50% of each subsidiary's voting securities.

Such control of the subsidiary boards empowers LTV to call its callable loans to subsidiaries at any time, though to their detriment; to raise money for acquisitions by issuance of equity or debt securities of the subsidiary; and to decide for itself the amount of earnings the publicly owned subsidiary retains or pays to LTV in dividends.

As an example, LTV planned to raise capital for acquiring Wilson & Co. by calling a $10 million loan, not due for two years, owed by Okonite. If interest rates had risen, of course, Okonite could have replaced the capital only at greater expense. Also, LTV planned to issue debt and equity securities of other sub-sidiaries (see Table 24).

The plan was not adopted. Okonite did repay the loan 14

TABLE 24
Ling-Temco-Vought, Inc.
Master Financial Plan

	(Dollars in thousands)
Accomplished to date:[1]	
LTV warrants exercised	$16,017
LTV Aerospace common stock	11,175
LTV Electrosystems common stock	5,500
Okonite common stock	7,900
Total[1]	40,592
To be accomplished:	
LTV Aerospace convertible debentures	25,000
LTV Electrosystems debt/equity securities	15,000
LTV Ling Altec debt/equity securities	5,000
Okonite debt/equity securities	15,000
LTV debt/equity securities	45,000
Total	105,000

1. Excludes $1,647,500 conversion of debentures, $415,800 exercise of stock options and $157,750 exercise of senior note warrants in 1966.
SOURCE: *Hearings on Conglomerate Corporations*, Part 6, p.417.

months before maturity of the note, but replaced the funds by borrowing at the lower interest rate of 4¾%. Ling acknowledged to the Antitrust Subcommittee that LTV's power to call subsidiary notes, or any other power over subsidiaries resulting from the parent's authority to place whomever it chose on the subsidiary boards, could possibly result in conflict of interest "because nothing is impossible." But, he continued, "all subsidiary directors . . . have to act in behalf of the minority shareholders as well as the management" whether they are chosen by the majority or minority stockholders, because "whatever is good for the management is good for the minority, and vice versa." Also, he explained,

> There could not be a problem because of the full visibility of these companies. Being publicly owned, and transactions are duly reported between the companies, and all transactions are reported in various and sundry agreements. Even if one were to have the temptation, one would resist it, because again, I think, most people, being basically honest, will make the proper decisions for the betterment of that particular company.[12]

If LTV were to act against the interest of a subsidiary, such as to call its loan and force the subsidiary to reborrow at higher interest,

> we would be liable to the minority shareholders and the independent members of the companies whose incentives for the future depend on that company. On the other hand, if you are saying that LTV can be irresponsible, well, anybody can be irresponsible. Conflict of interest among directors who are on both parent and subsidiary boards really hasn't developed.[13]

Ling eventually acknowledged, however, that LTV had appropriated to its own use proceeds from the sale of subsidiary securities and that LTV had converted subsidiary shares so that those securities began to pay dividends to LTV. He explained:

> You see, we have never sold any stocks . . . that I can recall, where LTV itself got the proceeds, you see. We have never done that. The underlying companies, in every instance, have received the funds for their own particular business purposes. We have never sold any Wilson stock in our behalf, or any Braniff stock, *until recently,* in our behalf, and so forth [emphasis added].[14]

That LTV converted Class B nondividend-paying stock of a majority of its subsidiaries into dividend-paying securities "is correct," the LTV chief executive stated. The earnings represented by that stock thus flow to the parent company. Ling continued:

> We did convert. In the original stages of Project Redeployment, we wanted the underlying companies to have the advantage of keeping all the funds generated through earnings for their benefit, so only the public shareholders received dividends with our objective through the years, as the subsidiaries grew, being that we in turn would participate. We did not participate for some period of years. This past year [1969], we have started participating through exercise of conversion provisions of a certain amount of the securities.[15]

Thus, whether the publicly traded subsidiaries retain their majority earnings for their own development or pay them to their majority shareholders is wholly determined by that shareholder.

A charge often leveled against corporate concentration is that it obscures the "visibility" of or the insight into the condition of the acquired company. An independent, publicly traded corporation must adhere to the Securities and Exchange Commission's disclosure requirements and expose to public investors' view information about its profitability and financial stability. Such knowledge tends to be indicative of the quality of management and enables the public to make more "informed investment decisions." Conglomerate corporations, with very few exceptions, do not reveal the income and stability figures of their acquired corporations after merger. The annual report of ITT, for example, does not show the revenue and profit of each of its more than 160 acquired companies individually, as each company reported before the merger. The ITT report discloses those figures only for the nine general divisions into which the companies have been conglomerated. Thus, investment information accessible to the public before acquisition is not available afterward.

LTV, however, contends that through the system of "redeployment" it affords the public better insight into operating conditions than do other conglomerates. Because the "redeployed" companies are publicly sold, they each must satisfy SEC disclosure requirements. LTV seemingly asserts that the public has a better view after conglomeration than before. The 1967 LTV Annual Report told the shareholders:

> the term 'visibility' indicates openness to public view. In a business sense, visibility leads to easy recognition of outstanding or sub-par performances. In this regard, we believe LTV is one of the most visible companies in the United States today. None of this is to say that we in any sense consider ourselves infallible. The perfect corporate structure does not exist, and it is likely that it never will. . . . Recognizing this, we have attempted not only to diversify LTV, but to make its component parts clearly visible.

To the House Antitrust Subcommittee on April 15, 1970, Ling elaborated: "Thus, it is not really too surprising that *Fortune* magazine declared in June of 1968 that LTV was the most visible American company out of the 500 or 600 listed in their Fortune Review."[16]

That reasoning is not clear. As already seen, the public was led to believe that the publicly traded Okonite subsidiary had increased its sales by 85% in 1968, while that increase came entirely from the simple addition of General Felt sales to the Okonite total. Reporting of income was no less obscure. The LTV and Okonite annual reports to shareholders showed only a decline of pretax Okonite profits from $16.4 million in 1967 to $12.1 million in 1968. Nowhere did they show that Okonite pretax profits, without the addition of newly acquired General Felt profits, declined $11 million, or 73%.

Eventually, the conglomerate's total earnings failed to increase even with the addition of acquired earnings. LTV's net income in 1965 — the last year before 1969 in which it made no acquisitions — amounted to $6 million. In 1967 income rose to $34 million. But although the incomes of the four companies acquired in late 1967 and 1968 were added to the 1968 figure, income fell to $28 million. In 1969 it fell to a $38 million loss (before estimated future income tax benefits).

Obviously then, the acquisition program did not increase return on assets. In 1964, total revenue equaled value of assets multiplied by 2.55. In 1969 that multiple had decreased to 1.28. In 1964, net income equaled 3.9% of assets; in 1968, 1%; and in 1969 of course, a negative figure.

In April 1970 LTV's income was not sufficient to pay the interest on its acquisition debt. James Ling was asked then whether that debt, soon due, exceeded LTV assets by over $150 million. The crowded hearing room was silent. Either the audience would hear the master of conglomerate finance admit that at last his back was to the wall, or hear another explanation of corporate restructuring which would shatter textbook rules:

> Mr. HARKINS. . . . does not in fact the debt of LTV exceed its salable assets by $170 million?
>
> Mr. LING. I am sure you will want a very honest comparison. If I may go to the chart——
>
> The CHAIRMAN. What was your answer about the parent company? Is it true that LTV's parent company long-term debt exceeds its salable assets?
>
> Mr. LING. No. If he is going to evaluate the stock market on the asset side, he has to stay with the market on the debt side. Our calculations show we have $210 million assets over debt. The debt

traded on the market does not trade at $800 million some odd but
trades on the order of $400 million some odd.

Mr. HARKINS. But the debt is a legal obligation as of the time
carried on your books.

Mr. GRIFFIN. That is correct.

Mr. LING. We have to pay it eventually but we are not obligated
to pay it today, by any stretch of the imagination. On the other
hand, we can buy it at 42 cents on the dollar as of yesterday.[17]

Each dollar represented by LTV debt securities was selling on
the market at 42¢ not only because of high interest rates but also
because investors had little confidence in LTV's ability to repay the debt. The conglomerate itself, then, could purchase its
debt securities, as Ling said, for far less than LTV sold them.

By that strategy a corporate acquirer first borrows the money
from the public to purchase other companies. Supported by those
acquisitions, it taxes but does not contribute to their operations.
The acquired companies, as a result, are less profitable under
the conglomerate's control. Public holders of the debt securities
the acquirer sold in order to purchase the companies lose confidence in its ability to repay the debt. They thus sell the debt
securities for 42¢ on the dollar. The conglomerate, if it has the
resources to buy them at that low price, can then pay off its debts
for less than half the amount it borrowed. By that strategy, an
acquisitor can reap advantage from, and augment the trend of
corporate concentration by virtue of, its management deficiency.

CHAPTER 9

The Purpose of Litton Industries, Inc.

We don't want anybody going up and down the highways and byways blasting out this information. This is the reason we are in the spot we are in here this morning. We are trying to get facts, not headlines. That is why we have the doors locked to the news media. I hope the mouths of the members of the committee will be closed to the news media.

> Chairman F. Edward Hébert at the outset of the House Armed Services Committee hearings on delays and cost overruns of Ingalls Shipbuilding Corp., *Armed Services Hearings*, p. 10575.

Litton Industries asserts that its management ability is transferable to all the multifarious industries it has entered by acquiring other companies. Its managers, allegedly, can operate those companies without specific training in the respective industries. That the acquiring management is capable of operating myriads of industries without experience before merger is the most common of conglomerates' claims. It is Litton's explanation for having acquired 119 companies in the nine years between 1960 and 1970. During that time Litton's total assets increased 1,228 percent, from $119 million to $1,580 million.

Litton's management purportedly improves the performance of acquired companies operating even in industries outside of its management experience. That is not to say, however, that acquired managements are at all dispensable to the conglom-

157

erate. Glenn McDaniel, chairman of the Litton executive committee and former president of Radio Corporation of America,
explained to the House Judiciary Committee on March 4, 1970:

> In our acquisitions we value good managers. We look to the
> existing managers for their specialized expertise and supplement
> them with Litton's broad management capabilities. We can de-
> velop their enthusiasm and expand their horizon. . . .
>
> Corporate central management works with each of our individ-
> ual managers in periodically setting business goals and the main
> strategies for realizing them. . . .
>
> Like a democracy, our organization is not perfect in its opera-
> tions. . . .[1]

Litton's management of acquired subsidiaries strengthens the
competitive process, Mr. McDaniel continued:

> We attempt with careful strategic planning to improve and broaden
> the products of acquired companies through the use of advanced
> technology.
>
> This is a long term process. We cannot emphasize too strongly
> that the process of strengthening acquired companies in this man-
> ner takes many years of product development and intense mana-
> gerial effort. . . .
>
> We have introduced beneficial competition into a number of in-
> dustries.

Illustrative of the transference of central management technique to untried areas of production is Litton's performance of
defense contracts. Military and naval production constitutes a
major portion of Litton operations, as it does for other large conglomerates. Litton's Defense and Marine Group derives 97% of
its revenue from government contracts. That group's revenue, in
turn, has amounted to at least one fourth or one third of Litton's total revenue during the period 1968 to 1972.[2]

Whether defense production standards influence Litton's entire mode of operations is subject to speculation. The House
Judiciary Committee voiced that concern:

> Has it been Litton's experience in dealing with the Government
> that delay, confusion, or resistance to requests tends to work to the
> advantage of the contractor?

Does Litton employ techniques and procedures in performing Government contracts different from those required for doing business with private industry?

Does the mere passage of time work to an advantage of the contractor in dealing with the Government?

Has it been Litton's experience that turn-over in Government personnel administering Government contracts and the resulting delay is advantageous to Litton?[3]

Such were the inquiries the committee addressed to Litton Chief Executive Tex Thornton. *Fortune* of April 1968 (p. 139) raised much the same issue while asserting that the government accepts a less competitive, lower standard of performance than do commercial customers. Defense contractors may thus, allegedly, profit in spite of malperformance:

the requirements for profitability in government work are less exacting than those of the private marketplace. In the advanced government projects where Litton has made its special mark, success depends almost solely on performance. Barring flagrant mismanagement, the company that can do the job can be reasonably sure of clearing a respectable profit. Minor delays and mistakes of judgment can be overlooked, and contracts are drawn to allow for unforeseen snags in research and development. Private customers are less forgiving, largely because in most cases there are competing suppliers of roughly similar products. If products reach the market late, or if costs rise unexpectedly, sales and profits may be irrevocably lost.

Pertinent to the committee's four questions – and to the claim of universality or adaptability of Litton's management ability to untried endeavors – is the conglomerate's operation of Ingalls Shipbuilding Corp. of Pascagoula, Mississippi. Litton had never built ships before acquiring Ingalls. The foremost reason Litton cited for that purchase was the opportunity to apply the conglomerate's electrical technology.

When Ingalls was first offered for sale in 1961, *Time* reported on October 4, 1963 (p. 107), Litton's chief executive, Tex Thornton,

brooded over the possibilities for weeks, finally concluded that the nuclear submarines that Ingalls was building were really just a collection of electronic machines and devices packed into a hull, and therefore an excellent destination for the products of Litton's expanding electronics complex.

Six years after the $20 million purchase, shipyard manager Ellis B. Gardner informed Roy Ash (then president of Litton) of Ingalls' inability to secure profits through the rigors of competitive bidding, of miscalculation of the true magnitude of operating losses, and of "the degree to which the . . . facilities have been allowed to deteriorate." He wrote on June 7, 1967:

> The operating loss experienced by Ingalls during 1967 and our obvious inability to have been able to predict its true magnitude I realize can produce a most skeptical frame of mind. . . .
> The situation in which we now find ourselves does not lend itself to successful strategic bidding for maintaining a continuing influx of reasonably profitable new business. . . .
> Another serious limitation at Ingalls is the degree to which most of the general purpose facilities have been allowed to deteriorate. Piers and shipways require major overhaul. We have just completed a comprehensive review of our electrical distribution system, the results of which indicate that much of this equipment will soon become completely undependable unless replaced, due to age and lack of care over the years. Of the ten original shipways at Ingalls, three have been unusable for a number of years and a fourth needs about $900,000 of repair work. . . .[4]

An alternative, however, to incurring expense by merely replacing Ingalls' limited facilities, Mr. Gardner continued, would be the more daring project of constructing a second, entirely new and larger facility for the construction of larger ships on the west bank of the Pascagoula River, across from the original yard. Competition for the building of smaller naval vessels was very intense, the memorandum read. But the larger the vessel the fewer contractors the navy had from which to choose. For instance, he wrote, "For certain classes of large complex ships such as aircraft carriers [Newport News] no longer has any competition."[5]

Ingalls presented no challenge to major shipbuilders such as Newport News and General Dynamics, the manager concluded in 1967:

The procurement officer for the DX Project . . . expressed astonish to hear that Litton intended to bid on DX. He was frankly dubious of our abilities, especially our "systems" and "electronics" capabilities. As to Ingalls' shipyard management and production capabilities, we have had to make strenuous efforts in recent months to restore confidence of the Navy in us.[6]

Convinced by the memorandum, the Litton management began construction of a new shipyard on the west bank which would employ a "modular" method of shipbuilding, said to have been originated by the Swedes and the Japanese. Rather than building a vessel all in one place, from the bottom up, the envisioned assembly operation would construct parts which would be fitted together later.

"By using modular techniques the new shipyard incorporates the world's most advanced marine production technology," Litton asserted.[7] In March 1973, however, the U. S. comptroller general reported that the Ingalls subsidiary had largely abandoned its ambition for modular construction and had reverted to "nearly conventional" methods.[8]

Litton announced to its shareholders in 1970 that in "building modern ship production facilities capable of achieving the highest possible efficiencies" the conglomerate had "invested more than $132 million."[9] That financing proves Litton's reputation as a master of money management. It had incurred less than $3 million—spent entirely on design—of the immediate cost of the shipyard. The State of Mississippi provided the funds, $130 million, by issuing bonds. According to the agreement, Litton leased the yard from the state but paid no rent for the first five years. In effect, Mississippi bore the rent obligation for Litton through 1972 by paying the interest on the bonds.

Litton had indeed chosen the more daring course (over the plan of mere facility replacement)—daring for the State of Mississippi.

By mid-1970 Litton's investment was succeeding stupendously on paper. The navy decided on a large-scale fleet replacement and anticipated annual shipbuilding budgets of $3 billion for the decade. The most coveted prizes for shipbuilders were contracts for building nine amphibious helicopter-carrying assault ships, designated LHAs (for Landing Helicopter Assault). Equally coveted were contracts for the construction of thirty DD-963 Spruance-class destroyers. Litton persuaded the navy that its not-yet-operating yard was capable of the production and won both sets of contracts. The vessels were to be built over a period of years. Even under the original contract, the cost would exceed the navy's entire current annual budget. The destroyer assignment alone, Litton told its stockholders in 1970, "is the largest single contract in the annals of American Shipbuilding."

An irate senator from Maine claimed that the bidding and qualifications of a major competitor, Bath Iron Works, had been ignored. The award amounted to overconcentration in one shipyard, Margaret Chase Smith declared. After the experience with Lockheed Aircraft Corporation and the C-5A, she wrote Secretary of the Navy John Chafee on April 24, 1970, "it is inconceivable to me that we would create a backlog larger than our annual ship-building budget in a single facility."[10]

The award amounted to a favoring of conglomerates and a threat to competition, the letter continued:

> As you know, throughout the McNamara era, large segments of industry believed that the Government was really interested in awarding its major defense contracts to the huge conglomerate enterprises. Award of all of the DD 963 ships to Litton Industries would, in my view, serve to confirm that this policy is being carried over into this Administration.
> . . . The award would undoubtedly discourage medium-size companies from attempting to compete with these industrial giants for other major defense contracts, thus restricting competition by eliminating some of our most highly qualified contractors, and thereby ultimately increasing the cost of our defense inventory.

The attempt to create production capability in a new and un-tried shipbuilding facility by shifting to it more than its capacity of production would result in atrophy of that capability in tried and proven yards, Mrs. Smith concluded:

> If the Navy fails to award at least some of these ships to Bath . . . , in all probability the shipyard's destroyer capability will be seriously diminished. The loss of this valuable national asset would

significantly reduce the Navy's ability to obtain first-line competition for destroyer construction.

But the navy was already swayed by the description of Ingalls' new yard conveyed by Litton Executive Committee Chairman Glenn McDaniel to the House Judiciary Committee in 1970. Again emphasizing Litton's founding purpose of strengthening competition in the industries it enters, he explained that though unfinished the yard would revolutionize world shipbuilding:

> Another distinguishing feature of Litton's history has been its ability to add new competitive strengths to companies it acquires. This is another implementation of the concept on which Litton was founded.
> Many industries which cling to traditional methods are facing a revolution due to technological change. One as moribund as any is the shipbuilding industry.
> Even as we entered that industry by the acquisition of Ingalls in 1961 we stated that it would have to undergo substantial innovative change. Four years ago we initiated a major effort to lead the shipbuilding industry in that change. We created a special division to apply whole new concepts to ship design and to engineer a unique ship production facility especially fitted for applying production line methods to complex ships.
> The new facility, the most advanced in the world, is now nearing completion.
> In competition with other large companies in the industry, Litton won the first major contract for serial ship production for the Navy. We believe this new industrial asset will benefit our nation and will be accorded world recognition for leading an old industry into a new era.[11]

To the stockholders went the information that:

> Litton's decisive innovation in American shipbuilding has been to unify engineering and production to design a ship not only for high performance but for economical production.[12]

Neither the Judiciary Committee nor the stockholders were told that the "economical production" was soon to result in a price increase of more than 100% of the LHA assault ship contract figure. Litton had secured the contract by promising to build the ships more efficiently than could its competitors, but with

the increase, Litton's price far exceeded the competing offers
which Litton's promise had eliminated.

As the price doubled so had the delay increased. As of April
1972, the assault ships were two years behind schedule. The delay was steadily increasing.

Commercial shipbuilding contracts entitle the customer to
claims against the contractor for such delay. For instance, *The
Wall Street Journal* of June 30, 1972 reported:

> BEVERLY HILLS, Calif. — Litton Industries Inc., beset by prob-
> lems at its Pascagoula, Miss., shipyard, said it will pay $5.5 mil-
> lion to two ship lines, thus settling claims against it for construc-
> tion charges and delays in the building of eight container ships.
>
> The conglomerate . . . said it reached agreement to pay $3.5 mil-
> lion to Farrell Lines Inc., New York, and $2 million to American
> President Lines Ltd., San Francisco, for "construction changes,"
> excusable delays and "liquidated damage" related to the construc-
> tion of the ships by Litton for the two lines.

However, a reverse generalization applies to defense contracts,
or at least to Litton's assault ship contracts. In spite of the two-
year, ever-increasing delay, Litton claimed $270 million under
those contracts alone from the navy, in addition to the more than
doubled price. Over and above the price increases, Litton's total
claims against the navy amounted to $450 million. One half of the
LHA claims alone far exceeded the cost of the new facility on
which the vessels were to be built.

The status of the LHA production thus raises the issue, em-
braced in the committee's questions to Litton's chief executive,
of whether a corporate acquisitor might develop and learn the
shipbuilding trade and profit in spite of malperformance not
tolerated by commercial customers, through securing U. S.
government contracts. The ambiguity of Litton's naval contracts,
the laxity of the navy's supervision of the construction, the navy's
system of divided authority which beclouds responsibility for
unwarranted contract awards, and the navy's protectiveness of a
failing contractor place the issue in focus.

The House Committee on Armed Services met on April 17,
1972 to question navy officials about Ingalls' performance. Litton representatives had received an invitation to the closed session but did not appear. Chairman F. Edward Hébert presided:

As you are aware, at our last meeting there was considerable discussion concerning reports that at least two of the Navy ship construction programs are in serious trouble. Specifically, the LHA and the DD-963 programs. . . . the committee now being aware of the production difficulties being experienced on the LHA and DD-963 programs must satisfy itself as to the contractor's capability to meet the cost, quality, and time schedule requirements initially established when the program was first presented to the Congress.

. . . these five ships [LHAs] are presently more than two years behind their production schedule, with very positive evidence that their costs, when delivered, will be substantially above the cost estimates originally provided the Congress.

Stated very simply, we have a very serious problem. . . .[13]

Admiral Isaac C. Kidd, chief of Naval Materiel Command, explained that the task entrusted to Ingalls was to replace equipment collapsing from overwear. The need was "catastrophic":

The military requirements for the LHA's and the 963's continue unchanged in the Navy's judgment. The increasing importance of these needs are manifest every day. . . . The 963 requirements . . . to replace aging ships are reaffirmed with each casualty report . . . from the fleet wherein old and tired equipment is breaking down. . . .

These catastrophic machinery derangements were due principally to old age, tired equipment. . . .[14]

He expected the delay of the LHA amphibious assault ship production to "impact" or delay the DD-963 destroyer production. Both types of vessels were to be built in the new West Yard. Work on the destroyers could not begin until the LHA's were finished and moved off the facilities. Nevertheless, the admiral continued, Litton was confident that construction of the destroyers would begin as scheduled in January 1973.

To add plausibility to its prediction, Litton began cutting metal for the destroyers in advance of schedule, on June 6, 1972. Les Aspin of Wisconsin, a member of the House Armed Services Committee, termed that initial work a

public relations device which will divert already scarce workers from the LHA project which is only 2% complete. By stretching out the LHA program the Navy and Litton are only increasing costs and delays while hoping that the metal-cutting motions will give the appearance of an early start on the critically impacted destroyer production.[15]

A major cause of the delay and the doubling costs (exclusive of the $450 million claims) of the LHA production was the inexperience of the Litton managers transferred from Pascagoula. Among the problems were "overoptimism" and "repeated changes in top management personnel, who came [to Ingalls] largely from the aerospace industry and knew little of shipbuilding."[16]

In response to questions concerning production, the Federal Maritime Administration received from Ingalls "irrelevant dissertations on what is done in the rocket and aircraft industries around the country." The FMA's report stated: "If the contractor would refrain from using superfluous slogans and get on with the job, it would be better off."[17]

Severe labor problems have beset the yard. The turnover of workers was double the normal rate of 30%. Also, the modular assembly system has worked poorly. The sections have not fit together. Admiral Kidd commented on the contractor's learning at government expense:

> Moreover, the contractor is learning that some of the management and technology planned for application of that mechanized shipyard is not adaptable. This learning process has produced errors, has caused delays, and is resulting in cost increases, but of an amount not yet determinable by the Navy.[18]

Under the original LHA contract, Litton was to secure a profit of $10 million for each vessel. After the delays and increased expenses became apparent, the navy reduced the order from nine to five vessels. The reduction was purportedly for the Navy's "convenience." Accordingly, it was obligated to pay Litton the contracted profit for the four never-to-be-constructed ships.

The amount of profit to be paid for the canceled orders was probably something less than $10 million for each. The exact profit figure was removed from the hearing transcript:

> Admiral KIDD. The profit was provided for at $10 million per ship.

Congressman CLANCY. And if we terminated for convenience, there would be an estimated payment of [deleted] million of profit?

Admiral KIDD. Correct.[19]

Had the navy declared the contractor to be in default of contract for delay, Litton could not maintain that the order for the four ships had been "terminated for [the Navy's] convenience." The U. S. government would not then be liable for the guaranteed profit.

The navy's hesitancy to declare default was the consequence of its excessive leniency in drafting the contract. The document did not specify the length of the contractor's delay which amounted to his default. In response to questioning of how default might be determined, the navy's attorney at the hearing confirmed that the contract contained no default definition which would render the contractor's reward proportionate to his performance:

Mr. PHELAN. . . . I can't answer your question. Some technical man has got to say he [the shipbuilder] is so far behind no matter what he does he can't meet that delivery schedule.

That is not a legal question [determinable by terms of the contract], that is a question for some expert to determine.[20]

The LHAs were costing more than twice the contracted price, were two years behind schedule, were thus "impacting" the destroyer production, yet the navy was helpless to declare that its obligation under the contract to pay profits for canceled orders was in any way altered.

Though the contracts might have been too simply written to hold the contractor for default, Litton nevertheless contended the documents were too complex.

Congressman MONTGOMERY. I had the opportunity to meet with the president of Litton, Mr. Ash, and I got the impression from him that the Litton Industries was completely behind the shipbuilding program down there. . . . He did say this, though, Mr. Chairman: Mr. Ash said, "It has gotten so you have such complicated contracts you spend more time working on the contracts, dealing with the Navy," than they do with engineering and researching. This has been the delay.[21]

In spite of the ambiguity of the contract, a contractor can maintain that he does incur a penalty for not progressing according to schedule. For each day of delay past the guaranteed delivery date he is liable for a certain amount of money. The delivery date, however, is not specified in the contract and is determinable only by extensive negotiation. Even then, if the delivery date is established, the absolute maximum penalty for delay is minimal; under the "impacted" DD-963 destroyer contract, for instance, it was but $1/79$ of the original contract price.

At least one reason that the contractor's penalty for delay is "infinitesimal," according to Admiral Kidd, is that the government, curiously, is liable for his insurance expense:

> Admiral KIDD. . . . I started digging into it as to why we have such an infinitessimal penalty, and I talked to contractors. I asked them—not just shipbuilders—why don't we make it tougher on you? And the answer I got back was very simple. "You can, but you will pay for it by the insurance rates that the contractors would have to take out." And in digging back through the files, I find indications that the Government insures itself, so this is about all we see in contracts of this sort. It is just a drop in the bucket, a kind of a slap on the wrist. It really doesn't amount to much.[22]

The navy has been writing shipbuilding contracts since its inception. That after 175 years its arrangements with contractors should fail to protect the public sufficiently from uncontrolled cost overruns and malperformance was, the navy's own spokesmen wholeheartedly agreed, inexcusable and reason for censure:

> Congressman PIRNIE. I gained an unmistakable impression this morning that the definition of "default," or the "time for performance" was so indefinite that you were dependent upon cumulative evidence in order to declare a default. . . .
>
> . . . I think it is deserving severe criticism of the form of the contract. It isn't as though we were just going into shipbuilding as an original project. This is something that has been incident to the performance of the Navy since its existence. And if we haven't learned how to draw a contract now that would cover these elements of performance, then there is something wrong.
>
> . . .
>
> So I hope there is one thing that is going to come out of this hearing, and that is that we in Congress are not going to any longer

accept these statements with respect to overrun, and indefinite advice as to the position of the Government. They can't blame this on inflation. Inflation can account for certain things. But when you double the costs or when we have to pay twice as much for half the number of ships, there is something wrong and it is wrong in the contract, or else the company would not be continuing in its relationship with this project.

Does the Admiral see what I mean?

Admiral KIDD. Oh, yes, indeed. I certainly do, Mr. Pirnie.

Mr. PIRNIE. You can understand the feeling of this committee as we go into this perpetual story of contractual misperformance, or nonperformance, without any apparent rights on the part of the Government in order to protect its interest, and then they begin to talk to us about prolonged litigation.[23]

Not just litigation of the navy's alleged liability for Litton's claims would be prolonged. Merely to comprehend the claims requires endurance. The contract is not as lenient to the government as to the shipbuilder. It holds the navy responsible for any delay of its own. To facilitate Ingalls' construction process, the navy itself agreed to furnish certain equipment for the assault ships. But Litton asserted that delivery of the equipment had been late and thus the cause of additional expense. Also on the basis of "Navy interference in Design Development and over Management" Litton submitted a 15-volume, 6,000 page "summation" of the claims against the government of $270 million for the LHA construction alone. That amount was not included in the price increase from $113 million to $288 million for each LHA assault ship.

The only valid claims against the navy, Admiral Kidd stated to the Armed Services Committee, were from losses and damages incurred at Pascagoula by strikes and hurricanes. "But in my humble judgment," he explained, "those two elements would justify but a minute fraction of the total size of his [Litton's] claim."[24]

The "summation" of claims took Litton a year to prepare. To substantiate it, the company explained, would require another year. The navy received its copy of the "summation" only ten days before the hearing. Thus, its spokesmen stated, the task of attempting to comprehend Litton's allegations had hardly begun:

> A substantial amount of the contractor's presentation are pure
> predictions, his own predictions. We will not be able to comment
> on them with any degree of accuracy, I would say, for some time.[25]

Thus, the shipbuilder troubled by purported complexity of his
government contracts wrote an intricate and voluminous document himself. Earlier, in response to the question of whether
Litton used a different procedure "in doing business with the
Government than doing business with the private sector," Tex
Thornton had complained: "The biggest difficulty of course is
the paper work. It is tremendous doing business with the Government."[26]

The selection of the Ingalls shipyard for construction of the
assault ships involved a miscalculation of the required man
hours by 200% to 300%. This mistake does not instill confidence
in the estimate of the cost of the destroyer construction. That
estimate had risen $10 million per vessel before construction
had even begun. Doubt now exists of Ingalls' capability to perform the contracts. Yet the navy selected Ingalls for the largest
shipbuilding award in history after a year-long "most comprehensive evaluation ever made by the Navy of a shipbuilding
program."[27]

"How could you be so wrong?" the committee asked the admirals.

> We've got to remember that we made a decision on the basis of a
> shipyard that was nonexistent at the time, and a technique for
> production that was still sort of a gleam in somebody's eye

was the reply of the chief of Naval Materiel Command.[28]

Explanations for selecting a nonexistent shipyard for the nation's most ambitious shipbuilding program over yards of proven
ability range from an account of patriotic inspiration to curious
and exceedingly optimistic defenses of Litton's promises. The
facileness of those defenses raises the question of whether an
agency of defense might still again award production contracts,
perhaps in a time of greater national peril, on the basis of promised rather than actual capability.

Patriotic rivalry was the justification offered by Admiral Kidd
for the "well-founded risk":

Congressman SPENCE. . . . how do you think we got into this mess in the first place?

Admiral KIDD. Overoptimism on the part of both the Government and the contractor in the beginning.

. . .

Congressman STRATTON. Admiral, I am aware that you . . . were not here when the decision was made but the statement was an incredible one . . . when you said . . . this contract was to a nonexistent shipyard to build a ship according to a technique that was also nonexistent. . . . It is hard for me to see how anybody in his right mind could have thought this was a desirable thing to do.

Admiral KIDD. Well, if I may, I would take issue with that, Mr. Stratton, because others abroad and in the Soviet Union were having success, and are making it work, and making it work well. So I think the risk was a well-founded risk. As I said earlier, I have got that much pride in Americans' ability to build things, and I don't see any reason why—

Congressman STRATTON. There is no point arguing it now, Admiral, because it wasn't well founded and we don't have that ability, whether the Soviets do or don't.[29]

The failure of technology, facilities, management, and manpower brought on a failure of capital. Although a stated purpose of Litton's conglomeration program is to inject financial strength (besides managerial strength) into companies it acquires, Ingalls lacked sufficient funds to perform the contracts. Consequently, the navy made payments ahead of schedule to Litton, thus paying for work that was not performed. The amount advanced was predicted to range from $100 million to $150 million by October 1, 1972. *The New York Times* reported on April 19, 1972:

The House [Armed Services] Committee was reported to have been told by Navy witnesses that Litton had already been paid 50 per cent of the contract price, whereas, even with the most generous calculation of engineering completed, only 25 per cent of the work had been done.

"Litton is confronted with a critical cash flow problem," a Congressional source said.

The company would not comment on these matters.

Under the terms of the contract, if the 24-month-delayed performance of the assault ships was not on schedule by September 1, 1972, Litton was to have repaid the advanced millions. When that time expired, the navy granted a six-month reprieve. When that extension expired on March 1, 1973, the navy granted another reprieve, extending the date to June 1, 1973. On announcement of the navy's second extension date, the conglomerate replied: "Litton believes such a repayment isn't due [even in June] and will oppose the Navy's claim."[30]

With that sword of Damocles hanging over the defense production, the navy's "on-site" inspector at Pascagoula, Admiral Charles N. Payne, turned to Ingalls' construction for private customers to find justification for the navy's "enthusiastic" acceptance of Litton's professed capability. He told the Armed Services Committee:

> I am Admiral Payne. I am supervisor of shipbuilding. I have been keeping up with the Farrell [Lines, Inc.] ships [under construction by Ingalls] on a regular basis with the Maritime Administration local representative down there. We have been very interested in the progress and the quality that the company [Ingalls] has been maintaining.
>
> My last reports indicate that although the progress is behind the original schedule and continues to be behind, and they are going to be delivering late, that the quality has improved tremendously on the last three ships. They did have quality problems on the first ship.
>
> . . .
>
> The outfitting which is proceeding on the first ship, they are still learning on it, and it is somewhat below the standards in the industry, but they expect improvements in the second, third, and fourth ships as they are showing improvements in their construction.[31]

Whether Farrell Lines shared the inspecting admiral's good feelings for Litton's "learning" efforts was not certain. The delays and cost overruns did not abate. *Time* of July 3, 1972 (p. 32) reported:

> The Pascagoula plant is also far behind on construction of eight container ships for the Farrell and American President lines. Now scheduled for completion next fall, the first such vessel will be 21 months behind schedule and will cost about double its contract

price of $21 million, making it the most expensive general cargo ship ever built. Litton will doubtless pay heavily for the overrun.

Litton would pay heavily, the article means, to its commercial, not government, customers, for on June 30 Litton had agreed to pay $5.5 million construction damages to the two lines.

The cost overrun alone on the first ship of the Farrell contract would equal considerably more than one quarter of the entire construction cost of the liner *Queen Elizabeth II*.[32] Six months before the damages settlement, *Forbes* of December 15, 1971 (p. 18) described the construction problems:

> The Austral Envoy's deckhouse was placed on the hull structure, but the main deck sagged because beams underneath had been left out. Litton jacked up the deckhouse, put in the beams, and set down the deckhouse again — still off kilter. "It's only nine-sixteenths of an inch off," says O'Green [Litton's new manager of Ingalls]. "It doesn't affect the ship's performance."

Litton had transferred manager O'Green to Pascagoula from its nonshipbuilding Defense and Space Systems Group.

A "lot of speculation, a lot of hypotheses that have been made of sand," Admiral Kidd stated, led responsible authorities to believe that Litton was capable of constructing the assault ships. Who those authorities were and where they are now, however, could not be ascertained:

> Congressman RANDALL. Who were the people that made this decision? Who were the people that went so wrong? One of the problems, it seems to me, is that when we try to get at any of these things we are dealing with mush. The flag officers are transferred every 2 years. The Assistant Secretaries rotate every couple of years. We have a new Assistant Secretary who comes up with a new plan for controlling cost growth, and he is replaced, and somebody else comes in with a plan.[33]

In reply to the question (phrased two years previously at House Judiciary Committee hearings) of whether the frequent turnover or rereplacement of government administrators of defense contracts resulted in an advantage to Litton as the contractor, Tex Thornton stated: "I don't think so. I never heard of that. No."[34] The fact that the persons to whom Litton sold its undeveloped and failing shipbuilding systems and concepts are no longer in places of conspicuous authority should cause little distress to the conglomerate.

None of the admirals in the Armed Services Committee hearing room could answer the question for which the hearing was specifically called, "Who made the decision to retain Litton?" The agency responsible is the Office of Naval Materiel Command. Its chief, not surprisingly, assumed command after the decision:

> Congressman RANDALL. . . . there is no one in the room that really made the decision [to award the contracts to Litton] is that right?
>
> Admiral KIDD. Made what?
>
> Congressman RANDALL. The original decision, the important decision here.
>
> . . . I am talking about back when the contract was let. That is my question. Who was that?
>
> Admiral KIDD. I don't know, Mr. Randall.
>
> Congressman RANDALL. You don't know? Are you standing on that answer that you don't know who made the decisions?
>
> Admiral KIDD. That is right. I wasn't here. I have no idea who made the decisions.[35]

Chairman Hébert explained:

> After you have been around Washington as long as I have been, you will find out it [the official responsible for mistaken contract awards] is the little man who isn't there, he went away the day before.[36]

Under the weight of questioning the navy admitted that the decision to award Litton the contracts was mistaken, being based on "a lot of hypotheses that have been made of sand." At the start of the hearings, however, the navy had attempted to defend the decision or at least to explain the deficiencies in the most ameliorating terms:

> Admiral KIDD. On the matter of Litton, and their performance at the new West Bank Shipyard, sir, there is no question in my mind that that new shipyard embodies the latest in mechanized improvements and ideas collected from around the world.

It has not yet measured up even closely to some of the expectations predicted of it. However, I have enough confidence in the engineering capabilities of these United States of ours to be comfortable in the prospect that American ingenuity and production potential can be able to do as well or exceed performance abroad, as has been done in the assembly line of high volume production ships in the Soviet Union. . . .

This contractor of ours is still learning to use his shipyard. He has a long way to go. . . . This contractor is pioneering an exciting new approach in ship construction. . . . We expected far too much of him at the outset, and the contractor was far and away overoptimistic in predicting his abilities to produce.[37]

The admiral urged indulgence. He expressed hope for Litton's billion-dollar "learning" program and pleaded that Congress not fire Litton. Worse than Litton's failing performance, the navy counseled, would be to remove the destroyer production to a competitor's shipyard, or to kill the project altogether. The chief of Navy Materiel Command stated:

There would, of course, be a possibility of having those ships built someplace else, if we find that the LHA impact on the 963 is too great. Moreover, if the Congress were to withhold funds for the . . . destroyers, this would remove a very important negotiating option from the hands of the Government as well as giving to Litton—mind you, giving to Litton cancellation charges which would be due Litton under the terms of the contract. . . .[38]

Although Litton would be fired only for its inability to perform the destroyer contract, the taxpayers' liability for such a measure could approach a billion dollars. The navy explained:

if the contract with Litton were canceled Litton would be entitled to collect a total of something between $400 million and $950 million from the government.[39]

Roy Ash resigned as president of Litton Industries in December 1972 to become director of the U. S. Office of Management and Budget. On assuming that office, which determines federal expenditure, Mr. Ash stated that he would not divorce himself from decisions affecting the navy. At the time, according to *The Wall Street Journal* of November 29, 1972 (p. 2), he also told reporters he plans to stress . . . sharper analysis of results in comparison with [government] costs. "We had better be sure we are getting our money's worth," he commented, because the federal government "is costing so much."

. . . "We want to keep our eye on the expected results rather than just the best efforts" to reach them, he said.

The budget office under Mr. Ash, the *Journal* continued, would "undertake a comprehensive examination of all government programs now in existence to determine whether they are actually meeting the purpose for which they were designated."

A report by Navy and Maritime Administration auditors released three weeks later described "poor workmanship and repetitive defects" of Litton's shipbuilding program. As stated by *The Washington Post* of December 19, 1972 (p. A 3), the report found that

> Senior managers of the Litton Ship Systems Division "diluted" their effectiveness "because of the large amount of commuting" they had to do between Pascagoula and [other conglomerate operations in] California.
>
> . . .
>
> "The planned allocation of manpower was inadequate for all ships."
>
> . . .
>
> The training program was "primarily subsidized by Government." The Company's own training program was "inadequate."

On December 20, 1972, the navy's director of Procurement Control, Gordon W. Rule, described the audit report as "the worst indictment I ever heard of a shipyard"[40] (see chapter 11). The Joint Economic Committee of Congress to which he spoke had invited Litton representatives to those same hearings at which the report was made public. Litton's Chief Executive Tex Thornton declined, however, replying: "a public discussion of the subject matter of these negotiations [of the conglomerate's claims against the navy] would be contrary to the best interest of both the government and Litton shareholders."[41]

The navy's insistence that Congress allow Litton to remain as contractor at all costs gives perspective to Tex Thornton's assertion to the House Judiciary Committee in 1970 that a private contractor's performance of government contracts is a competitive process. He stated then:

> Mr. Chairman, in the Government business that we compete on, most of our competitors, 90 per cent or more or them are the giants, the big companies. It is though competition. More often than not, it is your exposure, your investment, your profits, and your return is less than it is on the commercial business.[42]

Bidding on government contracts may be a competitive process. Once a contractor wins the contract, however, as Litton has secured the assault ship and destroyer production, apparently it is assured of keeping the assignment regardless of how disappointing its performance is and regardless of the number and the qualifications of competitors capable of finishing the project.

Mr. Thornton also stated that Litton's defense contracts were fixed in price, implying that the government could not be charged for price overruns:

> in the first place, most of our contracts for government work have been fixed priced. We have lost money on government contracts the same way that we have lost money on commercial projects. We operate under tight specifications at a fixed price. . . .[43]

The LHA contracts were "fixed price." As seen, Litton's charges against the government for an overrun in excess of 100% of the contract price and its claims of over a quarter-billion dollars represent only part of its 15-volume claim "summary."

A minute portion of the overrun consists of $7 million of navy funds which Litton misappropriated. That money, designated for the assault ship and destroyer production, Litton spent instead on its commercial projects.

In the Report to the Joint Economic Committee of Congress on Controls Over Shipyard Costs and Procurement Practices of Litton Industries, Inc., of March 23, 1972 (p. 16), in customary bland language the U. S. comptroller general stated:

> The Defense Contract Audit Agency found that, during the period 1969 through 1971, Navy contracts for the LHA's and DD-963's were charged about $7 million for overhead expenses applicable to Litton's commercial work.
>
> . . .

Although we did not review Litton's overhead-charging practices in detail, our selective examination indicated that they were
resulting in the Navy contracts' bearing some of the overhead expenses applicable to the West Yard's commercial work.

The wrongfully allocated funds reduced the contractor's expenses on his shipbuilding for commercial, nongovernmental
shipbuilding. Thus, the misallocation amounted to the contractor's placing the navy's $7 million in his own pocket.

Litton is not inclined to return the millions, but the navy, the
report happily assured, "has the matter under consideration":

The contractor believes that an adjustment should not be made for
prior years' [before July 1, 1972] costs.
 . . . Our limited review confirmed the DCAA finding that the
contractor's method of charging costs incurred by Marine Technology [a Litton division] had resulted in Navy contracts' bearing
certain overhead costs applicable to commercial work. The Navy
currently has this matter under consideration.[44]

Admiral Charles N. Payne, who spoke encouragingly of Ingalls' commercial production, is the navy's supervisor of Shipbuilding, Conversion and Repair at Pascagoula. He heads the
office, the comptroller general's report states, which is

responsible for administering the contracts at the East and West
Yards. . . . it exercises surveillance over the contractor's operations to ensure conformance with contractual requirements. To
carry out this surveillance, [the office] . . . as of November 1971
had a staff of 275 civilians and 19 military personnel. This staff
was involved in surveillance of such contractor operations as quality assurance, planning, control of materiel procurement, and cost
control.[45]

Cost control surveillance may well be a major obligation of that
staff. Congress, however, learned of the $7 million misappropria-
tion only because the Joint Economic Committee happened to
request that the comptroller general make an investigation. Had
the committee not requested the inquiry the misappropriation
would have remained undisclosed to the taxpayers' representatives.

A builder of ships who knows he can pass avoidable costs on

to an unquestioning customer has little incentive to curtail those costs. Depending on the degree of the customer's acquiescence, the shipbuilder might ignore federal laws enacted specifically for elimination of unreasonable expenses. Also, he might even ignore contract requirements for verification and proof of claims against the complacent customer who orders the ships. That a customer could be obliging enough to waive those requirements set forth for his own protection is difficult to conceive.

More specifically, a government contractor is unlikely to spurn safeguards against unfair subcontract charges if he is held responsible for the resulting cost overruns. If he does reject those safeguards he is apparently confident that the government, unlike commercial customers, will bear that unnecessary cost. According to the comptroller general's report, Litton "had foregone safeguards for determining whether it was paying fair prices":

> The purchase order files [of the East Yard] we examined, which covered larger buys, generally did not contain . . . [data] for determining the reasonableness of subcontract prices. Department of Defense regulations provide that the contracting officer, before soliciting quotations, develop, where feasible, an estimate of the proper price level or the value of the product or service to be purchased based on prior purchases and other data.
>
> We found that files for 122 of the 181 subcontractors for procurements of $2,500 or more showed no indications that price estimates had been prepared. In only a few cases did we find evidence that current quotes had been compared with prices paid in prior procurements. Although it does not necessarily follow that the subcontract prices were unreasonable, the contractor had foregone the opportunity offered by those safeguards for determining whether it was paying fair prices.[46]

The Truth-in-Negotiations Act (76 Stat. 528) requires that contractors performing for the government negotiate with suppliers or subcontractors to secure reasonable prices. The report continues:

> The shipyard [East Yard] apparently did not hold negotiation discussions for most of the subcontract awards we reviewed. As a result, the lowest available subcontract prices may not have been

obtained. The Truth-in-Negotiations Act provides that Government procurement officers hold such discussions. . . .[47]

Examination of 200 of the 224 total contracts revealed that the contractor had not complied with the act. Negotiations held in compliance with the act over the remaining 24 contracts had resulted in substantial price reductions.

Litton's $270 million claim against the navy involving the assault ship production was based, as seen, on alleged costs incurred from the navy's alteration of plans, or "change orders," and from late deliveries of equipment. The comptroller general reported, however, that Litton's "budgeting and cost control systems" were inadequate to determine the cost of the change orders. The navy agreed with Litton, he stated, that "to segregate the costs of changes" so that claims may be verified would be impracticable:

> the contracts at the West Yard required the reporting of budgetary data to the Navy. We could not evaluate the adequacy of the contractor's budgeting and cost control system, however, because it had not been fully developed and implemented. The LHA ships were in the early stages of production, and Litton officials told us that detailed budgetary data were not yet available. . . . We noted that the contractor's system did not provide for segregating actual costs of change orders to permit comparison with budgets in order to evaluate change-order prices and performance. The contractor and the Navy contend that it would be impracticable to segregate costs of changes and that to do so would be extremely costly.[48]

Litton's control system, the comptroller general indicated, was inadequate for verifying claims:

> the segregation of change-order costs, where feasible, is needed to provide a sound basis for negotiating change-order prices.[49]

Thus, by inadequate bookkeeping practices a contractor may thwart challenges to his claims and thereby profit from his contractual noncompliance. A customer who accepts such noncompliance should be ready also to accept a 15-volume claims "summation."

The West Yard's insufficient record keeping and cost analysis should have come as no surprise to the navy. Before the LHA assault ship and destroyer contracts were let, the navy itself had given the system in the East Yard a failing grade. The comptroller general reported:

> Approval of the contractor's purchasing system was withdrawn following a procurement review in August 1969 when the Navy determined that
> - the purchasing manual did not fully implement the requirements of the Truth-in-Negotiations Act,
> - the bidders' lists were incomplete.
> - criteria for conducting negotiation discussions were needed,
> - procedures and capability for making cost analyses did not exist, and
> - adequate documentation to enable reconstruction of purchase transactions was not present.[50]

More than a year later, after the award of the LHA ships and destroyer contracts, "the Navy found that most of the deficiencies previously disclosed had not been corrected."[51]

That the Litton headquarters contributes to the acquired subsidiary universal management ability adaptable to untried fields of endeavor may be, therefore, too sweeping a generalization. A safer deduction is that a distinct Litton purpose is to bestow the subsidiary with a particular technique for securing government awards. Through that technique the conglomerate won for the acquired company the most colossal production contract the navy ever granted—production to be performed by a "non-existent shipyard" with a "non-existent technology."

ITT secured anticompetitive advantage for its acquired subsidiaries through the mass of its acquired operations. Litton won such advantage for Ingalls through its technique for negotiating with government officialdom. If there is a lesson to be derived from the examination of the three acquirers it is strengthened by the fact that the one conglomerate which did not acquire for the purpose of securing anticompetitive advantage has fared least well. LTV has undergone reorganization and partial liquidation.

PART IV

The Counterattack in Disarray

Legislation of long standing exists to counteract the financial machination which aids and abets the present trend of industrial concentration. Laws even exist, as officials of the U. S. Department of Justice repeatedly asserted, to prevent directly that consolidation.

The extent to which such safeguards are applied is not uniform. Some enforcement agencies entrust their duties to the industry subject to the regulation. The Federal Reserve Board relegates to the New York Stock Exchange the responsibility of enforcing Federal Reserve Board regulation. The Securities and Exchange Commission, also believing in self-regulation for the regulated, does not keep abreast of the industry's interpretation of that responsibility (see p. 87). The question of the adequacy of enforcement, however, extends beyond the issue of stock exchange regulation.

If a physician were to minister to his patients, or a lawyer to defend the rights of his clients, only when he was in a particular frame of mind, his practice and income would suffer. No such discipline controls government regulatory agencies.

The analogy is none too strong. A government office which exists for the public's protection and which ignores the congressional grant of power for providing that protection harms far more persons than any physician who purposefully withholds from his patients obvious means of cure.

CHAPTER **10**

The Interstate Commerce Commission

[A] most prolific source of financial disaster and complication to railroads in the past has been the desire and ability
of railroad managers to engage in enterprises outside the
legitimate operation of their railroads. . . . The evil which
results, first to the investing public, and finally, to the general public, cannot be corrected after the transaction has
taken place; it can be easily and effectively prohibited.

> Report of the Interstate Commerce Com-
> mission's Investigation of the New Haven
> Company; The New England Investiga-
> tion, 27 ICC 560 (1913).

The Penn Central Railroad succumbed from injury inflicted
by its own hand. That injury was the drain of hundreds of millions of dollars incurred by its efforts to become a conglomerate
corporation. Had the Interstate Commerce Commission performed its most fundamental functions – and not thwarted basic
public protection against financial manipulation – the largest
bankruptcy in history could not have occurred.

By 1970, the Penn Central controlled over 190 corporations.
More than eighty of them operated outside the field of transportation. Its real estate holdings ranged from the Six Flags
Over Texas amusement park to the Waldorf Astoria Hotel. Consolidated assets surpassed $6.85 billion.

In the early 1960s the Pennsylvania Railroad's management
and Board of Directors reached the conclusion that to build a

184

conglomerate is better than to run a railroad. Stuart T. Saunders, chairman of the board and chief executive officer, had been in the railroad business for almost his entire working career, and admittedly was getting tired of it. His specialty, moreover, was not railroad operations but finance and public relations — especially stockholder relations.

He took control of the Pennsylvania Railroad in 1963 and by 1966 had increased its dividends from less than $7 million a year to more than $30 million.[1] Revenue increased also, though not at all by the same proportion. Part of Saunders' management technique was to issue stern directives to his subordinates to cut costs in any way they knew how. The railroad's steadily deteriorating service to the public was clear evidence that they obeyed.

By 1965 the Pennsylvania Railroad management and board had abdicated its responsibility and control by giving Finance Director David Bevan and Treasurer William Gerstnecker a free hand to dispose of assets necessary for railroad operations in order to acquire companies unrelated to the rail industry. The two officers freely spent millions of dollars not only without the board's express approval but without its knowledge.[2]

Funds for adequate roadbed maintenance grew steadily scarcer. Trains had to creep along over long stretches at speeds that would have been slow in 1890, just to stay on the wobbling rails. Nevertheless, derailments became endemic because of neglect and deterioration of track and roadbed.

Not surprisingly, then, in 1968 the Pennsylvania Railroad was enthusiastic about an exception to its diversification program — merger with another railroad, the more efficient and better-managed New York Central. The courts and the regulatory agencies, swayed by the argument that both railroads would somehow operate more effectively by combining their operations and management, permitted the merger — at that time the largest industrial combination ever — as an exception to antitrust legislation which generally prohibits combination of enterprises engaged in the same industry.

A prime consideration which induced the capable New York Central management to agree to the merger was the idea that the trains of one company could run over the rails of the other.[3]

FIGURE 4

PENN CENTRAL TRANSPORTATION COMPANY

Penn Central Company (*holding company*)

Penn Central Transportation Company (railroad)
(100% owned by Penn Central Company)

CARRIER COMPANIES OWNED

Baltimore & Eastern R.R.	100%
Beach Creek R.R.	79%
Boston Terminal Corp.	100%
Calumet Western R.R.	75%
Canada Southern Rwy. Co.	12%
Canadian Pacific Car & Pass. Tfr.	50%
Central Indiana Rwy.	50%
Cherry Tree & Dixonville R.R.	100%
Chicago River & Indiana R.R.	100%
Chicago Union Station Co.	25%
Cleveland & Pittsburgh R.R.	28%
Cleveland Union Terminals Co.	71%
Connecting Railway Co.	26%
Dayton Union Rwy.	33%
Delaware R.R.	85%
Detroit Terminal Railway	25%
Fairport, Painesville & Eastern	50%
Fort Wayne Union Rwy.	50%
Lakeport & Dock R.R. Term.	50%
Lake Erie & Pittsburgh Rwy.	100%
Mahoning Coal R.R.	83%
New England Transportation Co.	100%
New York & Harlem R.R.	94%
New York & Long Branch R.R.	50%
New York Connecting R.R.	100%
Nicholas, Fayette & Greenbrier R.R.	50%
Niagara Junction Rwy.	50%
Pennsylvania & Atlantic R.R.	100%
Penn-Ridge S.S. Lines	67%
Pennsylvania Truck Lines, Inc.	100%
Penna. Tunnel & Terminal R.R.	100%
Peoria & Eastern Rwy. Co.	30%
Peoria & Pekin Union Rwy.	8%
Philadelphia & Trenton R.R.	11%

CARRIER COMPANIES (CONT.)

Pittsburgh, Ft. Wayne & Chicago Rwy.	100%
Pullman Company	19%
Railway Express Agency Holding Corp.	26%
St. Lawrence & Adirondack Rwy.	100%
Shamokin Valley & Pottsville R.R.	29%
Toledo Terminal R.R.	32%
Toronto, Hamilton & Buffalo Rwy.	37%
Union Freight Co.	50%
Waynesburg Southern R.R.	100%
West Jersey & Seashore R.R.	57%
Wilkes Barre Connecting R.R.	50%

Northern Central Railway (80% owned)	
Shamokin Valley & Pottsville R.R. Co.	71%
Union R.R. Co. of Baltimore	58%

Lehigh Valley R.R. (97% owned)	
Bay Shore Connecting R.R. Co.	50%
Buffalo Creek R.R. Co.	50%
Ironton R.R. Co.	50%
Lehigh & Hudson River Rwy. Co.	22%
Niagara Junction Rwy. Co.	25%
Owasco River Rwy. Co.	50%

United New Jersey R.R. & Canal Co. (53% owned)	
Philadelphia & Trenton R.R.	65%
Associates of the Jersey Co.	100%

Richmond-Washington Co.	17%
Richmond, Fredericksburg & Potomac R.R. Co.	76%

Pennsylvania Company (investment company)
(100% owned by Penn Central Transportation Company)

Great Southwest Corp. (real estate development corporation; 90% owned)

GSC Apartments Inc.	100%
GSC Development Corp.	100%
GSC Industrial Properties Inc.	100%
GSC Properties Inc.	100%
Leadership Mortgage Investment Co.	100%
Six Flags Inc.	100%
Six Flags Inn, Inc.	100%

Macco Corporation (real estate)

Balmoral Homes, Inc.	100%
Bar-M-Bar Ranch Inc.	100%
Bonnie Valley Corp.	100%
Capistrano Highlands	100%
Castlebay Development Co.	100%
Courtyard Homes	100%
Custom Planning, Inc.	100%
Gleneagles Estates, Inc.	100%
Jamboree Land Co.	100%
Leadership Homes, Inc.	100%
Macco Business Properties Inc.	100%
Macco Distributors Inc.	100%
Macco Industrial Properties Inc.	100%
Newport Harbor Homes, Inc.	100%
Pentland Homes	100%
Rancho Santa Barbara	100%
Recreation Concepts, Inc.	100%
Richardson Homes Corp.	100%
Scripps-Miramar Development Co.	100%
Strathaven Estates	100%
Tartan Homes, Inc.	100%
Temecula Investment Co.	100%
Waverly Homes, Inc.	100%
Westcliff Advertising Co.	100%

Arvida Corporation (real estate development corporation; 58% owned)

Arvida Realty Sales, Inc.	100%
Frank B. Morgan & Co.	100%
University Park Water Co.	100%
Arvida Mortgage Co.	100%

Connecting Railway Co. (74% owned)

Akron & Barberton Belt R.R. Co.	25%
Akron Union Passenger Depot Co.	50%
Little Miami R.R. Co.	79%
Pittsburgh, Youngstown & Ashtabula Rwy. Co.	80%

Wabash R.R. Co.	77%
Illinois Northern Rwy. Co.	12%
Pullman Co.	16%
Norfolk & Western Rwy. Co.	23%
Penn Towers Inc.	40%
Toledo, Peoria & Western Rwy. Co.	50%
West Jersey & Seashore R.R.	28%

Buckeye Pipe Line Co. (100% owned)

Buckeye Tank Terminals, Inc.	100%
Everglades Pipe Line Co.	41%

187

FIGURE 4 *(continued)*

Penn Central Transportation Company (cont. from p.186)

Michigan Central Railroad (100% owned)
    Canada Southern Rwy.
      Co.   59%
    Detroit Manufacturers
      R.R.   81%
    Detroit River Tunnel
      Co.   100%
    Detroit Terminal R.R.
      Co.   25%
    Indiana Harbor Belt
      R.R. Co.   30%
    Mackinac Transporta-
      tion Co.   33%
    Toronto, Hamilton &
      Buffalo Rwy. Co.   22%

Penndel Company (100% owned)
    Mackinac Transporta-
      tion Co.   33%
    Norfolk & Portsmouth
      Belt. R.R. Co.   13%

New York Central Trans-
  port Co.   100%

Despatch Shops Inc.   100%
  Realty Hotels Inc.   100%

Providence Produce Ware-
  house Co.   100%
  New England Car Co.   100%

Clearfield Bituminous Coal Corp.
(100% owned)
    Cambria & Indiana R.R.
      Co.   40%
    Fort Wayne & Jackson
      R.R. Co.   27%
    Cambria Cty. Water
      Supply Co.   100%
    51st Street Realty Co.   100%
    Henrietta Water Supply
      Co.   100%

American Contract Co. (100% owned)
    Merchants Trucking
      Co.   100%
    Penntruck Co., Inc.   100%
    Delbay Corp.   100%
    Excelsior Truck Leasing
      Co. Inc.   100%

Cleveland, Cincinnati, Chicago &
St. Louis Railway (99% owned)
    Central Indiana Rwy.
      Co.   50%
    Union Depot Co.   50%
    Cleveland Union Term.
      Co.   22%
    Dayton Union Rwy. Co.   33%
    Indianapolis Union
      Rwy. Co.   40%
    Peoria & Eastern Rwy.
      Co.   50%
    Cincinnati Union Term.
      Co.   14%
    Chicago & Harrisburg
      Coal Co.   100%

Pittsburgh & Lake Erie R.R. (81% owned)
    Pittsburgh, Chartiers &
      Youghiogheny Rwy.
      Co.   50%
    Montour R.R. Co.   50%
    Lake Erie & Eastern
      R.R. Co.   50%
    Monongahela Rwy. Co.   33%

Manor Real Estate Company
(100% owned)
    C.I. West Virginia Corp.   50%
    Western Allegheny R.R.
      Co.   100%
    G.S.C. Leasing Corp.   50%
    Delaware Car Leasing
      Co.   40%
    General Car Leasing
      Co.   40%
    Greencar Corp.   40%
    Penna. Car Leasing Co.   40%

NON-CARRIER COMPANIES OWNED

Cleveland Technical Cen-
  ter, Inc.   100%
Fruit Growers Express
  Co.   24%
Green Real Estate Co.   33%
Merchants Dispatch
  Transportation Co.   100%
N. Y. Central Develop-
  ment Corp.   100%
Penn Central Park, Inc.   100%
Penndiana Improvement
  Co.   100%
Terminal Realty Penn Co.   100%
Western Warehousing Co.   100%

Pennsylvania Company (cont. from p.187)

Philadelphia, Baltimore & Washington R.R. Co. (PCT owns 65%, PC owns 35%)	
Union R.R. Co.	42%
Union Depot Co.	50%
Washington Terminal Co.	50%
Waynesburg & Washington R.R. Co.	100%
Indianapolis Union Rwy. Co.	60%
Tylerdale Con. R.R. Co.	50%
Chicago Union Station Co.	25%
Pittsburgh, Chartiers & Youghiogheny Rwy. Co.	50%
Montour R.R. Co. (50% owned)	
Youngstown & Southern R.R. Co.	100%
Montour Land Co.	100%
Detroit, Toledo & Ironton R.R. (100% owned)	
Ann Arbor R.R. Co.	100%
Manistique & Lake Superior R.R. Co.	100%
DTI Enterprises, Inc.	100%
Delaware Car Leasing Co.	60%
General Car Leasing Co.	60%
Greencar Corp.	60%
Penna. Car Leasing Co.	60%

SOURCE: Adapted from chart prepared by the House Banking and Currency Committee staff from December 31, 1969 Report Form A, filed with the ICC by Penn Central Transportation Company.
Percentages show what proportion of company is owned by corporation named above.

Thus the argument for concentration, facile as always, supposed that certain duplicate stretches of tracks of both companies could be eliminated. However, the Pennsylvania Railroad tracks, which hardly supported the trains of one company (and in some places not at all), held up no better under the weight of the trains of the combined companies.

Nor has the combination of managements resulted in economy of scale. The New York Central officers, more dedicated to the operation of railroads, did not enjoy losing control over the revenue generated by their formerly independently held assets and watching it being spent on nonrailroad properties.

> As the railroad operations deteriorated, the philosophical split already in being between the heads of the Penn Central's component railroads became virulent. Alfred E. Perlman, who had been president of the New York Central, did not believe in diversification.
>
> Even before the merger, Perlman loved to show visitors technological improvements he was making on the railroad. He would guide them through every part of a new electronic switching yard, for example, explaining how it would improve service for shippers while reducing costs so much that the Central would get its money back quickly.
>
> Then, in a slap at the Pennsylvania, he would say, "I'm putting every cent I can find into making this a better railroad. I'm not putting it into some silly amusement park" (a dig at the Pennsylvania's investment in the Great Southwest Corp. and the Six Flags Over Texas park).[4]

More unexpectedly, even the computer systems of the two companies could not be synchronized, and entire trains were lost for periods of a week and longer. The cost of replacing the two computer systems—both entirely adequate until the attempt to economize through combining—was estimated at $20 million.

Particularly galling to the former New York Central managers was the $21 million drain incurred by the acquisition and operation of Executive Jet Aviation. The Board of Directors of the Pennsylvania Railroad had approved Finance Director Bevan's and Treasurer Gerstnecker's purchase of the company in 1965 even though the railroad's control of an air carrier was without doubt illegal. Being a violation of the Federal Aviation Act, it was certain to be disallowed by the Civil Aeronautics Board.[5]

The decision to enter the air carrier industry unlawfully was only the beginning of the railroad's adventure into diversification for diversifications' sake. Whether the companies acquired (for the purpose of diversification) would return any income to the railroad appeared to be no concern of the Board of Directors. The stockholders would bear the loss. And because of the failure of the regulatory agencies to administer legislation designed to protect investors, the stockholders would never know their jeopardy until bankruptcy was upon them.

The First National City Bank of New York — eager for the millions of dollars the railroad would pay as interest — led the way in providing easy and ample credit with the greatest laxity. Like Chase Manhattan, it was not averse to helping conglomerates grow.[6]

The bankers' lending of their depositors' money was as automatic as the railroad's decision to diversify. Rather than investigate the soundness of the investments and determine whether the borrower or its subsidiaries would ever be able to repay the loan, the bankers dwelled instead on the railroad's reputation of invincibility. Eventually, the loans themselves were the very instruments which struck down the venerable reputation on which they were founded. Unable to meet its financial obligations in mid-1970, the Penn Central could not secure loans to avoid bankruptcy because its credit was already exhausted by the diversification loans.

Bevan and Gerstnecker enjoyed complete power in obligating the railroad for Executive Jet Aviation's purchases of aircraft — power as illegal as it was unbridled. Together with the president of EJA, Brig. Gen. Olbert F. Lassiter (U. S. Air Force, ret.), they purchased two 707s and two 727s from Boeing at a cost of $26.2 million.[7] The First National City Bank of New York made plain that it considered the borrowing to be the obligation of Penn Central.

General Lassiter, apparently even more confident than Bevan and Gerstnecker of the boundlessness of the railroad's financial reservoirs, later signed a letter of intent with Lockheed for delivery of its L-5000, the civilian equivalent of the Ç-5A military transport, the most gigantic airplane ever built. He needed six of them, he told Lockheed, for a total cost of $136.5 million. Boeing delivered. Fortunately, Lockheed did not.

To make use of its new jet fleet, Executive Jet Aviation needed to acquire customers. It decided to do just that—acquire by purchase a worldwide network of airlines, just as it had purchased the Boeing jets. EJA would then order the customer airlines it owned and controlled to lease its aircraft. Negotiations for the purchase of air transport companies were conducted in France, Germany, Indonesia, the Netherlands, Panama, Saudi Arabia, Spain, and Switzerland. Two purchases were Transavia Holland and International Air Bahamas, which flew between Nassau and Luxembourg. The transactions were so obscure, and Bevan's use of Penn Central funds for purchase so fast and free-wheeling, that $4 million transferred to a Lichtenstein shell corporation was simply lost sight of. Where those millions are today is unknown.

President Stuart Saunders explained in a public address early in 1967 that the railroad, by branching into the air transport business, intended to become "a department store of transportation."[8] He did not elaborate that for a railroad to control an air carrier is illegal, nor did he indicate that the millions of dollars of stockholders' money drained into it would not be seen again. After the address, the railroad's public relations director explained that Executive Jet Aviation, with its acquired airlines, was the instrument for the diversification to which Saunders referred. Immediately Treasurer Gerstnecker reprimanded the director. The railroad's control of the air carrier was not to be mentioned in public, the treasurer insisted, because the Civil Aeronautics Board might learn of it.

After devious and pointless maneuvers to hide the fact that it controlled Executive Jet Aviation—including sham sales agreements (in which Penn Central retained the right to repurchase EJA) with United States Steel and Burlington Industries—in the fall of 1969 Penn Central was ordered by the Civil Aeronautics Board to liquidate its holdings in the air carrier. The order found 13 separate violations of the Federal Aviation Act and levied fines of $5,000 on EJA and $65,000 on Penn Central—the latter being slightly smaller than the largest penalty ever imposed by the CAB.[9]

The management which incurred that fine never succeeded in finding a purchaser for Executive Jet Aviation. Today the company has no hope of recovering more than one million dollars of its $21 million investment.

That amount, of course, is only part of the entire conglomerate acquisition program. Two hundred nine million dollars was spent directly on acquisition. Millions more were distributed by Saunders through excessive dividend payments in efforts to boost the price of Penn Central stock so that it could pay for continued diversification through purchase of other companies.

Speaking as audaciously as he had spent, David Bevan told the Senate Commerce Committee on August 6, 1970 that income from the companies outside the rail industry which Penn Central had acquired enabled it "to keep the railroad running":

> In summary I believe our financial management over the years has been good. Even with all the adverse circumstances I have outlined, we were able to produce the money necessary for the operating people to keep the railroad running in the face of deficits and that was no small job.
>
> I might add that it would not have been possible without the income made available through our new diversification program. . . . Those dividends and income from other non-railroad properties, have served to blunt the losses from passenger service and have provided the margin necessary for continued operation of the Railroad. In other words, our investment in non-railroad companies yielded a much better return than the Railroad itself, which would have been in much more serious trouble without the benefit of diversification.[10]

That the railroad profited at all from the companies acquired after the beginning of the diversification program in 1963 is entirely erroneous. In fact, all the income those companies generated did not even surpass the interest the railroad had to pay on the money borrowed to acquire them. Thus, the return from the $209 million of capital directly invested in conglomerate diversification between 1963 and the time of bankruptcy in 1970 amounts to zero.

Finance Director Bevan's placing the blame for bankruptcy on the alleged nonprofitability of the railroad industry and his statement that the "non-railroad companies yielded a much better return than the Railroad" are, therefore, unsupportable. In-

TABLE 25

Penn Central Transportation Co.
Summary of Cash Impact from Diversification

	(In millions)
Cash expended by transportation group:	
Stock purchases	$157
Dividends paid downstream	19
Loans and advances	33
Total cash expended	$209
Cash received by transportation group:	
Dividends	$ 41
Proceeds received from sale of assets	15
Total cash received	$ 56
Net cash expenditures from the transportation group	$153
Estimated interests costs	56
Total cash expended from diversification	$209

Companies	Cash from transportation group	Cash to transportation group	Net cash from transportation group
Buckeye	$50	$37	$13
Arvida	22		22
Great Southwest	26	4	22
Macco	61		61
Madison Square Garden	5		5
Executive Jet	21		21
Strick	24	15	9
Total	$209	$56	$153

SOURCE: *The Penn Central Failure*, p.33.

deed, one Penn Central official stated that if the $25 million used to purchase the Great Southwest Corporation, a real estate developer, had been used to refurbish railroad yards and tracks, the investment would have paid for itself annually three times over. Invested in Great Southwest, the $25 million yielded 3%, rather than 300%, annually.[11]

On January 11, 1967, EJA President Lassiter wrote to Finance Director Bevan to express appreciation for his having secured the railroad's commitment for financing the jet aircraft purchase. "Thank you," he said, "for laying your career on the line."[12] His words were more apt than he meant. Five years later, Bevan, Lassiter himself, and Charles F. Hodge (a senior member of the investment firm of F. I. Dupont-Glore Forgan, which plotted the railroad's diversification program) were indicted in Philadelphia for having conspired to drain "substantially the resources of the Penn Central, contributing to its bankruptcy in June, 1970."[13]

Penn Central's rampant course of self-destruction should have been obvious to the public. Why its disastrous capital outflow in the late 1960s passed unnoticed is largely attributable to Saunders' use of misleading bookkeeping practices accepted by the Interstate Commerce Commission, the Securities and Exchange Commission, and the accounting profession. Also, his payment of exorbitant dividends did little to motivate the stockholders to investigate the condition of the operations.

The deception was for two purposes. First, stockholders would be lulled into a false sense that all was well. They would be less likely to question the assertion that diversification was profitable and certainly less likely to depose the management (as the company did when it finally – only as a result of impending bankruptcy – learned the facts). Second, by reporting false profits and paying high dividends – even while more cash flowed out of the company than in – Saunders and Bevan could inflate the value of Penn Central stock. So inflated, the stock could be used more easily to continue the conglomeration program of acquiring more companies.

Investors, misled by the inaccurate report of high earnings coupled with the payment of substantial dividends, would bid all the higher for Penn Central stock. With the increased market value of their stock, Saunders and Bevan then had greater resources with which to purchase other companies.

In 1968 Penn Central fortified public confidence in its operations by reporting a loss of more than $20 million as an $88 million profit. The next year the management told the shareholders it was sorry to report that the profit from operations had decreased to $4.4 million. The management did not say, however, that it was sparing them some details of the sorrowful story. Rather than earning $4.4 million as claimed, the company had lost at least $90 million, and possibly more than $110 million.

A two-edged sword for such reporting of inflated, or rather nonexistent, profits is the practice of adding to the income figure amounts which should not be added and of failing to subtract amounts which should be subtracted. That method should not be altogether unfamiliar at this point. Gulf & Western used it when the conglomerate added to operating earnings its non-recurring, nonoperating gains from the sale of securities on the stock market.

The method is especially valuable to a company which acquires other corporations because investors receive an exaggerated notion of the profitability of the acquirer's operations and mistakenly believe that the extraordinary gains will recur. They then place a higher value on the acquirer's stock, thus providing the acquirer with more paper wealth with which to purchase other companies.

Penn Central failed to deduct from its income figure vast sums paid in wages and the cost of depreciation of machinery—amounts which are no part of net income—and thereby reported profits it had not earned. Charging equipment repair costs to capital rather than to operating expenses (which should be deducted from income) alone inflated reported income by more than $20 million.

> Such normal operating expenses as wages and phase-out costs were taken out of capital rather than income, thus inflating Penn Central's reported profits by millions of dollars. Some bills for freight charges, which reportedly are uncollectable, were credited to income. Sales of real estate, which should have been designated as extraordinary items, were credited to normal income, as were the profits from securities sales. Assets were written off as extraordinary charges to avoid the annual depreciation, thereby enhancing earnings. When a large block of securities was exchanged, the paper profit from the transaction was credited to normal income in installments over the ensuing years, even though no cash had ever come in. In some transactions the railroad company sold assets to its financial subsidiary at many times their book value and credited the difference to its own income profit.[14]

Apparently the railroad accountants had only to gain from devising imaginative accounting techniques. While Penn Central revenue declined, the salaries of its executives steadily and sharply rose. Charles Hill, manager, General Accounting, received a salary increase of 100% between October 1967 and September 1969 – to $50,000 annually. The recommendation to Finance Director Bevan for Hill's salary increase of October 1967 states:

> He has been instrumental in the progress that has been made in the Accounting Department within the last several years. He is extremely creative, is an excellent manager and is very cost conscious. *His imaginative accounting is adding millions of dollars annually to our reported net income* [emphasis added].[15]

The Penn Central income figure given the public was further inflated by supposed dividend payments to Penn Central from acquired companies which it controlled. Traditionally, dividends come from a company's earnings. The payments, however, far exceeded the subsidiaries' income and came instead from capital resources which those payments depleted. Dispatch Shops, Inc., earned less than $3 million in 1969, but Penn Central took from it a dividend of $4.7 million. New York Central Transport Co. earned $4.2 million in 1969 but delivered to its parent company a dividend of $14.5 million and had hardly any assets left. Manor Real Estate suffered a $7,000,000 loss in 1969, but Penn Central took from it a $2 million dividend.

Such depletion of the acquired companies' resources impaired their earning capacities. With lower earnings or none at all, their alleged dividends to the controlling conglomerate headquarters could come again only from their dwindling capital assets. Of course the vicious cycle could not continue, because soon the subsidiaries had no more assets to give Penn Central under the guise of dividends.

The parent company, in turn, continued to pay supposed dividends in 1968 and 1969 to its stockholders, who thought they were receiving a distribution of income from operations, even though in those two years the company lost over $110 million from its operations. Saunders staunchly insisted that the railroad's appearance of profitability be maintained at all costs. Even Bevan advised him that the railroad, desperately short of capital, had exhausted all sources of resupply.[16]

If money is so scarce, Saunders replied, then borrow it. Book-keeping legerdemain still prevented disclosure to the investors of the company's deterioration, and Bevan managed to borrow $700 million in 1968 and 1969. Some amounts were at interest rates exceeding 10%. In the best of times the company's assets did not produce income at half that rate. Thus, Penn Central could not pay the interest, let alone the principal, without continued borrowing.

In April 1970 Bevan decided to sell bonds to the public (to be issued as a debt of the investment company subsidiary, the Pennsylvania Company). But by then every asset Penn Central owned was mortgaged. Investors rejected the bond offering, and in so doing undid the effect of Saunder's costly accounting gimmickry. The rejection was public indication that the company would not be able to pay its debts. At last, the Board of Directors was startled into realizing that the company was folding.

"Penn Central board chairman Stuart Saunders vigorously defended the solvency of his company today at the annual stockholders' meeting here," *The Washington Post* reported from Philadelphia on May 13, 1970. He admitted that the company could not continue to lose money at the rate it had been. But as usual, the scapegoat was the obligation to provide passenger service, "a dominant factor for keeping our railroad in the red." But Congress might relieve the company of that duty by creating a government corporation to run the passenger trains, Saunders informed the stockholders. "To emphasize the urgency Saunders feels over rail passenger operations," the newspaper concluded, "he asked all stockholders today to contact immediately members of the House Interstate & Foreign Commerce Committee, headed by Representative Harley O. Staggers and to urge passage of the rail transportation bill."

Finally, the Board of Directors was worried. It did not like the fact that the company could no longer sell bonds even at an interest rate above 10%. Undaunted, however, that same month it voted Saunders an increase in compensation. Other officers also received increases.

The public stockholders bore the expense of the management's diversification and acquisition programs. The value of their shares were to decrease from a high of 86 in 1968 to 5 and less after bankruptcy. Now the management, unable to borrow from regular sources, conceived the idea of keeping the company afloat by spreading the loss to an even greater public—the entire United States citizenry.

In May 1970 Saunders called on Secretary of the Treasury David Kennedy and Secretary of Transportation John Volpe to ask that the government come to the rescue by providing a loan guarantee under the Defense Production Act of 1950 (50 U.S.C. App. 2091). The purpose of the act is to prevent the collapse of corporations whose functioning is vital to the nation's defense. In such an emergency, the government is authorized to guarantee loans of private lenders to distressed corporations in defense industries. The guarantees are called Victory Loans.

Late that month the U. S. Department of Treasury outlined to an assemblage of 122 bank officials representing more than 70 banks its plan for granting Victory Loans to Penn Central. The government would guarantee the railroad's repayment of $225 million of loans from the banks. So as to fit the terms of the Defense Production Act, the Pentagon would act as the guaranteeing agency. More specifically, the Department of the Navy would shoulder the obligation.

A corporation the size of Penn Central—the nation's sixth largest—is bound to have considerable ties to defense production. If Penn Central by virtue of those ties was eligible to be rescued from bankruptcy by the Pentagon, then almost any defunct corporation which meets a similar test of size is entitled to Victory Loans. By that reasoning, any corporate management, no matter how derelict, reckless, or fraudulent, can be assured of government salvation so long as its operations are adequately gigantic.

The U. S. Department of Justice went a step beyond that reasoning by determining that Penn Central qualified for Defense Department assistance even though bankruptcy would not interrupt functions allegedly vital to national security—i.e., operation of the railroad. Assistant Attorney General William H. Rehnquist, soon to be appointed to the U. S. Supreme Court, informed Deputy Attorney General Richard G. Kleindienst that "insolvency is most unlikely to lead immediately to a cessation

or to any serious curtailment of services." Nevertheless, he concluded, the United States "is authorized by the Defense Production Act to make the guarantee in question."[17] If the company
then reportedly losing $700,000 a day could not pay the $225 million loan, as it admittedly could not unless another, much greater
loan was forthcoming, the U. S. taxpayers would pay instead.

The management congratulated itself for having ignored all
the old prescribed rules yet finding still another device for avert-
ing doom. Using railroad resources to purchase other companies,
depleting those companies' assets, resorting to artful accounting
techniques – all had only obscured or at best postponed the coming of Armageddon. Now, at last, a truly infallible device provided by the generosity of the American people would allow the
Penn Central managers once and for all to avoid the consequences of their efforts to turn the railroad into a conglomerate
corporation.

But this time the managers' sense of relief was short-lived.
Chairman Wright Patman of the House Banking and Currency
Committee, a framer of the Defense Production Act, disagreed
with the liberal interpretation of the act by the Department of
Justice. By no stretch of the language, he contended, was Penn
Central eligible for Victory Loans; "the Act was never intended,"
he maintained, "to prevent the insolvency of a large corporation
only tangentially involved in defense contracts, but rather was
intended as a way for small and medium-size contractors to expand their productive capacities so as to be able to meet critical
defense production needs."[18]

The railroad managers then flew in their company airplane
from Philadelphia to Washington (their regular means of con-
veyance for such hundred-mile journeys) to answer questions by
Mr. Patman. The session revealed that the $225 million Victory
Loan would tide the company over only for four months – i.e.,
until October, when more multimillion-dollar loans became due.
If the government did not guarantee loans of $500 million more
at that time, the first $225 million guaranteed by the taxpayers
would be lost and paid by them. Mr. Patman thereupon pledged
his opposition to the scheme.

For a while the administration continued to proceed with the
plan. But on Friday, June 19, 1970, in the face of mounting congressional opposition, the rescue attempt was abandoned. The

company was without means to pay its creditors, who would demand liquidation. To keep the railroad intact, the only recourse for the managers was to petition for bankruptcy. At 5:30 Sunday afternoon, hours before unpayable loans became due, Federal Judge William Kraft in Philadelphia signed the order for bankruptcy and rendered official the greatest corporate failure of all time.

As did the sinking of the *Titanic,* the collapse of Penn Central destroyed confidence in the judgment of experts. Safeguards thought to be infallible and the best that the mind of modern man could devise proved to be peculiarly ineffective.

The railroad industry is among those with the longest history of governmental regulation. It also appears to be among the most stringently regulated. With the exception of the gas and electric utilities, no industry reports as much data to regulatory authorities. On examination of the vast array of statutes setting forth the duties of the Interstate Commerce Commission and the Securities and Exchange Commission, the average purchaser of Penn Central stock would have thought his investment was protected against brazen corporate mismanagement. He would believe that before mismanagement could destroy his investment in the railroad and other properties represented by his Penn Central stock, the clearest legislative instruction would compel one of those agencies to expose and thwart improper deeds.

The Penn Central managers, however, were free to dissipate railroad resources on whimsical acquisition schemes, and to conceal from investors the calamitous state of the railroad's finances and performance because the Interstate Commerce Commission chooses not to act in two broad areas of responsibility which Congress entrusts to it.

First, the commission promulgates no regulations under its clear authority to require railroads and railroad conglomerates to disclose their financial condition upon sale of stock, bonds, and other securities to the public. Also, by indiscriminately classifying conglomerate holding companies as "carriers" it severs shareholders' rights to protection against financial manipulation.

Second, the Interstate Commerce Commission neglects to use

its authority to restrain railroads from the very type of conglomerate acquisition course which Penn Central pursued. Congress granted the ICC that power in 1920, after the commission
itself had explicitly requested the power in 1913.

The Penn Central managers also enjoyed circumvention of
Securities and Exchange Commission supervision. The ICC's
assertion of unexercised authority over the Penn Central's
nonrailroad (as well as railroad) properties nullified the Securities and Exchange Commission's power to disclose operating
conditions and uses made of Penn Central assets. Had either of
the two agencies publicly disclosed, as Congress intended, the
deterioration of Penn Central properties and operations, the
managers could not have continued their disastrous course to
the very end. Because the public did not know the facts, the
highest Penn Central officials were not deposed until bankruptcy was inevitable.

On September 24, 1970, the House Committee on Interstate
and Foreign Commerce convened to investigate the ICC's
failure to assert its authority in those two areas:

> Congressman MACDONALD (presiding). . . . Despite the Con
> gressional mandate 83 years ago that the [Interstate Commerce]
> Commission embark on a program that would establish an efficient
> and economically viable rail system in this country, the rail sys
> tem in this Nation is neither efficient nor economically viable.
> Therefore, we must question whether the Commission has
> lost touch with the economic realities of railroading today, and
> whether the tools which the Congress provided are being used
> . . . there is strong evidence of . . . misrepresentations to the
> public through incompete information prospectuses filed with
> the ICC.[19]

At issue was the commission's duty to require railroads to disclose their true financial and operating condition so that the
public will not be misled when investing in railroad securities.

ICC representatives at the hearing first insisted that the commission requires railroads to specify in any printed offer (or
prospectus) of public sale of securities the very same information which the Securities Act of 1933 (48 Stat. 881) requires of
other corporations. Schedule A of that act sets forth 32 funda-

mental information requirements—including a certified balance sheet, disclosure of management compensation, and management's interest in the transaction advertised—which are necessary for making an informed investment decision. Congress considered those 32 requisites to be so minimal that, upon enactment of the legislation in 1933, it stated that the channels of interstate commerce must be closed to any security issuer who does not supply investors with the specified information. At that time Congress elaborated:

> The items required to be disclosed, set forth in detailed form, are items indispensable to any accurate judgment upon the value of the security. . . . The type of information required to be disclosed is of a character comparable to that demanded by competent bankers from their borrowers.[20]

The Securities Act of 1933 does not apply to railroads. The ICC already had the authority to require carriers to disclose the information which the act specifies. There was no need to give the ICC that power a second time. Congress assumed that once it set forth the minimum disclosure standards, the ICC would extend those standards to issuers of railroad securities. But during the four decades since the passage of the act, the ICC has not promulgated a single regulation requiring railroads to divulge any item enumerated in the Securities Act.

The ICC explained to the committee that it nevertheless enforces the disclosure standard demanded by the Securities Act even though the commissioners have not set forth that standard in regulations. In a letter dated October 15, 1970, ICC Chairman George M. Stafford stated unequivocally that his commission secures from railroads the very same data for public investors' protection which the Securities Act requires from other corporations.[21] Also, ICC Supervising Attorney John M. Mattras asserted at the hearing:

> We require prospectuses [describing securities which railroads offer for public sale] to furnish substantially the same information as that required by the Securities & Exchange Commission [pursuant to the Securities Act of 1933 which that agency administers].[22]

The investigating committee hastened to test that assertion by asking for and securing eight railroad prospectuses approved by the ICC. Examination of those documents freely selected by the commission revealed that none of them satisfied the disclosure standard required by the Securities Act. The ICC's assertion that it enforces compliance with the act was thus disproven. The standard of disclosure enforced by the ICC (as shown by the examination of the eight prospectuses) is so uncertain, according to the Investigation Report, that:

> The decision whether to follow generally accepted accounting principles or to utilize ICC financial reporting rules apparently is a matter solely within the discretion of the issuer and its underwriter. . . . Of even greater significance to investors than the irregular financial reporting standards was the general reluctance of ICC-regulated carriers to disclose any information about management compensation, stock options or material interests in certain transactions involving management and the issuer.[23]

But even if information necessary for the public to make an informed investment decision is omitted from literature in which Penn Central or any other railroad advertises and describes the sale of securities, "it most certainly is included in the annual report form filed by the Pennsylvania Company with the Interstate Commerce Commission, at least in part,"[24] stated ICC General Counsel Fritz R. Kahn. With that remark the following colloquy ensued:

> Mr. LISHMAN [Investigating Subcommittee Counsel]. Is that annual report supplied to investors?
> Mr. KAHN. That annual report is available to investors; yes, sir.
> Congressman DINGELL. That was not the question that was asked; is it supplied to investors?
> Mr. KAHN. Upon request and payment of appropriate reproduction charges it will be supplied investors.
> Congressman DINGELL. So, the answer is very different. In effect, it is not supplied. If you have a most diligent and adroit investor who is willing to spend money and who is knowledgeable in ICC procedures he might be able to procure it. Perhaps you might indicate to the committee what number of requests have been made for this document by investors in Penn Central or any of its holding companies, affiliates, or subsidiaries.

Mr. KAHN. I have no idea, Mr. Dingell.

Congressman DINGELL. It would be fair to say probably none; would that be a fair answer?

Mr. KAHN. I do not say that would be; no, sir.

Congressman DINGELL. But a very small number.

Mr. KAHN. That is relative, yes, sir. . . .

Congressman MACDONALD. If I can interject, the answer is no, it is not supplied, it is made available.

Mr. KAHN. Yes, sir.

Mr. LISHMAN. Made available when?

Mr. KAHN. Upon request. . . .

Mr. LISHMAN. But there is no legal requirement that it had to be furnished to the prospective investor.

Thus, information essential to the public's appraisal of an investment and required by law to be supplied by corporations of other industries, was not and is not required by the ICC to be supplied investors in Penn Central and other conglomerate railroad corporations.

The Investigation Report evaluated the procedure described by General Counsel Kahn:

> The suggestion that investors desirous of discovering the information required by the Securities Act may purchase a copy of a carrier's annual report from the ICC is the grossest form of chimera. Based on ICC charges for reproduction, an investor interested in obtaining the reports of Penn Central and its subsidiary, the Pennsylvania Company, would be required to pay nearly $60, assuming, of course, his willingness to suffer the necessary time lag before receiving such reproduced data. It is a simple fact that the entombment of the missing data within the reports of a rail or motor carrier as filed with the ICC is a meaningless protection for investors. The prospectus, which by definition is a document designed to sell securities, forms the basis for analysis by professional investment advisers and the further dissemination of such information to the public. That document also frequently forms the basis for an investor's decision to buy a security in the aftermarket or, having bought, to retain his position.
>
> Because of the loophole available to rail and motor carriers, certain management personnel of Penn Central were able to avoid timely public disclosure of their self-dealing and outright fraud at the expense of the corporation.[25]

A natural consequence of the ICC's refusal to implement its authority to secure adequate divulgence of investment information by promulgation of regulations (under provisions of the Interstate Commerce Act which are commensurate with the Securities Act) is that the commission can require of the different carriers differing standards of disclosure. Its standards from one carrier to the next need not be uniform. It may decide not to demand of one company what it asks of others. A carrier's representative to the commission, therefore, has the occasion to plead for special leniency which may not be afforded other companies. Certainly, the representative would never receive the reply from the ICC that his request for special treatment (for circumvention of laws for the public's protection) is proscribed by uniform standards which restrict ICC officials from granting such treatment. Indeed, as already seen, the ICC approves prospectuses which vary in the extent of disclosure each affords the public. ICC Supervising Attorney John Mattras under questioning elaborated upon the lack of uniform standards:

Congressman ROGERS. Do I understand you do not have a set form [for disclosure prescribed by regulations] that you require of everyone?

Mr. MATTRAS. No, sir.

Congressman ROGERS. You kind of do it on an ad hoc basis? . . . But you never published it [regulations] to make this a set requirement?

Mr. MATTRAS. As I understand, sir, that is correct.

Congressman ROGERS. So, they [the security issuers] might have to furnish it [investment information] or they might not, depending on the attorney they deal with in the ICC.

Mr. MATTRAS. Well, they are required to furnish this prospectus and we, of course, look at the prospectus.

Congressman ROGERS. . . . but all of the material in the prospectus does not have to be the same for everybody; is that correct?

Mr. MATTRAS. It may vary with different people because of different carriers having different problems. Some may have to give more and others not as much, depending on what we see. But the basic information should be the same as with the Securities & Exchange Commission.

Congressman ROGERS. Hopefully so.

Mr. MATTRAS. Well, we look at them, sir.

Congressman ROGERS. But no set regulations are set forth.

Mr. MATTRAS. I believe that is correct.

Congressman ROGERS. It is amazing.[26]

The Securities Act of 1933 is only the earliest part of a broad series of statutes which, if applied to railroads, would have alerted the public to the danger of investing in Penn Central securities, provided protection to those who did, and most important, informed shareholders (and the rest of the public) of the damage to the railroad resulting from the diversification-acquisition program while there was still time to change the management and save the company. Those statutes are: The Securities Exchange Act of 1934 (48 Stat. 881), the Trust Indenture Act of 1939 (53 Stat. 1149), and the Investment Company Act of 1940 (54 Stat. 789).

As with enactment of the Securities Act of 1933, Congress largely excluded railroads from the protection that later legislation affords because the ICC already had power to apply to interstate carriers the safeguards which the statutes provide investors in securities of other industries. Also, as with enactment of the Securities Act, Congress assumed that once it established the minimum standards for investors' protection generally (by the passage of those acts) the ICC pursuant to its existing grant of congressional authority would extend the same standards to railroad investments. As seen, that assumption was mistaken.

The Securities Exchange Act requires industrial corporations to disclose extensive information indicating whether a management's interests or actions may conflict with or be inimical to the shareholders' interests in the corporation. Enforcement of the act to railroads, however, is left to the ICC. The Penn Central reports filed pursuant to the act contained no certified financial statements or sufficient data to reveal the railroad's accelerating deterioration.[27] ICC Acting Chairman Dale W. Hardin himself stated at congressional hearings that he was taken by surprise at the Penn Central bankruptcy.[28] His duty was to examine the railroad financial and performance data collected by his commission. If that data provided him with no indication of Penn Central's impending bankruptcy, at a time when rumors of imminent collapse were rampant, there is little reason to think that the commission's collection of the information could have forewarned and protected the average investor either. Doubt as to the utility of the information the ICC collects is shared by the staff of the House Banking and Currency Committee:

> On December 20, 1971, 18 months after the failure of the railroad, the ICC issued its "definitive study" of the Penn Central collapse. On the basis of this 1,760 pages of rehash, one would think that the ICC was a branch of the National Archives rather than a regulatory agency charged with the responsibility for seeing that the railroad industry is operated in the public interest. While the ICC's study might serve a useful purpose to historians, it is of little significance to the thousands of investors who lost their holdings because the ICC failed to perform its primary function of regulating the railroad industry.
>
> The ICC study consists of 1,760 pages of statements and exhibits, the vast number of which have very little meaning to the public. In addition, most of these documents had been in the ICC files for many months, and sometimes years, prior to the railroad's collapse. Why did it take the ICC so long to analyze these documents? Had the ICC performed its regulatory function and reviewed these documents at the time they were received, the railroad might not be in reorganization today.[29]

The Trust Indenture Act of 1939 protects small investors who make loans to corporations. The loans are often too small to warrant the individual creditor's (or debenture holder's) expense of suing the corporation if it does not repay the loan. Thus, the practice developed for many small creditors who aggregately have loaned a large sum to a corporation (by purchasing its debentures) to select a trustee, such as a bank, which would bring one suit against the borrower on behalf of them all.

The trustees, however, were not always vigorous in asserting the creditors' rights. Usually the creditors were dispersed over the country and had no effective way to oversee the trustee's performance of obligation to them, or—especially—to know when their trustee's interests were in conflict with their own. Indenture trustees at times even connived with defaulting corporations to defraud the creditors whom they were duty-bound to protect.

For the safeguard of such small creditors, Congress in 1939 enacted the Trust Indenture Act, but unfortunately it once again excluded the railroad industry from application because the ICC already had the authority to extend protection in that area. The act renders illegal those relationships between indenture trustees and corporate borrowers which might place the trustee's interests in conflict with the interests of the creditor-debenture holder.

But Penn Central, on the point of collapse, sought ICC sanction of just such a relationship. In April 1970 it submitted for approval a trust indenture for borrowing $100 million from the public through its investment company subsidiary, the Pennsylvania Company. The trustee was to be Manufacturers Hanover Trust Company, which itself was a creditor of Penn Central and its subsidiaries in the amount of $33.2 million. Section 310(b) of the Trust Indenture Act proscribes exactly that relationship, for the trustee and the debenture holder (whom the trustee owes the duty to protect) would, in the event of the borrower's bankruptcy, contend against each other for possession of the same assets. Manufacturers Hanover Trust did appropriate for itself the bank accounts of the Penn Central subsidiary — assets which the debenture holders also would have sought to appropriate.

The conflict never arose because, fortunately, the public rejected the subsidiary's $100 million debt offering. Nevertheless, the proposed indenture illustrates the jeopardy to investors which the Pennsylvania Company expected the ICC to approve. There is no indication that the ICC would not have approved the borrowing had it had the opportunity.

Impairment of the congressional design for the security of the investing public has resulted only, to this point in the chapter, from the ICC's fault of nonfeasance. The passage of the Investment Company Act of 1940, however, brings on a new dimension of administrative disregard. For since then the ICC has taken affirmative measures to short-circuit the lines of protection specifically designed for the public investor — protection he would have received but for the existence of the ICC.

The Investment Company Act provides protection for investors who purchase the securities of companies which, in turn, invest in securities of other corporations. Congress passed the act in 1940 after taking notice that manipulation of the public's

$7 billion investment in investment company securities during
the previous decade had been rampant and largely responsible
for the loss of over half that amount.[30]

A prominent provision of the legislation is that transactions
between the investment company and the corporation in which
it invests — particularly transfers of assets, loans, and loan
guarantees — are to be reported to the Securities and Exchange
Commission, which enforces the act. Also, the act seeks to prevent any investment company from acquiring excessive debt,
resorting to unsound accounting practices, or allowing more
than half its board to consist of bank officials.

Those safeguards are set forth as eight purposes (sec. 1(b)) of
the Investment Company Act. The railroad's subsidiary investment company, the Pennsylvania Company, violated all eight.

The $100 million attempted debt offering illustrates the liberal
attitude of the Pennsylvania Company (operated by the Penn
Central managers) toward transfer of its stockholders' assets. The
investment company was to shift $84.1 million of the proceeds
from the offering over to Penn Central in exchange for nonrailroad properties in which Penn Central had invested no more
than $29.3 million. On the basis of their 1969 earnings, it would
have taken those properties 150 years to have fully paid for
themselves by earning for the Pennsylvania Company their $84.1
million purchase cost.[31] Thus, any assertion that the transfer was
in the interest of the investment company subsidiary — shares of
which were traded to the public on the New York Stock Exchange — is difficult to comprehend.

The Investment Company Act, then, is another part of the congressional plan to provide investors with protection which
would have revealed the railroad conglomerate's mismanagement when the disaster course was still reversible.

A few days after the filing of the bankruptcy petition, and after
150,000 public stockholders had lost 95% of their Penn Central
investment, Harley O. Staggers, chairman of the House Committee on Interstate and Foreign Commerce, inquired of the
Securities and Exchange Commission why it had not required
the Penn Central subsidiary investment company, the Pennsylvania Company, to adhere to any of the eight general purposes of
the Investment Company Act.

The chairman of the Securities and Exchange Commission, Hamer H. Budge, replied two weeks later that the question was an interesting one but that he could not answer right away.[32]

On September 16, 1970, six weeks after the House Commerce Committee had raised the question, it received the response that the Investment Company Act "appears" to be inapplicable to the subsidiary investment company. The ICC had ordered that the Pennsylvania Company be classified as a "carrier," the Securities and Exchange Commission explained, because the company controlled a railroad (the Wabash), even though more than half of the investment company's assets were invested in noncarriers.[33] That order, the ICC declared, rendered the company subject to ICC regulation. Because the Investment Company Act excludes from its provisions any company subject to the ICC, the Securities and Exchange Commission could not apply the act's protection to the Pennsylvania Company.

Hence, the management of any investment company, mutual fund, or other enterprise which holds securities for the purpose of investment can deprive its stockholders of protection which Congress thirty years ago declared to be essential and absolutely minimal if the company or fund purchases 51% of the stock (controlling interest) of a railroad, regardless of that stock's proportion to the total amount of securities held.

When writing the Investment Company Act exclusions, Congress never supposed that shareholders would thereby receive less protection. It excluded ICC-regulated companies from securities legislation because it assumed that the ICC with its existing power would impose equivalent regulation. The ICC contends, however, that it has no such power, and that its affirmative orders can only take away and not replace provisions which guard the public from financial manipulation. That reasoning, disproven by the fact that the commission is empowered to authorize securities issuances (54 Stat. 907, Sec. 20(a)), defeats one purpose of the commission's existence.

Other conglomerate holding companies also have freed themselves of the act's minimal management standards by mere purchase of a carrier. International Utilities Corp., for instance, acquired Ryder Truck Lines in 1965. The Securities and Exchange Commission thereupon promptly declared that the entire corporation (represented on the Penn Central Board of Directors) was exempt from the Investment Company Act's restraints against financial manipulation.[34]

The ICC allows investment companies to sever shareholders' rights under the act by purchasing a carrier even though that purchase violates the agency's enabling statute, the Interstate Commerce Act. By virtue of such an illegal purchase, the Alleghany Corporation, acquirer of the nation's largest mutual fund, Investors Diversified Services (with assets of $6 billion), has removed itself from Securities and Exchange Commission supervision. In 1968, Alleghany purchased Jones Motor Co. The ICC itself determined that the purchase violated Sec. 5(4) of the Interstate Commerce Act. The commission nevertheless rewarded Alleghany with the prize it sought—the order for Alleghany's relief from adherence to the Investment Company Act. Jones Motor Co. constituted no more than 12.5% of the total assets of publicly held Alleghany.[35]

The greater the transaction the greater chance the conglomerate builder has for winning the ICC's acceptance of violation of public safeguards. After having approved Alleghany's purchase of Jones Motor Co., the ICC permitted Greyhound Lines' diversification transactions although the commission found them to be "not consistent with the public interest":

> Greyhound Lines . . . finds itself in a situation where its working capital is depleted by advances to affiliates, and its bus equipment encumbered essentially for the purpose of permitting applicant to expand at a greater rate into non-carrier investments. We find this situation not to be in the interest of Greyhound Lines, since it could in a financial squeeze seriously impair the carrier's ability to perform its service, and for other reasons as well, including good financial practice, is not consistent with the public interest.[36]

The transactions which caused the capital depletion and jeopardy to Greyhound's ability to perform its public service violated ICC regulations. The ICC, however, consented to the violations because Greyhound claimed that to undo the transactions would be costly. As the House Commerce Committee staff report warns, by such leniency an "agency's enforcement effectiveness and credibility will be severely limited."[37]

Worse, the regulated company has reason to understand that the possibility of obtaining the agency's permission to exceed regulatory standards is directly proportionate to the size of the proscribed transactions and, hence, to the extent of the company's infringement of the public's rights and protection.

The Investment Company Act's restriction of banker-directors to a certain percentage of the board indicates that bankers' prominent role in investment and holding companies is no new phenomenon. Even in 1913, decades before passage of the act, Louis Brandeis urged the same precaution while describing the danger to a corporation, and to the bank as well, from excessive interlocking between boards of the two entities:

> conflicting interests [of banker-directors] necessarily prevent single-minded devotion to the corporation. When a banker-director of a railroad decides as railroad man that it shall issue securities, and then sells them to himself as banker, fixing the price at which they are to be taken, there is necessarily grave danger that the interests of the railroad may suffer — suffer both through issuing of securities which ought not to be issued, and from selling them at a price less favorable to the company than should have been obtained. For it is ordinarily impossible for a banker-director to judge impartially between the corporation and himself. Even if he succeeded in being impartial, the relation would not conduce to the best interests of the company. The best bargains are made when buyer and seller are represented by different persons.

Besides dividing loyalty, Brandeis continued, the interlocking affects judgment:

> A complete detachment of the banker from the corporation is necessary in order to secure for the railroad the benefit of the clearest financial judgment; for the banker's judgment will be necessarily clouded by participation in the management or by ultimate responsibility for the policy actually pursued. It is *outside* financial advice which the railroad needs.
>
> . . . The proper function of the banker is to give to or to withhold credit from other concerns; to purchase or to refuse to purchase securities from other concerns; and to sell securities to other customers. The proper exercise of this function demands that the banker should be wholly detached from the concern whose credit or securities are under consideration. . . .

Is it conceivable that the great house of Morgan would have
aided in providing the New Haven with the hundreds of millions
so unwisely expended if its judgment had not been clouded by
participation in the New Haven management?[38]

Brandeis and the framers of the Investment Company Act
would not have been surprised, therefore, that the Interstate
Commerce Commission's own study of the Penn Central bankruptcy attributes largely to banker-directors the devastating policy that dividends be paid while the conglomerate incurred over-
all operating losses.[39] The banks represented on the board,
according to the study, held great quantities of Penn Central
stock in their departments and therefore voted for payments of
dividends. Also, as seen, banks represented by the conglomerate's directors, eager for the business from acquisition loans,
laxly extended credit for financing the completely unprofitable
Penn Central acquisition program. The Penn Central debt held
by banks which interlocked with the conglomerate's board far
exceeded the direct cost of the companies acquired.

Public confusion as to which investments the securities statutes protect, and which not, is justifiable. For the Interstate Commerce Commission classifies as carriers corporations which are
not carriers. Yet the Securities and Exchange Commission,
which is responsible for enforcing the Investment Company Act,
does not disclose which investment companies are free to operate outside of its enforcement. Chief Counsel Alan Rosenblat of
the Securities and Exchange Commission's Division of Corporate Regulation replied for Chairman William Casey to a public inquiry:

We do not have a list of publicly traded investment companies
which operate outside the Investment Company Act since there
is no legal requirement that they file anything with us.
    . . . As a matter of law any company designated by the Inter-
state Commerce Committee [sic] to be a carrier is a carrier. . . .[40]

Thus reads the public agency's response to a public request
for elucidation.

Evidence that legislators of the 1930s struck at the true causes
of the economic dislocation of the time is that circumvention
of their safeguards has given rise, in the bankruptcy of the Penn

Central, to the exact corporate failure which they sought to prevent. Rather than trying to prevent bankruptcies in the mid-1970s by the infusion of public credit—a remedy which even the U. S. government cannot long afford—a better solution would be the elimination of that inexplicable circumvention of proven and established safeguards.

The federal securities laws represent only one area of regulatory authority which if applied would have switched Penn Central off its suicidal route. The second area is the Interstate Commerce Commission's authority to estop a railroad from acquiring another corporation whether it be in the transportation field or not. By Section 5 of the Interstate Commerce Act (54 Stat. 907) a railroad may not acquire another carrier without the ICC's approval. Also, by Section 20(a) of that act, a railroad must obtain the approval of the ICC before issuing "any share of capital stock or bond or other evidence of interest in or indebtedness of the carrier." Congress enacted that section in 1920 in specific response to the commission's own request for power to halt conglomerate acquisitions by railroads. To foresee the consequences of its decision not to use that authority to halt the Penn Central conglomeration program, the ICC had only to read its own reports of 1913 explaining the need for that very authority:

> No student of the railroad problem can doubt that a most prolific source of financial disaster and complication to railroads in the past has been the ability of railroad managers to engage in enterprises outside the legitimate operation of their railroads, especially by the acquisition of other railroads and their securities. The evil results, first, to the investing public, and finally, to the general public, cannot be corrected after the transaction has taken place; it can be easily and effectively prohibited. In our opinion the following propositions lie at the foundation of all adequate regulation of interstate railroads:
>
> 1. Every interstate railroad should be prohibited from spending money or incurring liability or acquiring property not in the operation of its railroad or in the legitimate improvement, extension, or development of that railroad.
>
> 2. No interstate railroad should be permitted to lease or purchase any other railroad, nor to acquire the stocks or securities

of any other railroad, nor to guarantee the same, directly or indirectly, without the approval of the federal government.

3. No stocks or bonds should be issued by an interstate railroad except for the purpose sanctioned in the two preceding para-
graphs, and none should be issued without the approval of the
federal government.

It may be unwise to attempt to specify the price at which and
the manner in which railroad stocks and securities shall be disposed of; but it is easy and safe to define the purpose for which
they may be issued and to confine the expenditure of the money
realized to that purpose.[41]

In March of 1969 the commissioners received another warning strikingly similar to that of 1913, from their own staff;

Management [of the acquiring corporation] may very well strip
the carrier of additional assets reducing it to a corporate shell and
then dispose of it.[42]

Such casting off of a railroad nucleus on which a conglomerate
has nourished and grown is the sale in 1972 of the Chicago &
Northwestern Railway. The conglomerate holding company
secured capital for its acquisition program from the railroad.
After the conglomerate had substantially exhausted Chicago &
Northwestern's tax benefits and credits, and paid dividends by
selling the carrier's assets, Northwest Industries promptly began
negotiations to sell the railroad. The conglomerate retains the
name, but no longer the Chicago & Northwestern Railway.

The collapse of Penn Central has not prompted the ICC to
heed the advice of its own study of 1913 now any more than the
commission did before. On August 15, 1972 Commissioner Kenneth T. Tuggle informed the Sections of Public Utility Law and
of Administrative Law of the American Bar Association:

Today's Commission has not determined that diversification by
conglomeration is necessarily bad for transportation companies,
or inconsistent with the public interest. . . . Through the conglomerate structure, those lands and other rail assets can be released from certain government restraints, thereby facilitating
their use in enterprises promising more attractive returns. . . .
the conglomerate, like magic, makes the tax benefits [from railroads' deficits] materialize.[43]

Nor has the collapse called attention to staff reports, primarily of 1969, which warned the commission of that imminent bankruptcy and of specific pitfalls of diversification by merger. A Special Review of Railroad Conglomerates, of March 11, 1969, submitted to the commissioners stated:

> The serious financial manipulations set forth in this memorandum, whereby assets and earnings of railroads are being dissipated to noncarrier companies in the group, are definite indications of what may be expected in the future — all of which are detrimental to the carriers and hence to the national transportation needs of the public and national defense. . . .
>
> Regardless of all the glowing self-serving statements made in current merger proceedings, our belief is that when circumstances warrant, these managements will involve the railroad in similar transactions [to that committed by Bangor Punta in sapping the capital of its subsidiary, the Bangor & Aroostook Railroad]. For certainly, holding company managements, in addition to their own strong self-interests will owe their allegiance to the stockholders of the holding company and not to the railroad or to any individual part of the conglomerate.
>
> . . . we believe the Commission should immediately exercise all of its available power to stop abuses before the carriers' assets are dissipated.[44]

Commissioner Tuggle presented the very opposite conclusion to the utilities and administrative law specialists. Explaining "reasons why regulated carriers become affiliated with conglomerates," he stated:

> I believe it is conceded that diversification offers financial stability, especially to industries sensitive to economic fluctuations. The conglomerate can utilize the tax laws in dimensions not otherwise available; it can achieve economies of scale in management and administration; it can obtain credit on preferential terms and gain favor with investors; it has easier access to cash and capital.
>
> In turn, the conglomerate can provide ready financing at low interest to its affiliates — for equipment, maintenance, capital improvements, and upgrading of service.
>
> This would enable the carrier affiliates to reduce expenses; to

expand, innovate and improve as warranted by the business; to
establish long-range programs, and make their moves at the most
opportune times.[45]

The commissioner's speech did not substantiate those often-
repeated generalizations. His staff's conglomerate merger study
of 1969, however, substantiated direct refutations of them all
(except those concerning tax gimmickry).

On March 26, 1969, in its report "Conglomerate Mergers,"
the ICC Bureau of Economics told the commissioners that the

> conglomerate holding company device ... intensifies the Com-
> mission's regulatory and enforcement problems. The present
> threat to the public interest is ... the dilution of the interest of
> managements of the conglomerates in the provision of efficient
> transportation service and the potential dilution of the capital
> structure of the railroads. More specifically, the conglomerate
> holding company provides a convenient means for the transfer
> to other industries of assets now devoted to transportation. ...
>
> Of more immediate concern to the Commission is the certainty
> that the inclusion of railroads in conglomerate holding companies
> seriously impairs the Commission's ability to obtain information
> or to take timely action required for effective regulation of rail-
> road rates and services.[46]

Commissioner Tuggle listed eight "conglomerate affiliate"
railroads as examples of the good effects of conglomeration because those companies were not "in bankruptcy." Half of them,
however, the commission's Merger Studies described as exem-
plary of the "serious financial manipulations" committed by the
conglomerates which hold them.

"With Southern Pacific, Illinois Central and others, the story
is the same," the commissioner said. "As a parent railroad, they
enjoyed profits; but as subsidiaries in conglomerates, their profits increased."[47] But of the Illinois Central and its parent holding company, Illinois Central Industries, the ICC staff Studies
said:

> A variation of this inequity was demonstrated by *Illinois Central
> Industries* in its dealings with Illinois Central Railroad. The hold-
> ing company charges the carrier in excess of the consolidated
> Federal income tax liability. Illinois Central Industries thereby

took into income from 1963 through September 30, 1968, about $1.4 million more than its actual consolidated tax requirements.[48]

Another practice of the holding company, the Studies stated, is to lend Illinois Central Railroad cash for payments of dividends back to the holding company. "The practice of advancing funds with which to pay dividends," the staff explained, "is reminiscent of the abuses uncovered by the Federal Trade Commission in its investigation of the public utility holding companies during the 1930's. . . ."[49]

Mr. Tuggle had praise for diversification transactions which his commission found to be "not consistent with the public interest":

> Greyhound presents a unique chapter. Until 1963 it was content to be a bus line, and in many respects it was No. 1. But then it formed a holding company and began to diversify. In 1969, it took over a giant conglomerate already in being. That was Armour-Dial. With annual sales of $2 billion, it was the second meat packer in the country. . . .
>
> Today it holds investments with a net worth listed at three quarters of a billion dollars, of which the bus lines make up less than one-third.[50]

But the commission had specifically found (see p.212) that the Greyhound diversification-acquisition program so diminished the carrier's working capital that it jeopardized the carrier's ability to perform public service.

"Recognizing that the larger carriers are turning the conglomerate road," Commissioner Tuggle continued, "the ICC has proposed legislation to maintain the integrity of transportation regulation"—i.e., to protect railroads from their conglomerate acquirers. By so proposing, the ICC may add credibility to its disclaimer of authority already possessed.

It disclaims most authority outside the narrow confines of rate-making. According to *Forbes* of November 15, 1972 (p.29):

> The 11-member Commission says that transportation reform is not its business. "Our authority," says ICC Chairman George M. Stafford [former attorney for the American Trucking Association], "is basically economic regulation." In other words, to regulate rates and conditions of shipping.

The authors of the ignored staff warnings against railroad diversification and concentration do not agree:

> The ICC staff, many of them long-time professionals, hardly bother to hide their scorn for the commissioners.
>   . . . Said another staff member: "The commissioners are plain wrong in saying that we have only rate-making powers. We have the power to require the railroads to do anything — make improvements, change routes, the whole thing."
>   . . . The Commission itself is considered to be a kind of retirement home for old politicians. A commissioner is appointed for seven years, and gets $38,000 a year. . . . The job is not demanding. The temptation to use it to reward old allies is too much for most Presidents.[51]

The most recent appointee, Rodolfo Montejano, states that he does not know why he was appointed:

> I really don't know what all this is about. I was called by my friend Maramuto from the White House, who asked if I was interested. My background? The law firm I used to work for was the referral firm for the California Trucking Association. That's about all.[52]

American railroads derive wealth from land granted them from the public domain. The grants were an inducement for the original railway construction and its maintenance. Continuing his presentation to the assembled lawyers, Commissioner Tuggle — a former lieutenant governor of Kentucky and a member of the commission for over twenty years — explained that today that "vast acreage produces income from minerals, lumber, agriculture and other non-rail activities."[53]

According to the ICC Bureau of Economics, investment of that wealth in railroad facilities, as originally intended, "yields a substantially high rate of return."[54] Nevertheless, Commissioner Tuggle expressed his commission's position that such wealth best not remain devoted to the purpose of public transportation, for which it was granted.

A better use, according to that position, is the financing of conglomerate industrial concentration. The acquiring headquarters will decide how much of the railroad's wealth the railroad needs and keep the rest for itself.

Thus, "The important question . . . ," the commissioner summarized, "is not how much a conglomerate takes out of a carrier, but how much is left in."[55]

That property which is "left in" is scarcely adequate to pay its own taxation. The Association of American Railroads, in recommendations for "a more balanced transportation system," advised the public that "Railroads must be relieved of the burden of local property taxation":

> *The Federal government should exempt rail transportation from state and local property taxation and reimburse the states for the revenue loss.*
>
> *Permissible types of state taxes should not, as a matter of Federal law, discriminate against railroads* [original italics].
>
> The railroads' financial weakness demonstrates the burden on interstate commerce which local property taxation of some $300,-000,000 a year thrusts on the nation's rail arteries."[56]

The association also indicated that not enough revenue is "left in" to pay for total maintenance of rights-of-way originally granted. Its recommendations continued: "The Congress should require that the states devote 10 percent of Federal highway trust funds to grade crossing projects."

Retention by railroads of wealth granted from the public domain would enhance, as intended, their ability to shoulder their fair share of state and local obligations. The holding companies, however, adhere to their Association of American Railroad's advocacy of continued transference to them of wealth from those public grants. After the conglomerates have acquired the railroad assets, according to that plan, the government might just as well make subsequent bestowals of public wealth to accomplish the purpose of the original grants.

Holding companies are attracted to railroads, Mr. Tuggle indicated, not by an affinity for their operations, but by the chance to control their assets derived largely from railroad land grants. The conglomerate, therefore, is inherently motivated (as the commission staff Studies documented) to decide the question of how much it "takes out" in favor of the nonrail operations, to the detriment of the railroad and the public purpose for which the public wealth was granted.

According to available data (see p.112), performance of con-

glomerate subsidiaries deteriorates more often than not even under an acquiring management which seeks to strengthen the subsidiaries' operations rather than transfer and deplete their assets.
A subsidiary's future is bleak indeed, then, under such former
managers as Heineman of Northwest Industries, Salgo of Bangor-
Punta, and Saunders and Bevan of Penn Central, who held their
railroad subsidiaries' assets in higher esteem than the railroad
operations. For efforts to impress conglomerate shareholders
with earnings, or obscure declining earnings, induce transference, as the commissioner prescribes, of railroad assets to
nonrailroad subsidiaries.

Rather than fully recognizing such conflict of interest, Commissioner Tuggle cited unsubstantiated generalizations which
his audience could read in almost any conglomerate annual report. His and his colleagues' failure sufficiently to admit that
conflict — even after its clear demonstration by the Penn Central
suicide and by their own staff reports — does not augur well for
the industry and public interest which their commission exists
to protect.

CHAPTER 11

The Securities and Exchange Commission

Many corporations have caused a rise in the stock of another company merely by appearing to acquire control (see p.53). The method for creating the appearance and the method for profiting from it are one and the same. The supposed acquirer's purchases of large blocks of the supposed target company's voting shares creates a semblance of an attempt to gain control. The price of the purchased stock then rises, especially upon the purchaser's press announcement of its intent to acquire. The purchaser profits from the sale of those blocks of stock, which it includes in its report of regular earnings. The report of increased earnings creates the false impression that the purchaser's operations are correspondingly more profitable. That impression causes a rise in the value of the purchaser's own stock. The increased paper wealth in turn, gives the purchaser greater resources to acquire other companies.

Gulf & Western Industries reported operating earnings of $72 million for fiscal year 1969. In fact, $32 million of that amount came not from operations but from sale of fortunate stock market investments — investments in enterprises which, reportedly before sale, Gulf & Western was about to acquire.

On the morning of May 14, 1970, Securities and Exchange Commission Chairman Hamer Budge, General Counsel Phillip Loomis, and Chief Accountant Andrew Barr appeared in the House Judiciary Committee hearing room to explain why the commission allowed the practice, exemplified by Gulf & Western, of inflation of operating earnings reports by inclusion of stock market gains. The investing public had been led to believe, with the SEC's sanction, that the entire $72 million were earnings from regular and continuous operations. At the time of the earnings report the public had bid Gulf & Western common stock up to $53 per share. By the time of the hearings, when the public was becoming aware that the entire $72 million earnings of 1969 were not regular and recurring after all (1970 earnings declined to $44.7 million), Gulf & Western stock had fallen to $15.

To require adequate disclosure of corporate conditions and operations for the protection of the investing public is the reason for the existence of the Securities and Exchange Commission. The question of the lawfulness of Gulf & Western's addition of nonoperating earnings to operating earnings was directed to SEC Chairman Budge.

"I don't have a copy of your letter with me. . . ," he replied, explaining to the Judiciary Committee his inability to respond.[1]

"We just looked into it a little," stated SEC Chief Counsel Loomis. As to the propriety of a noninvestment company's reporting stock market gains as regular profit, he said, "There was no formal examination to determine whether there was a violation of law. . . . This was not pressed."[2]

SEC Chief Accountant Andrew Barr, however, met the issue head on. Gulf & Western's $32 million gain from the sale of securities was properly treated as regular, not extraordinary, income because, "I think you will find that that stock market gain has gone on for some time." The chief accountant was mistaken. During the previous fiscal year, 1968, Gulf & Western's gain from market investments was $4 million instead of $32 million. And before that, none at all.[3]

The questioning turned to Ling-Temco-Vought's reporting practices. Chief Accountant Barr was asked how LTV could report that all companies under its control produced an aggregate profit of $2.3 million in 1969 when that very profit computation included tax benefits from an overall loss for that same year. Included were $21 million refundable in federal taxes after a "carryback" of 1969 losses to previous years, and $19 million from predicted future tax savings, again from overall losses of the very same year for which the profit was claimed.[4]

How, through such reporting, could public investors know

that LTV subsidiary companies incurred a loss of $80 million instead of the $2.3 million profit that LTV claimed? How could the public know the extent of the loss?

"I will see what I can do," the chief accountant replied. "I can't analyze it from here."[5]

Nor could Mr. Barr analyze it back at his office with all information the files of the Securities and Exchange Commission might offer.

The inside cover of the SEC handbook admonishes:

WARNING TO INVESTORS!
INVESTIGATE BEFORE YOU INVEST

Avoid unnecessary losses in the purchase of securities by following this ten point guide to safer investments: Before buying—Think!

. . .

If you don't understand all the written information—*Consult a person who does.*[6]

If the friend the investor consulted in trying to comprehend the LTV income statement had been the SEC itself he would have been wasting his time. Two weeks after the hearing Mr. Barr succinctly replied by letter that a corporation's reporting of a $2.3 million profit in place of an $80 million loss is beyond the realm of the commission: "Our files do not have sufficient information to answer this question."[7] What information the SEC files do contain, he did not specify.

The commission did have available, however, a letter from LTV showing that the company had sought and obtained SEC approval for reporting the $19 million of its 1969 loss as profit for that same year (in claiming future tax benefits from that loss).[8] The letter, a plea for the commission's leniency in the performance of its public trust, exemplifies the efficacy of the procedure of unrefuted argumentation behind closed government office doors.

The letter and meaning of the law in question could not have been clearer. So clear that Mr. Barr himself said, "It is a factual matter." Bulletin 11, paragraph 45 of the Accounting Principles Board, agreed upon by all parties as the governing regulation, provides: "tax benefits of loss carry-forwards should not be rec-

ognized until they are actually realized, except in unusual circumstances when realization is assured beyond any reasonable
doubt at the time the loss carry-forwards arise."[9] Thus, it is per-
missible to reduce annual loss in the same year it is incurred by
the amount of the future tax benefit from the loss only if income
of future years to which the tax benefit can be applied is "assured beyond any reasonable doubt." A company's expectation
of profit from ordinary operations, according to established, unquestioned, absolutely unequivocal precedent, does not meet
that test. Nevertheless, the SEC allowed LTV to "carry the loss
forward" and in so doing ignored the accounting principle.

The commission could hardly have chosen worse circumstances for flouting the regulation, for LTV proves the principle's purpose. The conglomerate lost money on consolidated
operations in 1970 and 1971 also. No profit existed to which the
tax benefit could be applied. Since the tax benefit expires after
five years, LTV had, then, only 1972, 1973, and 1974 to produce
income which might authenticate the $19 million benefit al-
ready reported as profit.

Random examination by the House Judiciary Committee indicated that the SEC had permitted other companies besides LTV
to use the loss carry-forward. How often had the commission,
which according to its own literature had been created "to provide disclosure of important facts so investors may make realistic
appraisal of the merits of the securities and then exercise an
informed judgment in determining whether to purchase them,"
permitted the use of a device by which a multimillion-dollar
loss could be reported to the public as a two-million-dollar
profit?

This question drew no prompt reply. The agency assigned to
enforce rules of disclosure does not apply them to itself.

First Mr. Barr replied orally to the Judiciary Committee, "This
is an area in which we are often consulting, that is right. . . . I
would like to try [to inform you of the number of times the SEC
has allowed inclusion of future tax benefits in earnings reports
for the year in which the loss occurs]."

But two weeks later the written response was that the number
was anybody's guess, that such information just is not in the
SEC "index": "a search of the indexed cards can tax accounting

questions and recollections of the staff disclosed few instances of this question being raised. [But] The index would not necessarily include every case or telephone call where this question was raised."[10]

The SEC acquiesces to corporate accounting gimmickry even more than do the corporations' hired accountants. The auditing firm retained by LTV, Ernst & Ernst, refused to countenance the breach of the tax benefit principle.[11]

But the accounting profession, as well as the SEC, has permitted acquisitors ample "imaginative accounting" techniques. The bookkeeping of International Telephone & Telegraph exemplifies that liberality:

1. Merely by changing Continental Baking Co.'s depreciation accounting (from accelerated to straight line) upon acquisition, ITT reported for the subsidiary an additional $1.4 million of 1968 earnings.[12]

2. Solely by the same type of accounting change, ITT reported for the acquired Sheraton Hotel Corp. (and hence for itself) an additional $3.5 million of 1968 earnings.[13]

3. By reclassifying certain of Rayonier Corp.'s forestry expenditures as capital investment rather than as expenses (which diminish reported income), ITT reported additional 1968 Rayonier earnings of $1.1 million. "[I]nstructions from ITT World Headquarters Comptroller's Office" required the reclassification even though it "has a substantial adverse effect on our cash generation," wrote Rayonier's management in October 1968. "[T]he loss of cash generation from the accounting change," the memorandum concluded, "will make it increasingly impossible to generate funds internally to meet our [Rayonier's] needs."[14]

To Rayonier's profit for the year of acquisition total accounting changes added $2.27 million—over one third of the subsidiary's profit increase.[15]

4. ITT's income for 1968, the year in which it acquired the three companies, increased artificially, then, not only from the addition of their ordinary earnings to the conglomerate's earnings. It increased also in the amount of $7.2 million resulting merely from bookkeeping changes—changes which at least one acquired company resisted.[16]

5. ITT World Headquarters transferred Avis Rent a Car's $5.5 million bank debt to ITT Credit Corp.—a subsidiary *not* included in the conglomerate's balance sheet. Avis managers wrote President Geneen in February 1966: "ITT Credit Corp. now appears to be the vehicle to absorb this shift of obligations. . . ."[17] In August they elaborated: "This does nothing for Avis, but hopefully, is helpful to our parent company."[18] Thus, the debt disappeared from the public ITT balance sheet not because it was paid but because it was shifted to a different set of books.

The House Judiciary Committee staff reported: "None of these accounting changes [resulting in reported profit, and hence market value, increases] were disclosed in the notes to ITT's financial statements. . . ."[19] Neither the SEC nor the accounting profession required that the investing public know that bookkeeping ledgerdemain, rather than proclaimed management ability, produced the nonrecurring profit increases.

Perhaps the SEC officials themselves are not responsible for the standard of performance they described to the House Judiciary Committee. That the commission is understaffed is clear. In 1970 Chairman Budge told the House Appropriations Committee:

> It was not long ago that public investor complaints sent to the Commission could be numbered in the hundreds.
>   . . . An alarming 12,500 complaints were received for fiscal year 1969, and again the principal complaint was with the back office operations. . . . The public customer also expresses frustration that he is unable to get a simple response of acknowledgement to his inquiry [to the SEC]. . . . additional complaint processors are urgently needed to place complaint processing on a more current basis.[20]

Mr. Budge described the commission's inability to conduct even routine investigations of institutional investors:

> As I see it, we face two real administrative problems in the investment company area. The first is the failure of the Commission to be able to conduct the inspections of the investment companies,

primarily the mutual funds . . . and, second, the ability to process the filings for registration which are made with us.

The number of filings has increased dramatically just in the last 2 years particularly, and we simply have not had enough people in the division to process the filings for registration. . . .[21]

A committee member responded:

Mr. Chairman, there appears to be an alarming statement [in the testimony] under "Inspections and Investigations," in which you state in your budget estimate that, in fiscal year 1969, 72 inspections were conducted, as compared with 156 inspections in 1967. Now this . . . to the committee is a cause for concern.[22]

Mr. Budge answered that the commission had "nowhere near enough" investigators for adequate inspection of the institutions, although, "There is over $70 billion of the savings of American investors primarily invested in these investment companies."

Two years later, on February 23, 1972, Mr. Budge's successor, Chairman William J. Casey, presented similar testimony to the House Appropriations Committee. At first he had requested funds for 370 new staff positions, but then reduced the request to 94 positions. The reduction would result in curtailment of the agency's performance, the chairman explained. A member was curious as to why the request was reduced:

Mr. GIAIMO. The reason I am raising this point is this: There are many of us in Congress who are terribly concerned that the regulatory agencies are not keeping pace with the industries they are supposed to be regulating. I think this is clearly true in the case of the FCC and ICC. I am not so sure it is true in the case of SEC.

Mr. CASEY. It has been true, certainly.

Mr. GIAIMO. I suspect it has been true. There is no question that the markets are mushrooming in volume, particularly the New York market.

You recognized this problem when you originally asked for the . . . approximately 370 additional positions.

Now your request has fallen back to . . . 94 positions.

. . . What did you contemplate doing when you submitted your original request . . . that is not going to be done within the confines of the present budget? What is going to have to be deferred?

Mr. CASEY. Well, we will probably continue to examine the quarterly filings made by 10,000 corporations with respect to their financial operations on a spot basis rather than on a more intensive basis.

I think this could have serious consequences for the information to people in the trading market. We will have to defer inspection of investment advisors. Instead of inspecting investment companies every 3 years, we will probably inspect them on a 7-year cycle and it will be that kind of thing primarily that will account for the difference. . . .

Mr. GIAIMO. Are you, to a great extent, still depending on self-regulation?

Mr. CASEY. Primarily, but it is perfectly clear that the over-sight regulation has to be intensified and we give that a rather high priority.[23]

Chairmen Budge and Casey did not speak, however, as typically beleaguered administrators short on funds. The SEC traditionally and uniquely earns a large part of its appropriation itself. In 1968 it collected $14.6 million in registration fees—82% of its appropriations. In 1969 it collected in fees 118% of its appropriation, and was thus more than self-supporting, *giving* more to the U. S. Treasury than it received. Cost of operations, therefore, should not necessitate curtailment of performance of responsibilities.

A letter of July 14, 1972[24] from Chairman Casey, in reply to a question posed by the Joint Economic Committee, indicated, however, as did the testimony to the House Judiciary Committee, that the commission did not have the staff to determine whether its own rules were being violated. The Joint Committee had asked the commission on June 19 whether Litton Industries had included any part of its 15-volume claims "summation" in its earnings statement.

The question is even more fundamental than the issue of inclusion of stock market gains in earnings reports. If a corporation can add the amount of any unadjudicated claim, however questionable, to its income report, that report can indeed be unlimited. Elucidation of the commission's standards for reporting claims as income was also requested by the Joint Economic Committee.

The inquiry was especially pertinent, for on June 23, 1972 Acting Commander R. C. Gooding, Naval Ships Command, informed Litton that its claims summation concerning the cancellation of the four assault ship orders "is completely unsupported and is hereby rejected." Litton's "LHA Program Reproposal," which included the claims, the commander said, "is almost completely unresponsive to the [contract] obligations."[25]

But the Joint Economic Committee's attempt to determine whether Litton's earnings statement did include any of its navy claims was of no avail. The SEC could not definitely determine that matter.

The chairman's letter leaves no doubt, however, that Litton would have great freedom to inflate its income statement. The matter is for the company to decide, Chairman Casey explained:

> As to whether the inclusion of anticipated claim settlements as accounts receivable from the Government would violate any SEC rules, this would depend on numerous factors, the principal ones being the validity of the claim, the amount involved and the extent to which the company has a reasonable basis for believing it will be settled in a manner favorable to it. As you can recognize, this is basically an area involving the judgment of the company's management and its independent auditors.[26]

The chairman assured, however, that any assault ship claims figure in Litton's reported earnings was inconsequential. Confidently he said the claims were "only a relatively small amount (when compared to total current assets)." The basis of his comparison is not valid. A claim would have to be large indeed to be comparable to Litton's $1.976 billion of assets! Litton's entire earnings of 1971 amounted to less than 3% of that amount.

The indirection of the SEC chairman's response to the precise questions of the letter leaves little doubt that a corporate acquirer may indeed augment its public earnings report by imaginative or arbitrary claims figures. Those figures create the false impression of enhanced profitability, inflate the acquirer's market value, and thus add to its resources for acquiring more corporations.

The imaginative quality of Litton's claims figures began to come to light in December 1972:

Of a claim against the navy for $73.8 million, Litton reported $22.8 million as a "current asset." In fact, the navy agreed to pay no more than $7 million of the $73.8 million claim.

Of a claim for $94.4 million, Litton reported $10 million as "accounts receivable." The navy had agreed to pay not one cent of the claim.[27]

In 1971 the SEC staff had specifically designed rules to protect the public from such inaccurate reporting. Those guidelines would have warned investors of the exact defense production failures which gave rise to the imaginative claims. The following rules applicable to defense contractors were proposed:

> At any time a material cost overrun has been incurred, the aggregate gross amount of such overrun should be disclosed.
> [A government contractor] must inform its stockholders of known problems in meeting specifications or delivery schedules which could result in additional expense to the company.[28]

After a series of secret hearings on the proposed rules the commissioners rejected them. The Pentagon along with its contractors objected to the proposals for public enlightenment; not surprisingly, their objections, like the hearings, remain secret. Rather than requiring adequate disclosure, the commissioners thought it best to "appeal to defense contractors to make 'prompt and accurate disclosure.' "[29]

The commissioners actually professed to believe that their plaintive appeal would sway defense contractors. The General Accounting Office does not agree. It warns (Report B-163058 of July 26, 1973): "Litton is not likely to disclose [destroyer cost overruns and delays] until some time in the future when the full program seems committed" by Congress.

On December 20, 1972 the Joint Economic Committee of Congress inquired of SEC Commissioner Phillip A. Loomis and SEC Chief Accountant John C. Burton (who succeeded Andrew Barr a few months earlier) of the commission's reason for the rejection of the disclosure rules. Commissioner Loomis, general counsel at the time of the rejection, first denied and then admitted that he had been involved in the decision. He also acknowledged that the SEC "should do much more" to protect the public from the claims of defense contractors. The reasons for the rejection of the disclosure rules, however, he did not state. Chief Accountant Burton did say that a defense contractor might be injured by "too much disclosure."[30] He did not explain.

Less taciturn at the Joint Economic Committee hearings was the navy's civilian director of procurement, Gordon W. Rule. The appointment of Litton's former president, Roy Ash, as head of the United States Office of Management and Budget was, Mr. Rule stated, a "mistake." The procurement director testified that a few months before Mr. Ash's appointment, Mr. Ash had promised to go "on to the White House" to override the navy's reluctance to honor Litton's half-billion-dollar shipbuilding claims.[31] The promise carried increasing weight, for on December 14, 1972, Mr. Ash averred that he did not intend to disassociate himself from the Office of Management and Budget's decisions affecting the navy (see p.175).[32]

Mr. Rule referred to minutes of a meeting of June 6, 1972, recorded by navy officials, which state:

> Mr. Ashe [*sic*] indicated that it appears that some in the Navy have a built-in sense of selfrighteousness concerning Litton's performance and that the Navy would have to relax this view if Litton is expected to proceed with the contract. Mr. Ashe indicated that he intended to meet with Secretaries Sanders [Undersecretary] and Warner and then on to the White House to explain the problem.[33]

Along with that warning Mr. Ash urged, according to the same minutes, that the navy allocate one or two billion dollars "to help out the nation's shipyards."[34]

Procurement Director Rule continued that he "did not like to see the Navy pushed around" and that if Litton could not deliver the ships as scheduled, the contract "ought to be terminated for default." In reference to President Eisenhower's warning against the power of a "military-industrial complex," Mr. Rule stated that the appointment of Mr. Ash to head the federal budget office was cause for the former president to be "twitching in his grave."[35]

Within forty-eight hours after Mr. Rule concluded that testimony, the chief of Naval Materiel, Admiral Isaac C. Kidd, who had defended the selection of Litton for the ill-fated shipbuilding program before the House Armed Services Committee (see p.171), arrived at Rule's home with a form for him to sign terminating his navy employment and some letterhead stationery on which to write his letter of resignation.[36] It was less than two years since Mr. Rule had received the navy's highest honorary award for civilian service.

Admiral Kidd "had lost considerable confidence in the judgment of Mr. Rule" and requested his resignation because, asserted Jerry W. Friedman, deputy assistant secretary for Department of Defense public affairs, his remarks concerning President Eisenhower were disrespectful. Those remarks before the Joint Economic Committee, Mr. Friedman said, were "very nearly the ultimate in poor taste and bad judgment."[37]

The SEC's leniency extends not only to acquisitors who report as income their questionable claims against the government but also to those who consent to SEC suits for regulatory violations. On Friday, June 16, 1972, the Securities and Exchange Commission filed suit against International Telephone & Telegraph Corp., ITT Senior Vice President-Counsel Howard J. Aibel, ITT Secretary-Counsel John J. Navin, and ITT's servicing banking firms — Lazard Frères & Co. and Mediobanca di Credito Finanziario of Italy. On the following Tuesday the commission disposed of the litigation by accepting the defendants' consent to permanent injunctions which only forbid their further violations of securities laws. The injunctions thus require of the defendants nothing more than the law already requires of all persons.

The SEC alleged that ITT and its two officers had dealt illegally with ITT stock. ITT violated Sections 5(b) and 17(c) of the Securities Act of 1933, the complaint charged, by not disclosing in the registration of company stock its settlement with the Justice Department of the Hartford Fire Insurance Co. merger case (see chapter 13). That settlement entailed ITT's divestiture of major acquired subsidiaries on which the conglomerate relied for a substantial portion of its earnings.

Aibel and Navin violated Section 10(b) of the act, according to the charge, by the fraud of selling ITT stock while knowing as "insiders" of the undisclosed Hartford settlement. "Insiders" could accurately anticipate (as the suit for injunction claimed) that the requirement for divestiture, once known, would cause a sharp decline in the market price of ITT stock.

On June 17, 1971, the day after the settlement but before the public knew of it, Aibel sold his 2,664 ITT shares for $164,000. Navin sold 1,500 shares for approximately $100,000 on July 16.[38] On July 31, ITT publicly announced the settlement and the required divestiture of the profitable subsidiaries. On the first trading day thereafter, ITT stock fell by $7 per share.

ITT, Lazard Frères, and Mediobanca were further charged with violations of Section 5(a) and (c) of the act for unregistered transference of Hartford stock. The transaction accomplished the defendants' purpose of creating the semblance of a sale, which was sufficient reason for the Internal Revenue Service to free from taxation the conglomerate's acquisition of Hartford stock (see chapter 12).

The SEC did not inform the Internal Revenue Service of the violations against which it secured the injunctions because, the commission explained, "it was not the SEC's responsibility to call to the attention of another Government agency an action that might or might not be a violation of laws enforced by the other agency."[39] For that novel doctrine commission officials understandably cited no precedent.

The judgment to enjoin the defendants against further violations—to which they consented in a matter of hours—contained the incongruous provision that they did not admit those violations. That a person can agree to be enjoined against violations and not admit them is a legal fiction. The fiction served to allow the defendant ITT officials to retain the profits (approximately $7 per share sold) secured from the defrauded stock purchasers who bought before the announcement on July 31, 1971 of the required divestiture. Hence, the judgment entailed no penalty.

Conversely, previous SEC suits against "inside" dealing have required the restoration of profits (to stock purchasers who incurred losses because they did not have the confidential information known by the parties with whom they traded). The SEC's declared policy had been to require restoration. The commission gave no explanation for abandoning that policy.[40]

Section 15(b)(5)(c) of the Securities Exchange Act and Section

9(a)(2) of the Investment Company Act forbid enjoined parties from engaging as broker-dealers of securities. Granting further leniency, the SEC declined to enforce those provisions against ITT (owner of ITT Hamilton Management Corp., a manager of mutual funds, and of ITT Variable Annuity Insurance Co.) and Lazard Frères. The provisions constitute an automatic prohibition. In contravention of them, however, the SEC permitted the enjoined firms to continue to engage in the trading of securities.[41]

In reaction to that frustration of the law's intent, on September 21, 1972 the chairman of the House Committee on Interstate and Foreign Commerce, Congressman Harley O. Staggers, and the chairman of the Finance Subcommittee, Congressman John E. Moss, sought to examine the ITT documents on which the commission had based its suit for injunction. Congress created the SEC by delegating to it congressional power; therefore the commission is an agency of Congress. By requesting the documents the House Commerce Committee exercised its responsibility to oversee the SEC's performance of Congress' mandate.

SEC Chairman William J. Casey acknowledged Congress' right to the documents. Nevertheless, on September 22 he refused the congressional staff access to them. Only the whole commission could grant the permission, Mr. Casey explained. While the House Commerce Committee waited on that formal permission, the SEC without notice transferred the ITT documents to the Justice Department—an executive agency beyond the reach of Congress.[42]

Mr. Casey, informing the House Commerce Committee on October 6, 1972 of the transfer, stated that the Justice Department had suddenly requested the documents two days earlier. SEC Deputy Director of Enforcement Stanley Sporkin, however, not only testified to the committee that Justice Department officials never asked for the documents prior to the congressional request for them, but he also stated that on September 21, the day of the committee's original request, those officials had affirmatively informed the SEC that the Justice Department did not want the documents and had no use for them.[43]

"The Securities & Exchange Commission, in clear disregard of its duty to cooperate with the House Commerce Committee, has undertaken a most injudicious course of conduct," House

Commerce Committee Chairman Staggers and Finance Subcommittee Chairman Moss responded. They asserted:

> The Committee and its Subcommittees are required, by law, to
> see that the SEC administers the Federal securities laws the way
> they are written. This legislative oversight responsibility cannot
> be discharged if a regulatory agency can arbitrarily withhold rele-
> vant documents and records from Congressional review.
>
> . . . When the . . . House Commerce Committee sought access
> to those files . . . the Commission stalled and then wilfully ob-
> structed our investigation.

The dispute is not settled, they admonished:

> By hindering the [Committee staff] from gaining access to these
> materials prior to the time when the Members must recess, the
> SEC perhaps expects it has won the day. Let us disabuse it of any
> such expectation. This matter will be vigorously pursued. This
> development raises once again before the Congress an issue
> which has been persistently growing in recent years: Are the so-
> called "independent regulatory agencies" really independent of
> the Executive Branch of Government?[44]

In December of 1972, Mr. Casey announced plans to resign as
SEC chairman to assume international duties as a deputy under-
secretary of the State Department. If the congressional oversight
committee does pursue further its investigation of the application of securities laws to a conglomerate's acquisition process,
it well might then hear that familiar reply (see p.174): The
responsible official "is the . . . man who isn't there; he went
away the day before."

CHAPTER 12

The Internal Revenue Service

Conglomerate corporations commonly acquire companies by offering the owners of other enterprises quick market gains on their investments. Special tax treatment afforded corporate acquirers prevents taxation of that gain and constitutes a government subsidy which is fuel to the already thriving trend of industrial concentration.

A taxpayer who sells his investment in a corporation to reinvest in another must pay tax on any gain from the sale. Naturally, that requirement restrains the taxpayer from changing the form of his investment: since he must pay tax on any gain from the sale, he will not sell in order to purchase shares of another company unless that company offers investment opportunities that outweigh the tax liability. The fact that he sells and purchases not to realize gain but only to place his funds in a more diversified company or one that offers more liquidity (i.e., is more widely traded) makes no difference—he must still pay tax on any gain from the sale.

However, stockholders who transfer their investment to a conglomerate acquirer by an exchange of stock (not by selling and purchasing stock) for those purposes or even for sheer market gain are not required to pay tax on the gain at the time of the exchange. For instance, if shares selling for $10 on the market are exchanged one for one for the acquiring corporation's shares which are selling for $15, the tendering shareholders incur no tax liability from the exchange even though it increases the value of their investment by 50%. Thus, a restraint which applies to other forms of reinvestment does not apply to corporate acquisitions consummated by *exchange* of stock.

Not surprisingly, tax specialists refer to the exemption for such acquisitions, or "reorganizations," as a subsidy for economic concentration. The exemption is also known as a "tax avoidance leak," although the gain from the conversion of acquired-company shares into conglomerate shares is taxable upon sale of the latter. Former Internal Revenue Commissioner Sheldon S. Cohen in the *American Bar Association Journal* of January 1969 (p. 40) quotes an authority, Randolph Paul, who wrote in 1940:

> The exemption of corporate reorganizations has been called a subsidy; the question has been raised whether the net effect of the provisions, particularly as they stand in the statute with all their particularity, is not unfortunate, in that in actual effect they are a serious tax avoidance leak and one of the major and indispensable forces in the thrust toward economic concentration. . . .

The tax exemption for corporate acquisitions evolved after the First World War when Congress, fearful that industrial dislocation would result from conversion to a peacetime economy, actually sought temporarily to encourage mergers which served a business purpose. But once created, the exemption has proven to be durable.

The House Ways and Means Committee recommended elimination of the provision in 1933 after a study of tax avoidances. However, as Mr. Cohen wrote:

> [The Department of the] Treasury came to the rescue, arguing that because of the depression most reorganizations [mergers or acquisitions] were being undertaken to reduce corporate capital structures and the absorption of losses would result in net loss of revenues. In addition, Treasury felt that substantial corporate adjustments would have to be made in recovering from the depression and that imposition of a tax on such "legitimate" reorganizations would be poor economic policy.

The World War I aftermath and the Great Depression have come and gone; yet the exemption remains.

To qualify for the tax advantage, which is set forth in Section 368 of the Internal Revenue Code, the merger must amount to a "reorganization" which serves a "business purpose." Deputy Commissioner of Internal Revenue William H. Smith told the

House Judiciary Committee on May 15, 1970 that shareholders
cannot use the provision as a scheme for tax avoidance:

> As the law on reorganizations took shape, important judicial doc-
> trines and tests were also evolving. These included the "business
> purpose" doctrine. . . .
>
> In order for a reorganization [i.e., merger or acquisition] to
> qualify as tax free, the business purpose doctrine requires a show-
> ing of a bona fide business purpose. This rules out reorganizations
> conceived for the avoidance of Federal income taxes.[1]

Successful requests to the IRS for the exemption frequently
reveal, however, that if the IRS does not grant the exemption,
the parties will abandon the merger plan. Such statements alone
indicate that the proposed merger is "conceived for the avoidance of Federal income taxes" on market gain. That the merger
hinges completely on the granting of the exemption rules out
any other motivation.

Averments to shareholders by which managements win their
approval of merger also reveal the "business purpose" to be the
avoidance of the tax, which the deputy commissioner stated
"rules out" the reorganization exemption. The IRS nevertheless
grants the exemption.

For example, the management of Landis Tool Co. informed its
shareholders by a proxy statement of November 25, 1967, in
which it solicited their approval of a merger with Litton Industries, that the first of two purposes of the "reorganization"
was to double the market value of their investment by securing
Litton stock, which sold for more than "twice the price" of
Landis stock. The second purported purpose was the standard
unsubstantiated extollment of diversification: "Landis production is concentrated in grinding machines . . . Litton manu-
factures hundreds of different products."

In successfully seeking a ruling from the Internal Revenue
Service of nonrecognition of gain under Section 368 by asserting that the merger served a business purpose, the Landis
management made no mention of that prime purpose of market
gain. Nor was it mentioned to the Federal Trade Commission,
which heard from Landis that the reason for the merger was
only for shareholders to acquire an "equity interest in a larger,

more diversified corporation, the shares of which are to be listed on the New York Stock Exchange."[2]

To find a "business purpose" of a merger—and thus accelerate the pace of industrial concentration and create a tax revenue loss estimated by the Federal Trade Commission to exceed a billion dollars annually in 1968 and 1969—the government must, then, close its eyes to the reasons given to the stockholders to induce their approval. Hence, the IRS's nonrecognition of gain similarly entails nonrecognition of the actual reasons for conglomeration which are contrary to the rationale of the Section 368 exemption.

Other transactions of Litton Industries are cases in point. Had the IRS collected taxes on the market gain (to shareholders of acquired companies) from exchanges of stock vital to the conglomerate's growth and essential for the conglomerate's reporting of acquired income as steadily increasing income, Litton probably would not be a conglomerate today.

The assets of Litton Industries rose from $119 million in 1960 to $1.580 billion in 1969.[3] During those ten years Litton purchased more than a hundred corporations. The method of acquisition followed the classic (and by now oft-described) conglomerate cycle. The parent company inflated its earnings reports with the income of the companies purchased with Litton preferred, or preference, shares. Because the conglomerate determined its earnings per share by dividing total earnings only by the number of common (not newly issued preferred) shares, reported earnings steadily rose. Credulous investors thereby believed that Litton income would continue to rise even without mergers. They bid steadily higher for Litton shares, giving the acquirer more paper wealth with which to buy more corporations.

Litton common stock rose from $25\frac{1}{2}$ in the spring of 1964 to 114 in the fall of 1967. Reported income rose from $29.8 million in 1964 to $70 million in 1967.[4] Not disclosed was that the purported rise in earnings came from dumping the profits of the acquired companies onto the pile and not from the subsidiaries' heightened performance after merger.

Displaying that universal conglomerate characteristic, Litton does not release earnings statements of the individual acquired subsidiaries. For that information, showing deterioration of performance after acquisition, would dispel the myth of the parent's management ability, which is essential to acquiring the income of more companies, in turn essential to inflating more earnings reports, in turn essential to driving Litton stock prices still higher.

The excuse for keeping subsidiaries' performance secret is that competitors can use that information in some way. There was no fear of the Securities and Exchange Commission's questioning that excuse and disrupting the cycle. Hamer Budge, chairman of the commission while that cycle functioned most feverishly, believed that to require disclosure that so much as showed investors whether a conglomerate purchases earnings (by acquiring other corporations) or actually profits from operations might be too "complex." He explained to the House Judiciary Committee on May 14, 1970 that investors had

> asked us to go to the point that if you are manufacturing cookies, they would want a breakdown as to the sales and profits on vanilla cookies and on chocolate cookies. Obviously, that is no real importance to the investor in making his determination as to whether or not he wants to buy or sell the stock.[5]

In the eyes of the commission, subsidiary operations as diverse as machine tools, textbooks, myriad electronic equipment, food, submarines, typewriters, and cash registers (only to begin the list of Litton's acquired product lines) were no more worthy of distinction than baking processes for different flavors of pastry.

The committee's investigation disclosed that of the fourteen post-1964 acquisitions which had assets of $10 million or more each, Litton could show only one (Jefferson Electric Co., which operated at a loss before merger) which yielded more earnings from its assets under Litton management than before merger (see p.110).

While that fact was unknown, the myth that Litton management improves the performance of acquired subsidiaries easily persisted. Just as easily, stockholders of target companies agreed to exchange their ownership rights for ever-appreciating Litton shares.

So rapid was the appreciation that the market value of Litton stock received by the shareholders of some acquired companies

(Landis Tool Co., for example) doubled the value of the stock they gave in exchange. In all cases, the gain to the acquired shareholders, the inducement for the trade, was substantial.

The facile generalizations concerning diversification and conglomerate management ability cited to target-company shareholders to induce them to expect that market gain to continue and to agree to merger are essentially the same as those which the acquisitors cite to the IRS to explain "business purpose," and thus obtain a favorable tax ruling. The *Conglomerate Investigation Report* of the staff of the House Judiciary Committee of June 1, 1972 (p. 362) employs the term "overstatement" to describe that technique as applied by Litton:

> Litton's image making has developed flamboyant sham into an art. Overstatement is a way of life. It led Litton in the hearings to assert that even its organization chart was so special that it was imbued with business confidentiality. In the process of developing its image, Litton has utilized all of the sophisticated accounting techniques and statistical gimmicks available. It is adept at concealment, misdirection and incomplete statement.

On September 21, 1964 Litton informed the IRS that its acquisition of Hewitt-Robbins, a materials handler, was for "important business reasons." Hardly more explicitly, the letter continued, upon merger Litton would have greater opportunity to utilize "its electronic know how and equipment."[6] The Hewitt-Robbins stockholders would benefit from being able to "participate in a combined company having a substantially greater amount of assets, capitalization, earnings and sales volume and a greater degree of diversification." The IRS was not told that the Hewitt-Robbins shareholders consented to the merger only after being assured of a gain of 25%—paid in Litton stock—over the pre-merger market price of the target-company stock.

The "business purpose" of the acquisition of Rust Engineering Co., explained to the government in a letter of April 4, 1967, was that "Litton sees the opportunity to provide a real service to the people" by entering the heavy engineering-construction field in the United States and abroad—especially in underdeveloped countries.[7] The combination, it said, would create a

capability for "rebuilding of cities and construction of totally
new cities, combating water and air pollution, harnessing of
atomic energy and utilization of space and undersea explora-
tion." Neither that "opportunity" nor that capability has been
heard of since.

Further examination of explanations of merger (for which the
IRS granted the nonrecognition of gain ruling) from to-be-
acquired managements to their stockholders casts doubt that
the motivating purpose of "reorganization" was any other than
the speculative securing of the more highly valued Litton stock.

For example, the management of New Britain Machine Com-
pany, while urging its shareholders to approve merger with
Litton, made the following assertion in its proxy statement of
November 7, 1968:

1) Litton's stock will pay a higher dividend than the New Britain
   common shares [although the latter securities yielded greater
   earnings than the former];
2) New Britain owners will receive in exchange stock listed on
   the New York Stock Exchange;
3) The transaction will be tax free;
4) Employee benefits will be continued;
5) New Britain, as a subsidiary of Litton, will have substantially
   greater financial and technical resources for product development and other purposes;
6) Greater diversification will result from merger;
7) Value of stock received: $42.50 market value of New Britain
   share for $65.00 market value of Litton share.

Examination of these assertions leaves only one which could
be a motivating factor of merger. The first—that the Litton stock
to be received in exchange by New Britain shareholders paid a
higher dividend than New Britain stock—is self-contradictory
as a reason for merger. New Britain stock yielded higher earnings and thus was capable of providing a higher dividend than
Litton stock. If the New Britain management wanted to give
shareholders a higher dividend, they had only to declare it. Their
shareholders had greater resources for dividends before merger
than after.

The second assertion—that New Britain stock would be converted into securities listed on the New York Stock Exchange—

is only slightly less convincing as an independent reason for corporate "reorganization" than the fourth assertion—that employee benefits would be continued.

The fifth assertion—that New Britain after merger would have greater resources for research and development—is highly suspect as a purpose of merger. Litton has announced no New Britain product innovations since acquisition that were not possible before. Also, Litton management replied orally in answer to congressional inquiries that product development in its machine tool division was carried on not in separate research facilities but rather on the production line.

The sixth explanation—that merger would result in diversification—can be said, as it usually is, of any conglomerate acquisition.

One explanation stands alone as a convincing reason for the shareholders. Overnight, as a result of the merger, the market value of their investment would increase more than 50%—from $42.50 to $65.00 per share. And because the IRS was able to discern a "business purpose," tax on the gain would be avoided.

The opportunity which conglomeration affords for quick market gain renders the "nonrecognition of gain–corporate reorganization" ruling a greater force in the "thrust toward economic concentration" now than in past decades. With that ruling, combining shareholders secure their objective of financial gain and avoidance of tax—an objective for which, the deputy commissioner told the House Judiciary Committee, the IRS does not grant the ruling.

The IRS further contends that it applies the Section 368 "tax free" merger ruling only to legitimate corporate "reorganizations." A "reorganization" merger, according to the IRS's regulations, could result only from the *exchange* of voting stock between the owners of the two combining corporations—not from the acquisitor's *cash purchase* of the target company's stock.[8]

ITT Vice-President Charles T. Ireland thus informed ITT President Harold S. Geneen on January 2, 1969 that International Telephone & Telegraph Corp.'s cash purchase of 8% (1.74 million shares) of Hartford Fire Insurance Co.'s outstanding common stock would jeopardize their chances of securing the

TABLE 26

Acquisitions of Companies with Assets of $250 Million or More,
by Year of Acquisition, 1967 and 1968

Acquiring company	Securities exchanged	Acquired company	Securities exchanged	Acquired assets (in millions)	Tax consequences
		1967			
U. S. Plywood	Common & convertible preferred	Champion Papers	Common	$335.3	n/t
McDonnell	Convertible preferred	Douglas Aircraft	Common	564.7	n/t
Tenneco	Convertible preferred	Kern County Land	Common	253.9	n/t
Signal Oil and Gas	Convertible preferred	Mack Trucks	Common	303.0	n/t
North Amer. Aviation	Common	Rockwell Standard	Common	391.2	n/t
Studebaker	Common & convertible preferred	Worthington	Preferred	296.6	n/t
	Convertible preferred			2,144.7	
		1968			
Montgomery Ward	Convertible preferred	Container Corp. of America	Common	397.4	n/t
Colt Industries	Common & convertible preferred	Crucible Steel	Common	303.9	n/t

Company	Security	Acquired company	Type	Amount	
Singer	Common & convertible preferred	General Precision	Common		
	Common & convertible preferred		Preferred	322.7	n/t
Occidental Petroleum	Convertible preferred	Hooker Chemical	Common	366.5	n/t
Ling–Temco–Vought	Common, warrants & debentures	Jones & Laughlin Steel	Common	1,092.8	t
Loew's Theatres	Debentures & warrants	P. Lorillard	Common	375.3	t
Kennecott Copper	Cash	Peabody Coal	Preferred		
Northwest Industries	Cash		Common	315.6	t
	Convertible preferred	Philadelphia & Reading	Common	318.6	n/t
ITT	Common & convertible preferred	Rayonier	Common	296.3	n/t
Glen Alden	Debentures & cash	Schenley Industries	Common	570.7	t
Sun Oil	Convertible preferred	Sunray DX Oil	Common	749.0	n/t
American Standard	Convertible preferred	Westinghouse Air Brake	Common	302.7	n/t
			Total	5,411.5 7,556.2	

n/t – nontaxable
t – taxable
SOURCE: *Economic Report on Conglomerate Mergers*, p. 144; from *Capital Change Reporter*, Commerce Clearing House.

tax exemption for ITT's acquisition of Hartford.[9] For each of the
remaining outstanding common Hartford shares, valued at
$38.25, ITT would offer one ITT preferred share, valued at
$49.[10] The 28% market gain was the inducement to Hartford
shareholders to accept the trade and consent to acquisition. If
the IRS did not grant the exemption and thus required the tendering Hartford owners to pay tax on that gain in 1969, Vice
President Ireland envisioned that the stockholders would probably not accept the trade. Nevertheless, he recommended to
President Geneen that ITT continue, before the exchange offer, to acquire as much Hartford stock as possible with cash. The
IRS could be dealt with later.

His advice was sound. The gamble succeeded. In spite of
the cash purchase of stock the IRS recognized ITT's Hartford
acquisition as a "reorganization" and granted the Section 368
tax exemption. The granting was lawful and consonant with
regulations because ITT sold its cash-purchased Hartford stock,
the IRS said. The transaction which the IRS identified as a sale
was ITT's temporary transfer of the Hartford stock to an Italian
bank, Mediobanca of Milan. In fact, however, the shares passed
from ITT to Mediobanca—and after the ruling was secured, back
again from Mediobanca to ITT—without even the alleged purchaser's payment of a purchase price.[11]

Other elements of the transfer which indicate that Mediobanca
acted as ITT's agent for the temporary removal of the shares
rather than as purchaser are that:

> ITT paid Mediobanca an agent's fee of $1.3 million for under-
> taking the transfer.
> ITT and not Mediobanca, by their agreement, would incur
> all gain or loss upon any change of value of the Hartford stock
> after its transfer to Mediobanca.[12]

In spite of those elements which are inimical to a sales transaction, the IRS asserted with ITT that the transfer constituted
an "unconditional bona-fide sale to an unrelated third party."[13]

The application of the tax exemption to ITT's acquisition of
Hartford Fire Insurance Co. thus raises the question of when
does the IRS not grant the Section 368 "subsidy" for corporate

TABLE 27

Tax Treatment Accorded 411 Large
Acquisitions* in Mining and Manufacturing, 1963–1968

	Number of tax-free exchanges	Percent
1963	25	71
1964	36	84
1965	37	88
1966	47	96
1967	101	86
1968	104	83
Total	350	85

* "Large" acquisitions are defined as those involving acquired firms with assets of $10 million
or more.
SOURCE: *Economic Report on Conglomerate
Mergers*, p. 145.

concentration. The question is not easily answered, for the IRS
declined to make public the written opinion setting forth its
reasoning for applying the exemption to the Hartford acquisition.
To requests for such explanation the IRS replied only: "We believe that members of the American public justifiably have come
to expect the Service to observe this policy of confidentiality
and that it would be improper for us to deviate from it."[14]

Of 18 acquisitions in 1967 and 1968 of corporations with assets in excess of $250 million, 14 were "nontaxable" (see Table
26). Further, the number of "tax free" rulings increased with the
heightening intensity of the merger movement (see Table 27).

CHAPTER 13

The Department of Justice

The Penn Central managers sought government salvation when their corporate acquisitions led to their company's ruin. They failed and accepted bankruptcy. The managers of International Telephone & Telegraph avowed that their acquisition course was equally as ruinous, sought government rescue, and succeeded. They have since pursued the same course.

The price for the International Telephone & Telegraph rescue was higher than that proposed for Penn Central. The cost was the government's abandonment of its policies for restraint of industrial consolidation. The success of the one group of corporate officials and the failure of the other may well illustrate that selecting the right governmental bargaining technique is more important than the cause itself.

The decision to acquire Hartford Insurance Co. required ITT's confidence in its ability to deal with government officials. Relying on that talent alone, ITT assertedly laid its very existence on the line. Failure to surmount the government's obstacles to the merger, ITT declared after purchase, would have resulted in ruin. Those lethal barriers not only loomed but at times prevailed over the conglomerate. But along the harrowing course ITT never once admitted defeat, even when defeat was officially rendered.

Attorney General John N. Mitchell branded the attempt to acquire the second largest fire insurance company as illegal before ITT even announced the plan. The Justice Department would sue to prevent the merger, he said, between any of the largest corporations and any other occupying a dominant position in its industry. Federal prosecution, the conglomerate lawyers averred, would devastate ITT.

Besides that seemingly certain obstacle was the necessity of winning the consent of the Connecticut Insurance Commission. The commission's disapproval—at one point final and official—would be no less a disaster than the federal prosecution.

No matador ever walked into the ring with such overwhelmingly unfavorable odds as ITT avowedly assumed upon paying a $500 million premium for Hartford shares. Few matadors have risen and won, as did the conglomerate, after an initial failure to fend direct impact of double onslaught.

ITT prevailed where lesser challengers have failed because it convinced the government that the company had reached the ultimate heights of conglomeration. That is the point at which size is so great that any penalty to the corporation is a penalty to the nation. Because of the size and extent of its operations from acquisitions, the Justice Department reasoned, to prosecute ITT for its illegal actions would result in injury to the entire economy. The conglomerate officials successfully argued: better to allow an unlawful violation of public interest and not prosecute, for what harms ITT harms the USA.

In the process, ITT secured special dispensation by arguing, however contradictorily, that a first grant of leniency had paradoxically resulted in harm to the conglomerate. The government was therefore obligated, the conglomerate successfully pleaded, to grant further and greater leniency.

In 1968 ITT acquired at the rate of one corporation every two weeks. In 1969 the pace more than doubled, to an acquisition every six or seven days. Shortly before the start of that year, ITT purchased 6% of the outstanding stock of Hartford Fire Insurance Co. On December 23, 1968 the conglomerate proposed merger—the largest of all time. The Hartford management agreed on April 10, 1969.

The insurer was attractive to ITT in the same way as Great American was to National General and Reliance was to Leasco. Hartford possessed, as the Netter Report disclosed, great capital resources. Its investments in securities of other companies had substantially appreciated over the years. Income from them, paid as dividends and interest, had more than doubled between 1958 and 1968 when ITT began purchasing Hartford stock.

But far more important, the sale of the securities would result in a profit of over $200 million. Accounting rules would allow an acquirer to add any amount of gain from the sale of those securities to the income statement of any year it chose. Thus, ITT would obtain not just capital assets from the merger but nearly a quarter-billion dollars to report as increased profitability.

On August 1, 1969 the U. S. Department of Justice applied for an injunction against the merger, asserting that "it may substantially lessen competition . . . in violation of Section 7 of the Clayton Act." The U. S. District Court for Connecticut denied the preliminary application on October 21. Hartford shareholders voted to approve the merger in June 1970, and gave ITT 99.8% of the insurer's outstanding common stock in exchange for ITT preferred stock. Though ITT then controlled Hartford, the district court ordered the conglomerate to maintain Hartford's business separately from its own while the government's suit was pending. The federal prosecution, however, was only the second obstacle ITT was to confront. First there was the state barrier.

Insurance is Connecticut's basic industry. For its protection, the legislature enacted Public Act 444, which obligates would-be acquirers of insurance companies to disclose extensive information about themselves revealing whether the purchaser's control will be in the company's and the public's interest. The efficiency of the acquiring management is, then, a major issue, and performance data are subject to the required disclosure.

At hearings before Insurance Commissioner William R. Cotter on November 14, 1969, however, ITT gave no information about the revenue and income of its individual acquired subsidiaries which would indicate how well ITT managed them.[1] It did not supply the data, later obtained by the House Judiciary Subcommittee, which compare post-merger profitability and management efficiency of ITT-acquired companies with their pre-merger performance. Those data (see Table 18, p.111) indicate that ITT management does not enhance the operations of the companies it purchases and controls.

Nor did the conglomerate disclose that the preferred shares it proposed to issue in exchange would pay upon conversion (to common shares) smaller dividends than the common shares which the Hartford owners would surrender.[2] Also undisclosed was that once ITT possessed the Hartford shares, it would increase the dividends substantially and pay them to itself.

After public hearings in which all interested parties had the opportunity to argue for or against the merger, the commissioner ruled on December 13, 1969 that the proposed acquisition would be inimical to Hartford's as well as the public's interest. He formally and officially disallowed the merger.

In appreciation, the Hartford City Council passed a resolution in praise and commendation of the decision. The corporate headquarters of Hartford Fire Insurance Co. would not pass, as his ruling then stood, from the city of its origin.

Six months later, on May 23, 1970, Commissioner Cotter changed his mind. During those months ITT officials repeatedly met with him to urge him to reverse the decision. Their presentations to the commissioner in his judicial capacity were private and *ex parte*. Thus, there was no opportunity for representatives of the public to rebut ITT's innumerable arguments for a favorable second decision. The conglomerate, on the other hand, of course had had the opportunity to argue and rebut public representatives' arguments in the public hearings resulting in the first decision.

During the time of ITT's *ex parte* arguments, Commissioner Cotter became a candidate for Congress, and the conglomerate representatives proposed that their previously acquired Sheraton subsidiary build a hotel in the city of Hartford. The hotel would contribute substantially to the local economy, they assured. The ITT spokesmen also proposed that their company help construct the city's new convention center.

One day in May, Commissioner Cotter rode with ITT officials in the company automobile to examine possible sites for the Sheraton hotel.[3] The next day he approved the merger. As seen again, the acquisition process, like a rolling snowball, is not hindered by previous accumulations.

The commissioner based his about-face and consent to the merger on the same evidence on which he had based his refusal. No new evidence or substantial change of acquisition plans predicated his change of mind.

ITT did not rest on the laurels of victory. A professedly more

determined foe had already struck. The U. S. Department of
Justice had lost in the district courts, as expected, its attempts to
prevent ITT's purchase of Grinnell Corp. and Canteen Corp.
Those suits, also alleging violations of Section 7 of the Clayton
Act, were companion litigation to the Hartford suit. Assistant
Attorney General McLaren, apparently not at all surprised by
the lower-court decisions, prepared for an appeal to the Supreme
Court.[4]

Over and over again (see chapter 2), the U. S. Department of
Justice had expressed in unequivocal terms its resolution to
secure judicial interpretation of antitrust legislation which would
restrain the trend of conglomerate concentration. Its confidence
was well founded. Since the enactment of the Celler-Kefauver
Amendment twenty years before, the government had never
lost a merger suit appealed to the Supreme Court after an unfavorable decision in the lower court.

ITT soon admitted its despair of winning the Hartford suit in
the Supreme Court. But as demonstrated, the conglomerate was
not to be dissuaded from its chosen course. Thus there im-
pended, by all appearances, a struggle between implacable wills.

As with the Insurance Commission encounter, however, the
struggle was to occur not in a room of open and public argument,
but behind closed doors of administrative offices. The outcome,
too, was the same. ITT won.

For two years Justice Department spokesmen had been telling
Congress they would secure the ultimate judicial test of whether
the laws Congress had already enacted were sufficient to cope
with the most prolific trend of industrial consolidation. Further,
they expressed confidence that their arguments to the courts
would prove the laws to be adequate. Their words, then, tended
to negate any sense of urgency that Congress enact stronger
antitrust statutes.

Allowance of ITT to retain Hartford, without even having to
reduce conglomerated assets, should hardly convince conglomerate builders that they need fear enforcement of the Clayton
Act and the Celler-Kefauver Amendment. The Justice Department claimed, nevertheless, that the settlement restrained ITT
from further growth by merger. ITT's acquisition rate, true indeed, was down from a corporation a week. During the first nine

months after the Hartford settlement, however, the conglomerate easily acquired sixteen more companies, six of them in the United States. They included a producer of steel tubing, a manufacturer of packaging tools and supplies, a manufacturer of boiler controls, a bakery, a life insurance company, an exporter of hams, a pump production operation, a producer of toiletries and drugs, and a brassware firm.[5] A few days after the announcement of the settlement, *Business Week* of August 7, 1971 (p.84) editorialized:

> The ITT cases were promoted . . . as an attempt to establish a clear judicial definition of the limits on corporate growth in a modern society. By suddenly agreeing to accept the settlement, the government antitrusters have thrown away the chance to do that. . . .
>
> Antitrust chief Richard McLaren himself acknowledges that he missed a shot at a landmark decision because "it is a lawyer's job to get a satisfactory conclusion to a case as rapidly as possible."
>
> This is a perfectly proper attitude for a company lawyer—as ITT's legal team clearly concluded. But it is not right for the chief architect of the government's antitrust policy.
>
> If McLaren and his lawyers feel that the mushroom growth of the conglomerate corporations threatens the U. S. economy and infringes the antitrust laws, then it is their duty to push the point with the courts until the law is established beyond question. It is not fair either to the companies involved or to the public to keep on brandishing the antitrust gun without ever proving that it really is loaded.

Assistant Attorney General McLaren resigned his office in January 1972 and became a U. S. district judge in Chicago soon after. In March, when the Senate Judiciary Committee inquired of the considerations which prompted the ITT-Hartford settlement, Judge McLaren explained that, besides his own "background of 25 years," three factors predicated the decision not to seek divestiture of Hartford.[6]

The first was the opinion of ITT counsel Lawrence Walsh—a former U. S. district court judge and former deputy attorney general. At the time of the settlement negotiations he was chairman of the American Bar Association's Standing Committee on the Federal Judiciary, which passes on qualifications of candidates whom the Justice Department recommends for federal judgeships. The second factor was the opinions of other government agencies, namely, the Departments of Treasury and Commerce, and the President's Council of Economic Advisors. The third was the report of Richard Ramsden, a New York investment advisor.

On April 16, 1971 Lawrence Walsh urged Deputy Attorney General Richard Kleindienst to drop the department's suit, two years in the preparation, for Hartford divestiture. "To us this is not a question of the conduct of litigation in the narrow sense," he stated in a memorandum to Kleindienst.

> Looking back at the results of government antitrust cases in the Supreme Court, one must realize that if the government urges an expanded interpretation of the vague language of the Clayton Act there is a high probability that it will succeed.[7]

The ABA federal judiciary chairman/ITT lawyer argued to the Justice Department that the issue of ITT industrial consolidation was too important to be determined by the laws of the United States. An issue of such "economic consequence" was too far-reaching to be entrusted to the Supreme Court's interpretation of those laws: "the Supreme Court . . . will disregard any economic or other public benefits resulting from the merger," he informed Kleindienst.[8]

Further, the Justice Department learned, "It is our understanding that the Secretary of the Treasury, the Secretary of Commerce, and the Chairman of the President's Council of Economic Advisors all have some views with respect to the question under consideration."[9] Therefore, those gentlemen—to whom ITT representatives had *ex parte* access as they had to Commissioner Cotter and did not have to Supreme Court justices—should decide the question of divestiture, Walsh concluded.

Once again the spectre of the Stigler Report appeared. Two and a half years earlier its authors had recommended to the president "retrenchment" of antitrust enforcement. Quoting from the report, Walsh's memorandum urged that all opposition to conglomerate consolidation cease while the government undertook a "comprehensive"—i.e., protracted—investigation of mergers.[10] Whether the findings of that proposed study would serve any

better purpose than the investigation findings of the Federal
Communications Commission now kept under lock and key or
the investigation findings of the Federal Trade Commission that
were fed into a paper shredder (see p.11) (as were documents
from ITT files explaining negotiations with government leading
to the Hartford settlement[11]) the Walsh memorandum did not
say.

Though the Justice Department had been investigating and
preparing its Hartford case for over two years, Walsh felt no
awe in submitting to it unexplained generalizations which the
department's own evidence, set forth in its Grinnell trial brief,
refuted. With no countervailing evidence his memorandum
asserted:

> A ban on significant mergers and diversification would injure
> vital national interests.
>
> Diversification by merger is the most important guarantee that
> every economic resource of the Nation will in fact be used to the
> best advantage.
>
> Through diversification, scarce management skills, additional
> resources of capital and know-how, and most important, the will
> and ability to plan growth, can be brought to bear in new indus-
> tries.
>
> . . . a Supreme Court decision . . . would have exactly the same
> immediate impact as a statute and would be even more difficult to
> modify as experience showed its unwisdom.[12]

"[T]hus diversification by merger is often the only effective
means of stimulating new competitiveness in established industries . . . ITT is a case in point," Walsh informed the deputy
attorney general. But upon reading his department's trial brief
Kleindienst would see evidence directly to the contrary. It cited
specific examples of ITT's securing of reciprocal sales, which,
far from "stimulating," circumvent competitiveness. The brief
(Civil Action 13319, United States District Court, District of
Connecticut) stated:

> ITT has also engaged or attempted to engage in reciprocal prac-
> tices over the years. Although ITT has issued an "anti-reciprocity
> policy" directive, this directive . . . does not forbid the use of
> reciprocal practices when convenient and useful to ITT. In fact,

Mr. Harold Geneen, supposedly the strongest advocate of ITT's alleged "anti-reciprocity" policy, and Mr. Howard Aibel, ITT's General Counsel . . . have themselves resorted to the use of reciprocity when the opportunity presented itself.

The brief referred to the sale of electronics equipment:

> According to the testimony of Mr. Aibel, ITT had been trying to sell some of its equipment to General Telephone & Electronics Corporation (GT&E) with little success. However, when a GT&E subsidiary inquired about the possibility of selling some of its services to ITT in Puerto Rico, Mr. Aibel and Mr. Geneen seized upon this inquiry as a "golden opportunity" to suggest to GT&E that ITT would consider GT&E's offer and, in return, GT&E should consider ITT's offer to sell equipment to GT&E. GT&E correctly interpreted the offer from Mr. Geneen as an offer to enter into a reciprocal arrangement with ITT. Internal documents from GT&E's files reveal that GT&E considered various reciprocal arrangements with ITT, all of which involved the allocation of GT&E business to various ITT subsidiaries.

Avis Rent a Car, according to the Walsh memorandum, exemplified ITT's competitiveness and management ability. "The improved competitiveness of the companies ITT has acquired is illustrated by the growth and development of subsidiaries like Avis and Sheraton," it explained. "ITT in other words, has been able to apply modern management skills in such a way as to increase very substantially the efficiency and competitiveness of the companies acquired."[13] The memorandum, however, did not draw from the House Antitrust Subcommittee investigation, which disclosed that Avis' performance steadily improved before ITT assumed control and steadily declined after acquisition — in spite of envisioned anticompetitive advantages.

For substantiation of an opposite conclusion regarding Avis' competitiveness, the Justice Department officials again had only to read from their own brief:

> Maximizing of sales through use of ITT's purchasing power and influence was also a consideration in the ITT-Avis merger. . . . Various ITT subsidiaries have engaged in reciprocal practices. However, the only reprimand for such activities by ITT management resulted when the Government's discovery in this lawsuit

uncovered reciprocity within ITT. In fact, Mr. Aibel testified that the only way ITT would ever uncover reciprocity within its confines would occur if the perpetrator of the act brought it to the attention of ITT management.

Abrasive as the Walsh presentation may have been to the staff which prepared that brief, evidently it was not abrasive to Deputy Attorney General Kleindienst. He testified:

Mr. Walsh and I are very close friends and have developed a very close friendship over the three years as a result of our work together in the judicial program [for selection of Federal judges].[14]

In fairness to Judge McLaren, the former Antitrust chief, one must cite his averment to the Senate committee that he found the Walsh presentation — regardless of its effect on other officials — unconvincing:

For example, he [Walsh] said in there, as I recall, that our policy was stopping perfectly normal, legitimate mergers that had nothing to do with effects on competition, and I strenuously argue with that. . . .

I say again, I strongly objected and was not persuaded as to the legal aspects of it [Walsh's argument].[15]

The only factors, then, which could have caused his change of mind (according to the aforementioned testimony) were the opinions of the three government agencies and of the financial analyst Richard Ramsden.

The heads of the three agencies, however, Judge McLaren explained, were in favor of the suit to force ITT to divest Hartford. In contradiction of Walsh's information to the deputy attorney general, Judge McLaren testified:

I thought that Dr. McCracken [Chief of Economic Advisors] . . . was very much in favor of our antitrust policy, and I have never heard . . . that [Commerce] Secretary Stans or the Treasury people were against it, and I subsequently turned out to be right.[16]

The Ramsden Report, then, remains as the predominate, if not sole factor for the decision to allow ITT to keep Hartford. The Justice Department retained Richard Ramsden to evaluate the merits of the Walsh memorandum. Although the department had

its own staff of economic advisors, already well versed on the
subject of ITT finances, the officials thought it best that an "outside" analyst determine the issue.

A prominent conclusion of the Ramsden Report and of the
memorandum which it evaluates was that divestiture of Hartford would hinder ITT's ability to contribute to the U. S. balance of payments. The Walsh memorandum did not attempt to
explain how Hartford's inclusion or exclusion from the ITT
syndicate could affect the amount of dollars returned to the U. S.
from abroad. Ramsden's explanation, however, was that ITT's
obtaining of the Hartford assets would be so beneficial to the
conglomerate that Europeans would buy more of its stock.[17]
By that reasoning, no multinational corporation should be denied
any anticompetitive advantage. President Geneen summarized
the point of view to the Senate Judiciary Committee on March 15,
1972:

> Any company such as ITT which is scheduled during the next
> ten years to bring back something on the order of $5 billion from
> abroad without imports to the credit side of the United States
> balance of payments cannot be said to be working against the na-
> tional interest in these trying times.[18]

Ramsden also observed that "fundamental changes in the insurance industry suggest . . . earnings improvement" because
insurers are assuming less risk. The reduction he described of
insurers' capability to perform their public service results pre-
cisely from the phenomenon of which he wrote—acquisitors'
take-over of insurance company assets. He explained:

> The amount of insurance capacity in certain markets has been
> reduced. One estimate is that $1.5 billion of capital has been taken
> out of fire and casualty companies (mostly in the form of dividends
> paid to holding companies). Such capital would support net writ-
> ten premiums of $4.5 billion as compared with the industry's
> current level of premiums written of $2.9 billion.[19]

Consequently, insurance companies have "radically reduce[d]
their exposure to unprofitable markets such as high risk urban
areas." In the industry, Ramsden told the Justice Department,
"excessive competition has been reduced."

The predominate consideration, however, was not the effect of acquisition on Hartford's operations, but rather on ITT's balance sheet:

> The effect of the acquisition of Hartford on ITT's balance sheet was an increase in the asset and stockholder equity accounts for both the parent company and ITT consolidated of approximately $500 million. Prior to the pooling, at Dec. 31, 1969, ITT's consolidated balance sheet showed $1.1 billion of long-term debt and $2.1 billion of equity; after the pooling long-term debt was $1.1 billion and equity was $2.6 billion. Thus, ITT consolidated was able to improve its capitalization with long-term debt decreasing from 34% to 30% of the total.
>
> For the parent company balance sheet the effect was even more dramatic. . . .
>
> Most likely it [divestiture] would result in further concern as to ITT's ability to manage consistent earnings increases and such concern would probably be reflected in a diminished multiple on the common stock.[20]

That concern, Ramsden wrote on May 17, 1971, would be likely to result in a decline of ITT's stock value from $64½ to $54, or 16%. The paper loss to the conglomerate investors would be approximately $1.2 billion. His reasoning persuaded the Justice Department to accept the Walsh recommendations. Such a decline resulting from a court-imposed divestiture would be so harmful to the U. S. economy and ITT's investors, the department agreed, that its antitrust policy must be halted and the suit abandoned. In return, ITT consented to acquire no more U. S. corporations with assets exceeding $100 million. Also, the conglomerate agreed to divest itself of four subsidiaries. By selling them, however, ITT will only exchange those assets for other assets, such as cash. Thus, there will be no diminution of ITT's total assets as a result of the divestiture order.

No precedent exists for the government's reversing its course to prevent a 16% fluctuation in a stock's quoted value. And fortunately not, for in April 1972 ITT's market performance proved the futility of the government's compassion. At the very time that the Senate Judiciary Committee hearings were examining the events leading to the abandonment of the suit, the conglomerate's stock fell to the exact forecasted $54 level. The stock thus

incurred the 16% decline in spite of the allowance of the combination which was supposed to prevent it.

Although the decline did not then result in the economic dislocation which the Walsh and Ramsden memorandums had forecast a year earlier, ITT director Felix Rohatyn summarized that
previously envisioned effect to the committee in April 1972:

> It had been our belief that a forced divestiture of Hartford Fire
> could raise fundamental issues of national policy transcending
> both the narrow scope of traditional antitrust philosophy and
> the narrow interest of ITT. Several points were involved, includ-
> ing possible United States balance of payments effects and gov-
> ernment policy toward preserving the underlying strength of
> domestic companies competing overseas. In addition, as chairman
> of the New York Stock Exchange Surveillance Committee during
> that period of financial crisis, I was concerned that so massive a
> divestiture might unsettle our securities markets, and with pos-
> sible impact on some financial organizations.[21]

Accepting that general conclusion (as later expressed), Mr.
McLaren informed Deputy Attorney General Kleindienst on
July 17, 1971:

> We have had a study made by financial experts and they substan-
> tially confirm ITT's claims as to the effects of a divestiture order.
> Such being the case, I gather that we must also anticipate that the
> impact upon ITT would have a ripple effect — in the stock market
> and in the economy.

Thus he concluded reluctantly that the acquisition must be
allowed:

> I say reluctantly because ITT's management consummated the
> Hartford acquisition knowing it violated our antitrust policy;
> knowing we intended to sue; and in effect representing to the
> court that he need not issue a preliminary injunction because ITT
> would hold Hartford separate and thus minimize any divestiture
> problem if violation were found.[22]

ITT, Mr. McLaren explained, had represented to the district
court in late 1969 that it would operate Hartford separately from
other conglomerate activities. Hartford would not, therefore, the
acquirer asserted, incur disruptive ill effects in the event of a

later divestiture order. On the strength of that argument, the court in late 1969 had denied the government's request for an injunction which would have held merger plans in abeyance until final adjudication of the suit.

Having obtained that dispensation which allowed the merger to proceed, however, ITT adopted exactly the opposite argument for opposing divestiture. In mid-1971 the company successfully argued that undoing the combination would result in injury to the conglomerate, to Hartford, and to the nation.

The consented final judgment which permitted ITT to retain Hartford contained only two restrictions: it enjoined ITT for ten years from acquiring more U. S. corporations with assets over $100 million and restrained the conglomerate from forming reciprocal sales agreements with its suppliers. The government thus closed its eyes to the greatest anticompetitive advantage ITT intended to secure for itself and Hartford. That oft-described benefit, carefully explained in other ITT merger documents, is the use of the nation's third largest mass of corporate employees as captive customers of their employer's goods and services.

At the same time that Justice Department officials were reading and acting on Walsh's denials of anticompetitive intent, they had in their possession the ITT merger plan of November 2, 1968, entitled "Tobacco — ITT Joint Opportunities." "Tobacco" was the acquisitor's code name for Hartford Fire Insurance Co. The unpublished document read:

1. MARKETING OPPORTUNITIES WITHIN THE ITT SYSTEM
    1. ITT is a vast consumer of insurance products. Most of our 300,000 [400,000 by 1972] employees in the United States and overseas are covered by various types of group insurance. In addition, the corporation has a substantial volume of property and casualty insurance in the United States and overseas.
    2. ITT has 150,000 employees in the United States with a similar number overseas. This total places ITT about fourth [by 1971, third] in the lists of largest employers. We have developed a combination life insurance/mutual fund program for sale to those ITT employees in the United States through payroll deduction. Virtually all of these people require various forms of casualty insurance which could be readily included in the salary savings program.

Again, the merger plan was to increase the acquired company's profitability not from improved service but from its membership in a syndicate which generated captive clientele—an anticompetitive luxury for which other insurance companies would pay by their loss of customers.

Besides subsidiaries' employees, subsidiaries' customers would tie in as Hartford's "captive audience." The document continued:

> 6. There are several opportunities for the marketing of insurance programs to special ITT interest groups:
>
>   a) Sheraton has 1.2 million credit card holders.
>   b) Avis has 1.5 million credit card holders.
>   c) 100 million APCOA [an ITT subsidiary] parking transactions.
>   d) ITT has over 200,000 shareholders.
>   It is suggested that various types of insurance programs could be offered that may or may not prove advantageous (Avis cars for salesmen, Sheraton hotel arrangements, etc., TDI, travel advertising locations, etc.)
>
> 7. Levitt has sold homes to 80,000 homeowners and building new homes at the rate of 6,500 per year. Within five years this figure will exceed 11,000. These purchasers require homeowners and mortgage insurance which may be offered through special marketing programs.

Also, the document proposed that Hartford receive the business of financing various conglomerate operations.

In essence, it described the formation of a self-contained economic domain, an insulated generator of self-patronage.

At the end of 1971, ITT allayed the Justice Department's fear for the acquisitor's ability to report consistent earnings increases. Its income for 1971 was $44 million more than the 1970 figure. The 12% increase was right within the area of ITT's traditional objective. The department, then, should be all the more satisfied with its allowance of the combination. For $36 million of that $44 million rise is the amount which ITT secured as profit from the sale of Hartford investment securities.[23] Thus, it was the sale of Hartford assets that produced the sizable earnings increase which ITT attributed to management ability. As seen, the Hartford acquisition supplied the acquirer with almost a quarter-billion dollars of asset appreciation that can be used for ready profit in future years.

In reply to the question in 1970 of whether ITT planned to acquire continuously, President Geneen told the House Antitrust Subcommittee:

> No; I think our fundamental objective [has been accomplished]. . . .
>   Chairman CELLER. When do you think the saturation point will be reached?
>   Mr. GENEEN. That is a good question. In my opinion, the saturation point is reached when we feel that we can't manage things properly that we would be acquiring, and I think we are getting to a point — [24]

ITT's reliance on acquired earnings to maintain its history of increasing profits, however, does not add to the credibility of its president's suggestion that the acquisitor might some day reach a "saturation point" of acquisitions. Neither does his advocacy, at the May 10, 1972 ITT shareholders' meeting, of "transformation" of antitrust laws to allow more mergers so as to prevent "weakening of the nation's economic strength." Quoting former Secretary of the Treasury John B. Connally, President Geneen called then for: "Turning antitrust policy inside out, so that in many cases the government would *encourage* mergers instead of *discouraging* them [original italics]." [25]

ITT's power, as Napoleon said of his own (p.1), may well hinge then on the continuation of the expansion which created it. As long as the conglomerate, like the Emperor, can convince the right people that its expansionary course and the nation's destiny are one, the cycle should continue unimpeded.

The forces of concentration surge through the remaining unobstructed channel. Legislation largely disallows mergers of competitors and of customers with their suppliers. Acquisitors thus assert that conglomerate mergers—those between industrially unrelated companies—do not result in monopolization of industries. Nevertheless, Department of Justice officials, while themselves permitting unquestioned violations of the department's merger regulations, warned that conglomeration embodies age-old dangers historically inherent in all merger movements.

The significance of that warning becomes clear as one gains insight into acquisition techniques, the purposes of the acquirers' headquarters, and government agencies' effectiveness in protecting the public (directly and indirectly) against industrial consolidation:

1. The increased size of acquiring corporations resulting from their take-over of other companies' assets is no guarantee of heightened productivity and efficiency. Nor does greater corporate size yield greater resources for product development and research. In 1970, former Antitrust Chief Richard W. McLaren summarized empirical studies:

> The bulk of the available evidence runs counter to the hypothesis that high concentration, huge size, and substantial market power are prerequisites for research and innovation. Indeed, some of the most careful studies find that if anything, market power and the security of bigness, with the concomitant vested interest in the status quo, may have a stultifying effect. And I submit that this should not be surprising.[1]

Acquisitors, nevertheless, expound the theory of "economy of scale." Concentration of industrial control within ever-larger corporate units, they assert, provides capability for more advanced and more economical production. Data of acquired companies' performance after merger, most reluctantly revealed,

266

contradict that claim. The data indicate instead that the proficiency of acquired companies declines more often than not under conglomerate control.

Also, acquisitors most often take control not to provide financial resources to companies they acquire. Conversely to their claim, they acquire them to transfer those companies' financial resources to themselves. Thus, capability for improved performance – such as reduction of cost to consumers – generally diminishes rather than improves upon a company's loss of autonomy to conglomeration.

2. The increased mass of operations and heightened industrial control of acquiring corporations, while not resulting in more efficient production, does provide profitable opportunities for circumventing free-enterprise competition. The securing of anti-competitive advantages is the one contribution which conglomerate managements may bestow on acquired subsidiaries.

From sheer vastness of acquired assets, an acquisitor will arrange to increase the sales of acquired companies by delivering to them a clientele composed of conglomerate subsidiaries, conglomerate employees, companies beholden to the conglomerate for its patronage, and even of those companies' employees. If the acquisitor has acquired to the extent that it is the third largest employer in the nation, the captive clientele may be a greater sales factor than the quality of its products and services.

3. Conglomerate corporations obscure management deficiencies through production for the U. S. government. Defense contracts, easily secured outside the confines of competitive bidding, may be performed at a standard unacceptable for commercial production.

A primary tenet of corporate concentration is that the acquiring headquarters possesses management excellence which it transfers even to acquired companies of industries in which that management is inexperienced. Post-merger performance data of acquired conglomerate subsidiaries disprove that claim, as seen. Because the government is not an exacting customer, however, a corporate acquirer which fails the test of commercial production may yet expect to profit from like production performed for a government agency. The Defense Department, rarely critical of a private contractor's failure to perform as contracted, neglects to enforce required contract provisions which would insure that the public receives what it pays for.

4. The "hidden asset value" which acquisitors discern in target companies most often is an opportunity for reporting increased profits through simple bookkeeping alterations. By merely changing the acquired company's conservative methods of accounting for inventory and depreciation, the acquiring corporation shows overnight multimillion-dollar paper profit increases. Public reporting of these increases, which do not represent actual increases in income, is nevertheless the basis of the acquisitor's widely publicized claims of superior management ability. Those assertions, founded on accounting gimmickry, are the traditional basis for a rise in the public market value of the acquiring corporation. That rise stimulates the acquisition spiral. With the artificially increasing value of its market shares, the acquisitor has greater wealth with which to continue to acquire.

Acquisitors report increased profits and claim management proficiency also by adding earnings of acquired companies to their own earnings figures. By purchasing those companies with preferred stock or debt securities rather than with common stock, acquisitors avoid having to issue new common shares. Thus, acquisitions cannot but increase such acquisitors' reported earnings per share.

After acquisition acquisitors may shift the purchase debts (represented by debt securities) to the acquired companies. Ultimately, only the public consumers pay those debts through the prices they pay for the acquired companies' products.

5. Lending banks and borrowing acquisitors are able to form virtual acquisition trusts through actual or de facto interlocking of officers. Federal statutes prohibit commercial banks from using their depositors' money to gain control of other corporations. In return for the favor of acquisition loans, however, the acquisitor may transfer to the bank the banking business of the corporations it purchases with the bank loans. The concert between the conglomerate corporation and the commercial bank thus results in a breakdown of public protection against corporate concentration.

Also through such circumvention of laws designed to prevent a bank from acquiring industrial control by lending its customers' money, both the bank and the acquisitor secure near-infallible methods for stock market manipulation.

6. Interlocking of officials between acquisitors and traders of securities can also foment conglomeration. By serving on the board of directors of an acquiring company, officers of a broker-age firm persuade the company to acquire a corporation whose stock the brokers already own. When the acquiring company begins to purchase that stock (at a premium above the market price) the brokers have created for themselves the opportunity to sell at an increased price.

The arrangement of corporate consolidations is also profitable to the brokerage firm because it serves as the agent for the trading of securities between the purchasing and purchased companies. It receives commissions for shares both bought (by the acquisitor) and sold (by the former owners) of the target company.

Corporate consolidations are often instigated by the broker's informing failing or debt-saddled corporations of companies which over the years have built up great amounts of cash or easily liquidated reserves. After merger those acquisition targets, having lost their capital resources to acquisitors, are unable to provide their former quality of service to the public.

7. Acquisitors' anticompetitive practices often boomerang. Acquisitors would then shift resulting losses to the taxpayers. Roy Ash, formerly president of Litton and now U. S. budget director, says that the U. S. should undertake a multibillion-dollar program of direct aid to failing shipbuilders; Penn Central won administration support for its plan to transfer acquisition losses to the taxpayers; and LTV-Memcor salvaged itself, after undercutting competitors' bids, by shifting its losses to the Pentagon. The chairman of the board of Gulf & Western, Charles Bluhdorn, is quoted in the company's "Report for Nine Months Ended April 30, 1973" as urging "Legislation giving small investors up to perhaps $5,000 of tax-free earnings from gains in stock market securities, to attract the millions of individual investors back to the nation's capital markets." Acquisitors largely attribute the decline of their stocks to the market exodus of "the millions of individual investors" who lost confidence in the stock market upon its decline beginning in 1969.

Concerts such as the one between Gulf & Western and Chase
Manhattan, which resulted in the predictable and confidential
market fluctuations which they both engineered, may well have
contributed to that decline, loss of public confidence, and
exodus. The recommended billion-dollar plan of tax-free
earnings for small investors would result in increased market
values and greater gains to acquisitors from any future abandoned
take-over bids.

8. The public's right to protection against corporate concentration is thwarted by the regulatory agencies' domination by the
industries they are created to regulate. Assistant Attorney General of the Antitrust Division Thomas E. Kauper explained on
October 27, 1972:

> there have been instances in our history in which the industry
> to be regulated may at first view the regulation as inhibiting, but
> over the years learns to control such regulation to its own pur-
> poses either by reason of its expertise in dealing with the intri-
> cacies of the regulatory scheme or due to the fact that it eventually
> becomes the primary "constituent" of those who regulate.[2]

Merger advocates unabashedly describe to government officials the decline of public service resulting from conglomeration
even while requesting a suspension of antitrust enforcement
which would allow the greatest corporate consolidation of all
time. And the officials grant the request.

Government regulatory agencies permit mergers which their
professional staffs unequivocally advise against. Contrary to the
laws and regulations they exist to enforce, the agencies permit
the acquisitor to report inaccurate and misleading performance
data. The public is denied, then, its right to know the true financial condition of companies in which it invests. Keeping that
knowledge from investors enables a conglomerate corporation
to acquire until it is bankrupt.

By claiming jurisdiction over an industry but failing to assert
it, a regulatory agency negates the authority of other regulatory
agencies over the industry. Investors consequently lose protection which Congress fully assumed it had provided.

Pleas to government agencies to permit corporate concentration—by nonenforcement of antitrust laws and indirectly by non-

enforcement of investor protection statutes — are couched in descriptions of emergencies. Former Secretary of the Treasury John B. Connally warned, for example, that if antitrust enforcement is not curtailed so as to permit more mergers and more anticompetitive practices, the nation may face outright "revolution."[3] Conversely, the opposing principles of free competition cannot be expressed in similar terms of immediacy. The protection of a future competitive market structure requires enforcement even without the commission of anticompetitive practices.

The public's legal safeguards against corporate consolidation are suspended after public officials hear behind closed doors uncontested pleas that enforcement of that protection will cost the conglomerate its $500 million gamble that the protection will not be enforced. Pleas citing the acquisitor's loss of stock premiums paid, the supposed loss of the shareholders' market value, and the supposed contribution to U. S. balance of payments — however spurious — are always clothed in concrete monetary terms. The granting of those urgent pleas is only at the cost of an abstract principle — the ideal of future competitive market structure.

Certain changes of laws and accounting rules are thought to restrain the proliferation of corporate mergers. Widely heralded Public Law 91–172, December 30, 1969, amends the Internal Revenue Code to disallow deduction from taxable income of interest incurred on debt to finance corporate acquisitions. For example, an acquisitor can no longer deduct interest paid on debentures it issues in exchange for a target company's controlling (common) stock. That alteration, however, will not restrain conglomerates which acquire by the issuance of preferred stock. Litton Industries, among the most prolific acquirers of all time, asserted: "Consequently, we are not affected by the provisions of the Tax Reform Act of 1969 which were designed to discourage acquisitions which use debentures or other debt."[4]

Other alterations said to affect the pace of acquisitions are:

Public Law 91–607, December 31, 1970, which restrains commercial banks from acquiring control of corporations through the formation of a holding company;

Securities and Exchange Commission Release of July 14, 1969, 34 Federal Register 12176, which requires that companies with annual revenues of $50 million or more report separately the earnings of each line of production which contributes at least 10% of total revenues;

Opinion 15, May 1969, and Opinion 17, August 1970, of the Accounting Principles Board of the Institute of Certified Public Accountants, which require that computation of per-share earnings account for outstanding convertible preferred shares and that the excess over book value paid for acquired companies be amortized in the computation of reported earnings.

It is doubtful, however, that the changes will affect the rate of consolidation for long. *Dun's Review* of June 1972 (p. 49) reported:

some of the inhibiting forces have become less inhibiting. Washington's opposition to mergers, according to most sources, is less formidable than it once was. And most companies have now become familiar with the new accounting rules, which for a time slowed the pace of acquisitions. Says John Castle, executive vice president of the Wall Street firm of Donaldson, Lufkin & Jenrette: "You can play the game by almost any rules, once you get used to them. It's only when somebody changes them in the middle of the game that things necessarily slow down for a while."

The article quotes further from Castle: "'Just let that Dow [Jones Industrial Average] climb to 1,200, and you'll see the wild times of the 1960's all over again.'" Quoting from an unidentified authority, it concludes: "'Unless you are a particularly inviting target, you can go about your acquisitions business nowadays without much fear from Washington.'"

An accounting authority, Alexander Briloff, asserts:

The public now has a false sense of security that the worst is behind us in terms of accounting mischief. It's like a drug that has cleared the FDA — the public doesn't bother to read the fine print.[5]

One half of all independent manufacturing corporations with assets over $10 million that were in existence during the period

1948 through 1968 are no more.[6] As the number of autonomous industrial units diminishes, so declines the power of the people to regulate their economy naturally by granting or withholding patronage through choosing among market rivals. As the control of industry gravitates into fewer and fewer hands, so increases the opportunity of industrial suzerainties to thwart the workings of an open market by self-engendered and reciprocal patronage and by concerted manipulation. Through heightened concentration, industrial assets are regrouped to the disadvantage of the needs of the public and to the advantage of the financial motives of the concentrators.

Acquisitors profess to altruistic use of their concentrated power as though their benevolent disposition were fair exchange for the public's loss of authority. Their easy conversion of concentrated economic power into political power over agencies of government does not attest to that professed benevolence.

ITT, "Serving People and Nations Everywhere" (according to its advertising motto), asserted to the Senate Foreign Relations Committee on March 22, 1973 that the purpose of a projected $1 million expenditure in Chile in 1970 was for "low cost housing . . . and other ventures" similar to "Marshall Plan aid" "to help the Chilean economy and reaffirm that the company had confidence in Chile."[7] The committee revealed ITT documents of September 1970 which showed the true purpose to be, rather, "to induce [through concert with other international corporate control centers] economic collapse in Chile" in order to prevent the Chilean government from exercising its lawful authority over ITT operations.[8]

The public's decline of control over the economy envelops even the conglomerate managers themselves. In 1969 Litton Industries insisted that the House Judiciary Committee maintain the secrecy of Litton's organization chart. The committee repeatedly inquired why a document of the type often set forth in corporate public reports should be a secret. Finally, on March 4, 1970, the reply came that the purpose of secrecy was to prevent the company's own managers from viewing the chart. The sight of the vastness of the scheme of acquired operations, the executive committee chairman explained, would demoralize Litton executives:

Mr. McDANIEL. [Litton executives] are proud, jealous of their prerogatives. . . . By looking at the box where they go on the organization chart, they become dissatisfied with their status in the organization and it affects their morale. This is the reason we do not like to see the organization chart made public.

. . . There are men who run organizations that are not shown on the chart, who pride themselves on having direct access to Messrs. Thornton and Ash. . . . They look at this chart, and they see two or three layers in between and it affects their morale.[9]

If corporate concentration demoralizes even the conglomerate managers, whom but the acquisitors can it inspire?

The staff report of the House Antitrust Subcommittee's examination of acquisitors' internal documents concluded:

Explosive growth by acquisition by our largest corporations has resulted in changes that confront the public with a situation where the American economy will be dominated by virtually self-contained economic domains. Growth of these vast corporate structures . . . presages imposition of cartel-like structures throughout American business.[10]

Perhaps assurances by Justice Department officials in 1969 and 1970 convinced Congress that existing laws were adequate to cope with that threat. Or perhaps the failure of enforcement of those laws further convinced Congress of the futility of new enactment. In any case, no legislation has resulted from the investigation.

NOTES

Frequently Quoted Sources in Order of Reference

Economic Report on Corporate Mergers, Staff Report to the Federal Trade Commission, 1969.

Economic Concentration, Hearings before the Subcommittee on Antitrust and Monopoly of the Committee on the Judiciary, United States Senate, 91st Cong., 2d sess., 1969 and 1970.

Report of the Attorney General's National Committee to Study the Antitrust Laws, 1955.

Louis D. Brandeis, *Other People's Money and How the Bankers Use It* (New York: Harper and Row, 1967 [1913]).

Investigation of Conglomerate Corporations, Hearings before the Antitrust Subcommittee of the Committee on the Judiciary, House of Representatives, 91st Cong., 2d sess., 1969-70.

Investigation of Conglomerate Corporations, Report by the Staff of the Antitrust Subcommittee of the Committee on the Judiciary, House of Representatives, 92d Cong., 1st sess., June 1, 1971.

Hearings on Military Posture before the Committee on Armed Services, House of Representatives, 92d Cong., 2d sess., Apr. 17, 1972.

Controls over Shipyard Costs and Procurement Practices of Litton Industries, Inc., Pascagoula, Mississippi, Report to the Joint Economic Committee, Congress of the United States, B-133170, Department of the Navy. By the Comptroller General of the United States, Mar. 23, 1972.

The Penn Central Failure and the Role of Financial Institutions, Staff Report of the Committee on Banking and Currency, House of Representatives, 92d Cong., 1st sess., Jan. 3, 1972.

Investigation into the Management of the Business of the Penn Central Transportation Co. and Affiliated Companies, Interstate Commerce Commission, Docket No. 35291, Mar. 8, 1972, p. 112.

Emergency Rail Services Legislation, Hearings before the Committee on Interstate and Foreign Commerce and the Subcommittee on Transportation and Aeronautics, House of Representatives, 91st Cong., 2d sess., June, July, and Dec. 1970.

Penn Central Transportation Company: Adequacy of Investor Protection, Hearing before the Special Subcommittee on Investigations of the Committee on Interstate and Foreign Commerce, House of Representatives, 91st Cong., 2d sess., Sept. 24, 1970.

Inadequacies of Protections for Investors in Penn Central and Other

275

ICC-Regulated Companies, Staff Study for the Special Subcommittee
on Investigations of the Committee on Interstate and Foreign Commerce, House of Representatives, 92d Cong., 1971.
*Hearings before the Committee on the Judiciary on Nomination of
Richard G. Kleindienst to be Attorney General,* United States Senate,
92d Cong., 2d sess., March and April 1972.

Introduction

1. *Economic Report.*

2. For reviews of the merger movements, see Ralph L. Nelson,
Merger Movements in American Industry, 1895–1956 (Princeton:
Princeton University Press, 1959); and Samuel R. Reed, *Merger,
Managers, and the Economy* (New York: McGraw-Hill, 1968).

3. This idea comes through in a number of articles in *Fortune.* See
Editors of Fortune, *The Conglomerate Commotion* (New York: The
Viking Press, 1970).

4. See Oscar Schisgall, *The Magic of Mergers: The Saga of Meshulam
Riklis* (Boston: Little, Brown and Company, 1968).

5. Editors of Fortune.

6. See, for example, J. Harvey and A. Newgarden, *Management
Guides to Mergers and Acquisitions* (New York: John Wiley, 1969).

7. The State of Wisconsin commissioned a study of the effect of
mergers in that state. See Jon C. Udall, "Social and Economic Consequences of the Merger Movement in Wisconsin" (Madison: University of Wisconsin, May 1969), mimeographed.

8. Neil Jacoby, "The Conglomerate Corporation," *Center Magazine,*
July 1969.

9. A. A. Berle, Jr., and G. Means, *The Modern Corporation and Private Property* (New York: Macmillan, 1932).

10. As examples, see Robin Marris, *The Economic Theory of
Managerial Capitalism* (New York: Basic Books, 1964); and Oliver Wil-
liamson, *The Economics of Discretionary Behavior: Managerial Objectives in a Theory of the Firm* (Englewood Cliffs, N. J.: Prentice-
Hall, 1964).

11. John K. Galbraith, *The New Industrial State* (Boston: Houghton
Mifflin, 1967).

12. See Editors of Fortune.

13. For more on public policy, see I. M. Grossack, "Public Policy
Views on Conglomerate Mergers," *Academy of Management Proceed-
ings,* 1969. It is worth noting that public agencies other than those in
antitrust have been concerned with mergers.

Part I: The Forces of Concentration
1. The Offensive Intensifies

1. *Economic Report*, p.669.
2. *Fortune*, Feb. 1969, p.80, quoting Nicholas Salgo, chief executive of Bangor Punta.
3. *Economic Report*, p.3.
4. Ibid., p.4.
5. Ibid., p.39.
6. *Dun's Review*, Jan. 1972, p.31.
7. Senate Select Committee on Small Business, Hearings Mar. 8, 1973.
8. Ibid.
9. *Economic Report*, p.51.
10. *Economic Concentration Hearings*, p.4760.
11. *Economic Report*, p.111.
12. Ibid., p.130.

2. Mounting the Counterattack

1. *Economic Concentration Hearings*, p.5123.
2. Ibid., p. 5177.
3. Ibid., p.5180.
4. *Attorney General's Study of the Antitrust Laws*, p.2.
5. Transcript of Joint Economic Committee Hearings, Feb. 21, 1973.
6. "White House Task Force Report on Antitrust Policy," *The Congressional Record*, May 27, 1969, p.S 5643.
7. *Senate Report No. 1326*, 62d Cong., 3d sess., p.17.
8. *Other People's Money*, p.152.
9. *Attorney General's Study of the Antitrust Laws*, p.117.
10. *Economic Concentration Hearings*, p.5123.
11. *Senate Report No. 1775*, 81st Cong., 2d sess., p.3.
12. *House Report No. 1191*, 81st Cong., 1st sess., p.2.
13. *Economic Concentration Hearings*, p. 5123.
14. Ibid., p.5177.
15. *Economic Report*, p.35.
16. *Economic Concentration Hearings*, S 5122.
17. Ibid.
18. Ibid.
19. Ibid.
20. *Economic Report*, p.462.
21. Civil Action No. 13320, United States District Court, District of Connecticut, filed Aug. 1, 1969.

22. *Hearings on Conglomerate Corporations*, Part 7, p.1.
23. Ibid., p.15.
24. Ibid., p.7.
25. Ibid.
26. *The Congressional Record*, June 16, 1969, p.S 6475.
27. Ibid.
28. Ibid.
29. Ibid., p.6476.
30. Ibid., p.6479.
31. Ibid., p.6478.
32. Ibid.
33. Ibid., p.6471.

Part II: How to Build a Conglomerate Corporation

1. *Hearings on Conglomerate Corporations*, Part 1, p.150.

3. Make Friends with a Bank

1. *Fortune*, Mar. 1968, p.124.
2. *G & W*, 1971 [a Gulf & Western publication], p.17.
3. 12 U.S.C., Sec. 24.
4. *Other People's Money*, p.103.
5. *Hearings on Conglomerate Corporations*, Part 1, p.743.
6. Ibid., p.468.
7. Ibid., p.338.
8. Ibid., p.340.
9. Ibid., p.339.
10. Ibid., p.37.
11. Ibid., p.361.
12. Ibid., p.43.
13. Ibid., p.47.
14. Ibid., p.481.
15. Ibid., p.123.
16. Ibid., p.173.
17. Ibid., p.71.
18. Ibid., p.77.
19. Ibid., p.774.
20. Ibid., p.74.
21. Ibid., p.449.
22. *G & W*, 1971, p.32.
23. 68 S. Ct. 915 (1948).
24. *Hearings on Conglomerate Corporations*, Part 1, p.467.
25. Ibid., p.149.
26. Ibid., p.147.

27. *G & W*, 1971, p. 27.
28. *Hearings on Conglomerate Corporations*, Part 1, p.103.
29. Ibid., p.737.
30. Ibid., p.738.
31. Ibid., p.454.
32. Ibid., p.81.
33. Ibid., p.124.
34. Ibid., p.84.
35. Ibid., p.455.
36. Ibid., p.456.
37. *Hearings on Conglomerate Corporations*, Part 1, p.125.
38. *Conglomerate Investigation Report*, p.205.
39. Ibid., p.204.
40. Ibid.
41. *Hearings on Conglomerate Corporations*, Part 1, p.474.
42. Ibid., p.472.
43. Ibid.
44. Ibid., p.126.
45. *Conglomerate Investigation Report*, p.198.
46. *Hearings on Conglomerate Corporations*, Part 1, p.474.

4. Shift the Purchase Debt to the Purchased Company

1. *Hearings on Conglomerate Corporations*, Part 6, p.66.
2. Ibid., p.416.
3. Ibid., p.418.
4. Ibid., p.575.
5. Ibid., p.576.
6. Ibid., p.426.
7. Ibid., p.156.
8. Ibid., p.421.
9. Ibid., p.158.
10. Ibid., p.431.
11. Ibid., p.736.
12. LTV 1967 Annual Report.
13. Letter of C. Skeen, LTV president, to George Griffin, vice president for finance, Jan. 11, 1967. House Judiciary Committee files, unpublished.
14. *Hearings on Conglomerate Corporations*, Part 6, p.574.
15. House Judiciary Committee files, unpublished.
16. *Hearings on Conglomerate Corporations*, Part 6, p.434.
17. Ibid., p.162.
18. LTV 1967 Annual Report.
19. LTV 1965 Annual Report.
20. *Hearings on Conglomerate Corporations*, Part 6, p.736.
21. Ibid., p.13.

5. Acquire One Company with the Treasury of Another

1. *Hearings on Conglomerate Corporations*, Part 4, p.25.
2. Ibid., p.12.
3. Ibid., p.11.
4. Ibid., p.12.
5. Ibid., p.22.
6. Ibid., Part 4, p.25; Part 2, p.244.
7. Ibid., Part 2, p.181.
8. Ibid., p.805.
9. Ibid., p.179.
10. Ibid., p.244.
11. Ibid., p.77.
12. Ibid., p.181.
13. Ibid., Part 4, p.45.
14. Ibid., p.60.
15. 12 C F R 220.
16. *Hearings on Conglomerate Corporations*, Part 4, p.65.
17. Ibid., Part 2, p.875.
18. Ibid., p.880.
19. Ibid., p.882.
20. *Conglomerate Investigation Report*, p.229.
21. *Hearings on Conglomerate Corporations*, Part 7, p.98.
22. Ibid., Part 4, p.299.
23. Ibid.
24. Ibid., p.87.
25. Ibid., p.380.
26. Ibid.
27. Ibid., p.33.
28. Ibid., p.349.
29. Ibid.
30. Ibid., p.31.
31. Ibid., p.33.
32. Ibid., p.27.
33. Ibid., p.39.
34. Ibid., Part 2, p.224.
35. Ibid., p.44.
36. Ibid., p.46.
37. Ibid., p.48.
38. Ibid., p.54.
39. Ibid., p.55.
40. Ibid.
41. Ibid., p.56.
42. Ibid., p.75.
43. Ibid., p.288.
44. Ibid., p.293.

45. Ibid., p.195.
46. Ibid., p.126.
47. Ibid., p.6.

6. Accept Delivery from the Pentagon

1. *Hearings on Conglomerate Corporations*, Part 6, p.480.
2. Ibid., p.482.
3. Ibid., p.484.
4. Ibid., p.491.
5. Ibid., p.490.
6. Ibid., p.173.
7. Ibid., p.493.
8. Ibid., p.179.
9. Ibid., p.508.
10. Ibid., p.509.
11. Ibid., p.510.
12. Ibid., p.183.
13. Ibid., p.518.
14. Ibid., p.521.

Part III: The Purpose of the Conglomerate Headquarters

1. *Economic Concentration Hearings*, p.4584.
2. *Conglomerate Investigation Report*, p.408.
3. Ibid., p.411.
4. *Armed Services Hearings*, p.10569.
5. Ibid., p.10593.

7. The Purpose of International Telephone & Telegraph

1. *Hearings on Conglomerate Corporations*, Part 3, p.249.
2. Ibid., p.161.
3. Ibid.
4. Ibid., p.158.
5. Ibid., p.158.
6. Ibid., p.16.
7. Ibid., p.22.
8. Ibid.
9. Ibid., p.23.
10. Ibid.
11. Ibid., p.94.
12. Ibid., p.71.
13. Ibid., p.405.

14. Ibid., p.101.
15. Ibid.
16. Ibid., p.10.
17. Ibid., p.251.
18. Ibid., p.113.
19. *U. S.* v. *Penick & Ford, Ltd. Inc.,* 242 F. Supp. 518; *U. S.* v. *Northwest Inds. Inc.,* 301 F. Supp. 1066.
20. *U. S.* v. *International Telephone & Tel. Corp.,* 306 F. Supp. 766.
21. *Hearings on Conglomerate Corporations,* Part 3, p.481.
22. Ibid., p.496.
23. Ibid., p.502.
24. Ibid., p.121.
25. Ibid., p.515.
26. Ibid., p.523.
27. Ibid., p.529.
28. Ibid., p.129.
29. Ibid., p.585.
30. Ibid., p.787.
31. Ibid., p.804.
32. Ibid., p.786.
33. Ibid., p.787.
34. Ibid., p.804.
35. Ibid., p.213.
36. Ibid., p.215.
37. Ibid., pp.215, 217.
38. Ibid., p.216.
39. Ibid., p.215.
40. Ibid., p.735.
41. Ibid., p.217.
42. Ibid., p.219.
43. Ibid., p.879.
44. Ibid., p.225.
45. Ibid., p.219.
46. Ibid., p.198.
47. Ibid., p.196.
48. Ibid., p.203.
49. Ibid., p.200.

8. *The Purpose of LTV, Inc.*

1. *Hearings on Conglomerate Corporations,* Part 6, p.261.
2. Ibid., p.90.
3. Ibid., p.279.
4. Ibid., p.683.

5. Ibid., p.261.
6. Ibid., p.262.
7. Ibid., p.130.
8. Ibid., p.131.
9. Ibid., p.511.
10. Ibid., p.216.
11. Ibid., p.83.
12. Ibid., p.153.
13. Ibid.
14. Ibid., p.144.
15. Ibid.
16. Ibid., p.6.
17. Ibid., p.73.

9. The Purpose of Litton Industries, Inc.

1. *Hearings on Conglomerate Corporations*, Part 5, p.43.
2. 1970 and 1971 Litton Annual Reports.
3. *Hearings on Conglomerate Corporations*, Part 5, p.60.
4. Ibid., p.998.
5. Ibid., p.1012.
6. Ibid.
7. Ibid., p.46.
8. *The Wall Street Journal*, Mar. 2, 1973.
9. Litton 1970 Annual Report, p.18.
10. *The Congressional Record*, Apr. 13, 1972, p. S 6124.
11. *Hearings on Conglomerate Corporations*, Part 5, p.60.
12. Litton 1970 Annual Report, p.19.
13. *Armed Services Hearings*, p.10547.
14. Ibid., p.10550.
15. Press release of June 16, 1972.
16. *Forbes*, Dec. 15, 1971, p.18.
17. Ibid.
18. *Armed Services Hearings*, p.10572.
19. Ibid., p.10603.
20. Ibid., p.10658.
21. Ibid.
22. Ibid., p.10653.
23. Ibid., p.10665.
24. Ibid., p.10666.
25. Ibid., p.10669.
26. *Hearings on Conglomerate Corporations*, Part 5, p.61.
27. *Armed Services Hearings*, p.10635.
28. Ibid., p.10608.
29. Ibid., p.10610.

30. *The Wall Street Journal*, Mar. 2, 1973.
31. *Armed Services Hearings*, p.10659.
32. *The Journal of Commerce*, Mar. 4, 1969, p.5.
33. *Armed Services Hearings*, p.10636.
34. *Hearings on Conglomerate Corporations*, Part 5, p.61.
35. *Armed Services Hearings*, p.10618.
36. Ibid.
37. Ibid., p.10572.
38. Ibid., p.10574.
39. Ibid., p.10612.
40. *The Washington Post*, Dec. 23, 1972.
41. *The Wall Street Journal*, Dec. 19, 1972.
42. *Hearings on Conglomerate Corporations*, Part 5, p.62.
43. Ibid., p.60.
44. *Report on Controls over Shipyard Costs*, p.16.
45. Ibid., p.17.
46. Ibid., p.4.
47. Ibid., p.5.
48. Ibid., p.11.
49. Ibid., p.13.
50. Ibid., p.17.
51. Ibid., p.18.

Part IV: The Counterattack in Disarray

10. The Interstate Commerce Commission

1. *Fortune*, Aug. 1970, p.106.
2. *The Penn Central Failure*, p.55.
3. *Fortune*, Aug. 1970, p.107.
4. *Business Week*, June 27, 1970, p.98.
5. *The Penn Central Failure*, p.72.
6. Ibid., p.33.
7. Ibid., p.67.
8. Ibid., p.61.
9. Ibid., pp.55, 71.
10. Ibid., p.25.
11. *Fortune*, Aug. 1970, p.165.
12. *The Penn Central Failure*, p.77.
13. *The New York Times*, Jan. 4, 1972.
14. *Fortune*, Aug. 1970, p.164.
15. *The Penn Central Failure*, p.273.
16. *Investigation into the Management of the Business of the Penn Central*, p.112.
17. *Emergency Rail Services Legislation Hearings*, p.711.

18. *The Penn Central Failure,* p.12.

19. *Adequacy of Investor Protection Hearing,* p.5.

20. House of Representatives Report No. 85, 73d Cong., 1st sess., 1933, p.3.

21. *Adequacy of Investor Protection Hearing,* p.137.

22. Ibid., p.112.

23. *Inadequacies of Protections for Investors in Penn Central,* p.9.

24. *Adequacy of Investor Protection Hearing,* p.112.

25. *Inadequacies of Protections for Investors in Penn Central,* p.10.

26. *Adequacy of Investor Protection Hearing,* p.113.

27. *Inadequacies of Protections for Investors in Penn Central,* p.25.

28. *Emergency Rail Services Legislation Hearings,* p.192.

29. *The Penn Central Failure,* p.xi.

30. *Hearing on H.R. 2191 and H.R.5220 before a Subcommittee of the House Committee on Interstate and Foreign Commerce,* 76th Cong., 1st sess., 1939.

31. *Fortune,* Aug. 1970, p.165.

32. *Adequacy of Investor Protection Hearing,* p.29.

33. Ibid., p.35.

34. *Inadequacies of Protections for Investors in Penn Central,* p.36.

35. Ibid., p.37.

36. Ibid., p.39.

37. Ibid., p.40.

38. *Other People's Money,* p.134.

39. *Investigation into the Management of the Business of the Penn Central,* p.112.

40. Letter of July 6, 1972 to Morris Goldman.

41. *The New England Investigation,* 27 ICC 560 (1913).

42. *Emergency Rail Services Legislation Hearings,* p.949.

43. Address of Kenneth H. Tuggle before the American Bar Association, Sections of Public Utility Law and Administrative Law, Aug. 15, 1972.

44. *Emergency Rail Services Legislation Hearings,* p.952.

45. Commissioner Tuggle's address of Aug. 15, 1972.

46. *Emergency Rail Services Legislation Hearings,* p.1041.

47. Commissioner Tuggle's address of Aug. 15, 1972.

48. *Emergency Rail Services Legislation Hearings,* p.969.

49. Ibid.

50. Commissioner Tuggle's address of Aug. 15, 1972.

51. *Forbes,* Nov. 15, 1972, p.29.

52. Ibid.

53. Commissioner Tuggle's address of Aug. 15, 1972.

54. *Emergency Rail Services Legislation Hearings,* p.1048.

55. Commissioner Tuggle's address of Aug. 15, 1972.

56. *The American Railroad Industry: A Prospectus* (Washington, D. C.: America's Sound Transportation Review Organization, June 1970), p.21.

11. The Securities and Exchange Commission

1. *Hearings on Conglomerate Corporations*, Part 7, p.88.
2. Ibid.
3. Ibid., p.89.
4. Ibid., p.92.
5. Ibid.
6. *The Work of the Securities and Exchange Commission*, Nov. 1971.
7. *Hearings on Conglomerate Corporations*, Part 7, p.92.
8. Ibid., p.93.
9. Ibid., p.96.
10. Ibid., p.91.
11. Note I to Financial Statement, LTV 1969 Annual Report, p.27.
12. *Hearings on Conglomerate Corporations*, Part 3, p.526.
13. Ibid., p.358.
14. Ibid., p.513.
15. Ibid., p.616.
16. *Conglomerate Investigation Report*, p.139.
17. Ibid., p.124.
18. Ibid.
19. Ibid., p.139.
20. *Hearings before the House Committee on Appropriations for 1971*, 91st Cong., 2d sess., Part 2, p.1092.
21. Ibid.
22. Ibid., p. 1114.
23. *Hearings before the House Committee on Appropriations for 1973*, 92nd Cong., 2d sess., Part 1, p.164.
24. Joint Economic Committee files, unpublished.
25. Ibid.
26. Letter of July 14, 1972, ibid.
27. *The Washington Post*, Dec. 21, 1972.
28. Ibid.
29. Ibid.
30. Transcript of Hearings of the Joint Economic Committee, Dec. 20, 1972, p.37.
31. *The New York Times*, Dec. 20, 1972.
32. *The Evening Star*, Washington, D. C., Dec. 15, 1972.
33. Ibid.
34. Ibid., Dec. 23, 1972.
35. Transcript of Hearings of the Joint Economic Committee, Dec. 19, 1972, p.16.
36. *The New York Times*, Dec. 23, 1972.
37. *The Washington Post*, Dec. 23, 1972.
38. *The Wall Street Journal*, Mar. 16, 1972.
39. *The New York Times*, June 21, 1972.
40. Ibid.

41. Memorandum of Law, House Commerce Committee, Investigations Subcommittee, Oct. 12, 1972, p.8.

42. Ibid.

43. Transcript of House Commerce Committee Hearings of Dec. 15, 1972, p.108.

44. Joint Press Release of Oct. 12, 1972.

12. The Internal Revenue Service

1. *Hearings on Conglomerate Corporations*, Part 7, p.261.

2. Letter of Oct. 25, 1967, House Judiciary Committee files, unpublished.

3. *Hearings on Conglomerate Corporations*, Part 5, p.158.

4. Ibid.

5. Ibid., Part 7, p.97.

6. By letter, House Judiciary Committee files, unpublished.

7. Letter to the Federal Trade Commission, House Judiciary Committee files, unpublished.

8. 26 C. F. R., Sec. 1.368.

9. *The Wall Street Journal*, Oct. 12, 1972.

10. *Kleindienst Nomination Hearings*, p.103.

11. *The Wall Street Journal*, Oct. 12, 1972.

12. Ibid.

13. Letter of Sept. 25, 1972 from IRS Assistant Commissioner Peter P. Weidenbruch, Jr., to Prof. Boris Bittker.

14. Letter of May 5, 1972 from IRS Acting Commissioner Raymond Harless to Ralph Nader, Alan Morrison, and Reuben Robertson.

13. The Department of Justice

1. Plaintiff's brief, *Nader, et al.* v. *Cotter, et al.*, No. 166205, Connecticut Superior Court, Hartford County, Jan. 27, 1972, p.23.

2. Ibid., p.31.

3. Ibid., p.12.

4. *Kleindienst Nomination Hearings*, p.118.

5. *The Washington Post*, Mar. 25, 1972.

6. *Kleindienst Nomination Hearings*, p.118.

7. Ibid., p.265.

8. Ibid., p.268.

9. Ibid., p.265.

10. Ibid., p.268.

11. ITT 1972 1st Quarter Report.

12. *Kleindienst Nomination Hearings*, p.266.

13. Ibid., p.267.

14. Ibid., p.289.

15. Ibid., p.328.

16. Ibid.
17. Ibid., p.110.
18. Ibid., p.644.
19. Ibid., p.104.
20. Ibid., p.109.
21. Ibid., p.114.
22. Ibid., p.111.
23. ITT 1971 Annual Report.
24. *Hearings on Conglomerate Corporations*, Part 3, p.21.
25. ITT 1972 1st Quarter Report.

Conclusion

1. Address of Richard W. McLaren before the Federal Bar Association, Council on Antitrust and Trade Regulation, Sept. 17, 1970.
2. Address of Thomas E. Kauper before the American Bar Association, Section of Corporate, Banking and Business Law, Oct. 27, 1972.
3. *The Wall Street Journal*, April 24, 1972.
4. *Hearings on Conglomerate Corporations*, Part 5, p.43.
5. *Dun's Review*, June 1972, p.49.
6. *Economic Report*, p.670.
7. Transcript of Senate Foreign Relations Committee hearings, March 22, 1973, p.47.
8. Ibid., March 21, 1973, p.23.
9. *Hearings on Conglomerate Corporations*, Part 5, p.50.
10. *Conglomerate Investigation Report*, p.439.